The Mississippi Chinese

Harvard East Asian Series 63
The East Asian Research Center at Harvard University
administers research projects designed to further scholarly
understanding of China, Japan, Korea, Vietnam,
and adjacent areas.

James W.
Loewen

**The Mississippi
Chinese**

Between Black
and White

Harvard University Press
Cambridge, Massachusetts
1971

"You're either a white man or a nigger, here. Now, that's the whole story. When I first came to the Delta, the Chinese were classed as nigras."

["And now they are called whites?"]

"That's right!"

Conversation with white Baptist minister, Clarksdale, Mississippi

Acknowledgments

I wish to thank the many Chinese-Mississippians who shared parts of their lives and histories with me and made possible this book. Nothing that I have written here has been intended to injure or embarrass the Chinese as a group or any individuals among them. Those who shared the most information with me expected me to tell the truth, and that is what I have tried to do. I hope they will approve the result.

I am also indebted to many other Mississippians — blacks, whites, and others — for suggestions and data. Several students and faculty members at Tougaloo College and Harvard University read all or parts of the book and made valuable suggestions. Patricia Hanrahan, now Loewen, read and edited the entire manuscript; Jan Hillegas and Mrs. Agatha Bradford were expert retypists. Finally I owe thanks to many others for advice and assistance, among them Dorothy Heid Bracey, Peter F. Loewen, Gerald Globetti, Anthony Layng, Michael H. Schwartz, Harrison White, Bruce Nicholas, Joe C. Huang, Rev. Jachin Chan, and especially Ezra F. Vogel.

The research was partly supported by a National Institute of Mental Health predoctoral fellowship and accompanying research grant and by a grant from the Field Foundation to the Department of Social Relations of Harvard University for studies in the area of race relations. The East Asian Research Center at Harvard was also generous in its assistance.

James W. Loewen
Tougaloo, Mississippi, June 1970

Contents

Tables

Figures

The Mississippi Chinese

Introduction

In the northwest corner of the state of Mississippi lies a vast alluvial plain, formed from the rich black flood deposits of the Mississippi and Yazoo rivers. Almost perfectly flat, rimmed by low bluffs to the east and south, the basin is called the Yazoo-Mississippi Delta. The Delta stretches over nearly the entire 185-mile distance from Memphis to Vicksburg, though it includes neither of those cities, and at its widest point it extends sixty miles east of the Mississippi River. Divided into plantations often several square miles in area, the land is tilled by black sharecroppers and owned by white planters. These two groups are all that most persons know of the Delta; indeed, they form the stereotyped image of its population. But in fact, other ethnic groups have lived in the Delta almost from its first settlement, including Lebanese, Italians, Mexicans, Jews, and a substantial number of Chinese.

Although they form the largest population of Chinese in any Southern state, the existence of the 1200 Delta Chinese is virtually unknown outside of Mississippi. They came to the state in 1869 or 1870, at a time when planters were recruiting agricultural labor, and they entered the plantation system at the bottom, as sharecroppers. Partly for this reason, white Mississippi considered them to be of roughly Negro status and barred them from white schools, organizations, and other social interaction.

Soon after their arrival, however, the Chinese forsook the cotton fields to become merchants — small grocers — and over the ensuing decades they rapidly improved their economic position. They became richer, and their social position showed corresponding improvement. No longer were they clearly of "Negro" status. As a group, their racial definition gradually shifted upward.

For a time they were considered neither white nor black, and the segregation system attempted to deal with them as exceptions. During the 1930's and early 1940's, Cleveland, Greenville, and several other towns operated triply segregated school systems, with separate buildings for Chinese pupils, as well as for whites and blacks. These schools still stand, but they have been abandoned for some twenty years. Since that time, the Chinese have been admitted into the white public schools and into other institutions. Today they are very nearly, and in some respects entirely, equal in status to Caucasians.[1]

Ten decades have passed since the Fourteenth Amendment to the Constitution was enacted, but Delta society is still rigidly segregated. A vast social and economic gulf yawns between the dominant white and subordinate black. Yet one group in Mississippi, a "third race," the Chinese, has managed to leap that chasm. Originally classed with blacks, they are now viewed as essentially "white." The color bar stands, but they have crossed over it. Moreover, in some communities they bridge it anew every day, for they still stand in a sense as an intermediate group. Negroes do not consider them exactly white; Caucasians do not consider them black. They are privileged and burdened with an ambiguous racial identity.

This book focuses on the causes of their change in status, the processes by which it came about, and the opposition it engendered. Therefore the emphasis is always on race relations; only in part is the book an ethnography of the Chinese as an ethnic minority. The history of their status transition and the complexity of their present relations with the other races pro-

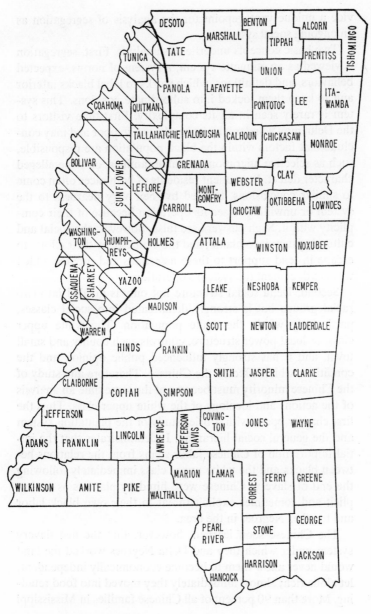

1. The Mississippi Delta.

vide a unique vantagepoint for the analysis of segregation as an ongoing social system.

Two basic concepts underlie this analysis. First, segregation is viewed as an etiquette system, a system of norms, expected behaviors, and definitions, which works to label blacks inferior and to keep them locked into subordinate positions. This system is rarely seen in all its complexity. First-time visitors to the Delta may wonder why its blacks are so poor and may conclude that factors within the black population are responsible, such as selective migration, unstable families, or some alleged character defect. Permanent residents of both races often come to similar conclusions, blinded by their very nearness to the system or unwilling to see its operation because of their complicity with it. Such answers are false, however; the social and cultural system is to blame; and the Chinese, by their efforts to escape it, lend support to these assertions and provide added ways to document the system's operation.

Second, Delta social structure not only is divided into two racial groups but is strongly demarcated into social classes, particularly within the white population. The white upper class, or local power structure, controls each county and small town, and it has strongly influenced public opinion and the conditions which affected the Chinese. Therefore any study of the Chinese minority must become at the same time an analysis of the actions and ideology of the white upper class. Thus the first chapter opens with a brief study of the plantation system and the general social hierarchy. It demonstrates that the initial importation of Chinese labor stems from the relations between blacks and the white upper class immediately following the end of slavery. Chinese were hired by planters as an implicit and sometimes explicit threat to their own black labor and to other Negroes in the area.

The Chinese soon learned, however, that the neo-slavery system under which they and Delta Negroes worked the land would never allow them to become economically independent, let alone rich; almost immediately they moved into food retailing. More than 90 percent of all Chinese families in Mississippi now operate groceries — an incredibly uniform occupational emphasis. Chapter 2 argues that the concentration and economic success of the Chinese groceries indicate that something was amiss in the segregation system, that segregation seemed to create a profitable niche for the Chinese which neither blacks nor whites could exploit.

In turn, the economic advance of the Chinese made possible their later social rise, though not in any simple way. Chapters 3 and 4 define their earlier, near-black status and analyze the process by which they came to be defined almost white. Money alone, of course, was not the answer and has done little for the racial status of the black middle class. The Chinese had to use their cash to establish a life style and image different from that of the black majority. Otherwise, whites would say, "But if we let in the Chinese, won't the 'niggers' be right behind?" Having thus dealt with this main ideological objection to their advance, the Chinese utilized ministers, wholesalers, and other Caucasians to whom they had close ties in order to persuade the local white power structure to admit them to schools, hospitals, and other white public institutions.

However, as Chapter 5 observes, there was a great deal of opposition to the Chinese in the earlier parts of this century, and it continued to manifest itself whenever the minority attempted to break another social barrier. Almost no whites are in a position to have strong personal interests, economic or symbolic, in keeping the Chinese "down." Consequently, it is not obvious why the Chinese have almost always been opposed. The explanation invokes processes related to anti-black opposition, and Chapter 5 assesses parallels between anti-Chinese and anti-Negro discrimination.

As the Chinese rose in status, gradually attaining membership in the white caste, one group was left behind: those members who had married or lived common-law with black wives and families. These families are the subject of Chapter 6. Like the group as a whole, they have lived in an uneasy ambivalence between white and black sides of the segregation barrier. But while the majority of the Chinese have now been clearly placed on the white side of that barrier, the Chinese-Negro families are definitely on the black side. Their relations with Negroes and with Caucasians are not exactly those of "pure" Negro families, however, and the contrasts afforded by this small group shed more light on the values held by both blacks and whites resulting from segregation.

Finally, the concluding chapter projects present trends and tries to assess the future of the group. Ironically, now that white Mississippi has begun to accept the Chinese more fully, the Chinese themselves are leaving. Occupationally oriented toward large Western cities, most will not remain much longer in the land of their youth. And at the same time, vast changes in the system under which they have made their living may threaten the incomes of those storeowners who stay. Segregation is slowly dying, but not without violence, and some of that violence is directed toward the race which for so many decades stood in the middle. And as segregation ends, the special place it created for the Chinese ends as well.

It should be clear, then, that this book is both historical and contemporary, both a study of the Chinese minority and an analysis of the system with which the group interacted. Accordingly, not only the Chinese experience but also white and black relations to the Chinese had to be surveyed. The most important tool in this work was the free-ranging interview, not confined to a written schedule or rigid set of questions. In all, I interviewed 321 different people — Chinese, Negroes, Caucasians, and others.[2] Nearly as important was participant observation among the Chinese and in white institutions in which Chinese participate. My field experience ranged from pure observation, such as attendance at an all-night mah jongg game in which high stakes and a limited research budget combined to make me solely an onlooker, to participation in the bass section of the Chinese Baptist Church Choir of Cleveland, Mississippi, in which my preoccupation with the musical notes at hand precluded notes of any other kind. In addition, current records and historical sources proved useful in a number of ways. Finally, five-page questionnaires were given to twenty-seven Chinese college students and to seventy-five Caucasian students at Mississippi State University. Most of the research was carried out in Greenville, Clarksdale, Vicksburg, and the small towns and rural areas of Bolivar County. I first learned of the Mississippi Chinese when I met and became acquainted with several Chinese students when I was enrolled at Mississippi State University in 1963. All other field research was conducted in January–February and May–September of 1967, with occasional one-day visits in 1968, 1969, and 1970.

Because of the sweeping changes caused by school desegregation orders in early 1970, this book is perhaps the last field study of segregation in its "pure" form that will ever be written. Already segregation is passing into history. In some areas, public schools are no longer "white" or "black"; in other districts the public schools are overwhelmingly black, while whites have retreated to new private schools. What new social and cultural system will replace segregation is not yet clear, but changes have already occurred since the research for this book was completed.

Entry of the Chinese 1

The Plantation System and the Social Hierarchy

The Delta includes only about a sixth of Mississippi's land area and less than a fifth of its population; yet, except for a handful of teachers and students at the larger state universities, virtually all of Mississippi's more than 1200 Chinese residents live in the Delta. This is the area of greatest Negro concentration. More than that of any other region of the state, its social structure is still dominated by the cotton plantation, and the white planter stands at the top of the status hierarchy. It is not by chance that the Chinese have settled in the plantation area and no other. Their entry, their occupational focus, and the later shift in their status are all intricately bound up with the plantation system. Furthermore, outlines of the system still persist. Without an introduction to the social structure with which the Chinese had to contend, then, little could be understood of their subsequent history.

The Mississippi Delta remains one of the least urbanized areas of the United States. The 1970 census shows only nine cities of more than 3000 people in the entire Delta, and nearly three out of every four residents live in towns smaller than that minimum or in rural areas. And as that statistic indicates, the economy of the Delta is still based on agriculture.

The richness of the soil is outstanding — it is the finest land in the South, equaled elsewhere in America only by a few counties in Iowa and Illinois. On some farms, cotton crops have been produced annually for seventy-five years, yet only moderate fertilization is required. Highways and crop rows are laid out perfectly straight on the basin's flat floor, and only man-imposed acreage restrictions keep the land from being wholly under cultivation.

This area was settled late, from river towns eastward into the interior. Although a few settlements had been established well before the Civil War, Grant found the Delta north of Vicksburg an impassable wilderness in his siege of that city in 1863. Even by 1900, except for the river towns and a few large plantations, the area was largely undeveloped.[1] Blacks and whites entered the area simultaneously, with the former a few feet behind, carrying the white man's burden. "This land is first and last his handiwork. It was he who brought order out of primeval wilderness, felling the trees, digging the ditches, and draining the swamps. He erected the homes which shelter him and the white man. He built the schools, the court houses, the jails, the factories, and warehouses. Everything in the Delta sprang from the sweat and brawn of the Negro."[2] As soon as the land could be cleared, it was planted in cotton. A pattern of large landholdings developed, and the Delta became populated by a heavy majority of Negro farm laborers, mostly on a furnish-sharecrop system, and a small minority of white planters, amounting to one-fifth to one-tenth of the population. To be sure, some plantations have comprised only a hundred or so acres, and a considerable number of independent operators, including Negroes, have owned individual farms of only forty or eighty acres. But the system has always been dominated by the larger planter, whose holdings may stretch into the thousands of acres.

In past decades, each step in the growing of cotton — the planting, the "chopping" or weeding, and the final picking at harvest — was done by hand. Many hands were required: large planters employed fifty to a hundred families to work their land. Mechanization began to make serious headway in about 1950, however, and family sharecropping in its traditional form is now an anachronism. Table 1 shows the rapid growth of the Delta's population in its early years and the major decline accompanying mechanization since 1940.

Table 1. Population by Race, Mississippi Delta, 1880–1970[a]

Year	Total population	Negro	Caucasian
1880	178,700	118,000	60,650
1900	367,400	301,600	65,600
1920	394,200	310,700	83,200
1940	479,700	345,500	133,500
1960	409,300	262,400	145,800
1970	341,100	202,700	137,200

Source: The United States Census of Population for the respective years. For Chinese data, see Table 3.

[a] Included in the Mississippi Delta are ten counties (Bolivar, Coahoma, Humphreys, Issaqueena, Leflore, Quitman, Sharkey, Sunflower, Tunica, and Washington) and parts of seven additional counties (Grenada, Holmes, Panola, Tallahatchie, Tate, Warren, and Yazoo). Populations are estimated in accordance with the proportion of these counties which are within the Delta.

Sharecropping operated so as to keep tenants poor and make landowners rich. In 1937, for example, sharecropping families received an average total of $300 for their combined labor during the year. However, even this was not usually paid in cash, but as "furnish" — food, seed, and other supplies loaned to the families until autumn. Interest rates on this credit extension averaged 36 percent; thus it is not surprising that many tenants were never out of debt, even at harvest. The planter, meanwhile, who had distributed approximately the equivalent of $3000 income to his average of ten working families, retained about $5500 for himself and his own family, excluding income from commissary, gin, or other nonfarm operations. In 1937, in the midst of the Depression, the average plantation was worth $150,000.[3]

Plantation families were furnished from March 1 through autumn picking season. In the fall, if they had a cash income coming, they were paid it; this supported them during part of the winter. For the rest, they lived essentially without income, occasionally managing to get an odd job on the plantation or in town. Most but not all plantations operated commissaries, through which the croppers were given their furnish. Where the commissary system operated in full force, tenants were locked in to the plantation quite effectively; both their selling and buying had to be done through the same white landowner. Increasingly during the 1920's and 1930's, however, the smaller plantations were eliminating their commissaries, and the larger plantations, faced with pressure for a wider selection of goods, were giving out some cash or trade guarantees, to be used in town.

The rural service-center towns sprang up in the last century, with a somewhat higher percentage of whites, but with Negroes still in the majority, as domestics and manual laborers. In addition to businessmen catering to the population's basic needs, town-dwellers included cotton factors, bankers, and the many lawyers produced by planter families in their second and third generations. The towns now are also centers of concentration of those in society other than the white upper class and Negro lower caste, including several other ethnic groups. Between 1900 and World War I, planters brought in many Italian farm laborers to work their land as sharecroppers. Since then the Italians have managed to establish small and sometimes large farms and small businesses. In a few of the smaller towns they constitute up to 45 percent of the white population — and there they are beginning to make themselves felt in local decision-making. Lebanese and Syrian merchants entered the Delta several decades ago, and a substantial Jewish population has also lived in the Delta for several generations. Both groups are now concentrated in the larger cities in mercantile occupations. Mexican and Mexican-American farm workers have been introduced occasionally, and some have remained as permanent residents, with status very near that of the Negro, though they are for the most part in white schools.

There are also many whites who are not planters or businessmen or professionals. First there is what might be termed a lower-middle class, including teachers, barbers, and owners of such small businesses as drycleaning establishments. However, they look so intensely toward the upper-middle-class establishment that they can be discounted as a source of independent action in society. Below them come the working-class whites, until recently a much smaller group in the Delta than in hill counties. They work in the new industries in the area or as mechanics, truck drivers, filling-stations attendants, and so forth, in establishments owned by others. In addition, through the years one sharecropper in ten to twenty has been white. Finally there are a few "river whites," extremely poor, who fish or hold occasional jobs.

The various groups can be ranked roughly as shown below:

Planter; landed businessman; old-resident professional
Established small businessmen; old-resident whites in various
    middle-class occupations; city officials
Jewish merchants; highly successful businessmen from other
    ethnic groups
Italian farmers; Italian and other ethnic small businessmen;
    working-class whites
Chinese merchants
Poor whites; white sharecroppers
Negro teachers, businessmen; other Negro middle class
Mexican farm laborers
Negro manual and farm laborers; domestics; unemployed

Such a listing is inevitably crude, for it generalizes far too quickly. In one or two small towns, a Chinese grocer with a very successful store may be admitted to the very top group, at least in some respects. More broadly, there is no "social status," quantifiable on a single continuum. Depending upon the issue at hand, a Chinese merchant may be considered of far greater eminence than an unemployed white, or he may be barred where the white may freely enter. And the placement of poor whites, as the adjective indicates, is highly dependent upon their economic situation; they can rise over time, and some do, while such groups as the Chinese, already much higher economically, may be unable to progress because of their immutable racial and ethnic identification.

To understand the forces underlying the status hierarchy, we must survey the amount of inequality in the system, its general level of wealth in comparison to other areas in the United States, and the rigidity of its stratification. In the following analysis Bolivar County, a prototypical Delta county, is contrasted with national averages and with a comparison unit, Livingston County in north central Illinois. These two counties are remarkably similar topographically in size, population, size of major towns, and in urban-rural ratio. Their differences, which are profound, stem from their diverse historical development, one a large cotton-growing plantation land with Negro work force, the other a family-farm grain-raising area, overwhelmingly white.[4]

Bolivar County has an overall median household income of $1416. This compares with $4597 for Livingston County, Illinois, and a national median still higher. In some ways, however, Bolivar is not a poor county. It possesses vast soil resources, the equal of the Illinois county, and the cash value of all products extracted from its soil is higher per acre than in most other areas of the United States. The white population is not on the whole poor. Indeed, there is such an air of affluence among those whites who influence public decisions that poverty program publicists in the Delta must expend substantial energy merely to establish that *any* whites are poor. In short, Bolivar County is a highly stratified system in which the Negro, roughly, forms the bottom half, the white the upper. As Table 2 indicates, the white median income for the county, $4042, begins to compare favorably to the national median, especially since living expenses in several categories of ex-

Table 2. Selected Socioeconomic Characteristics, Bolivar County, Mississippi, Compared to Livingston County, Illinois, and to U.S. National Averages, 1959

Characteristic	Bolivar County	Livingston County	United States
Area (square miles)	917	1,043	
Number of families	11,290	10,024	
Total population	54,464	40,341	
Population of largest city	10,172	8,435	
Percent of total population	18.7	20.9	
Percent urban	18.7	36.0	70.4
Percent rural nonfarm	34.6	37.3	22.5
Percent rural farm	46.7	26.7	7.5
Density, rural (rural population/square mile)	484	248	
Percent white	32.7	99+	88.6
Percent foreign born	0.7	1.9	
White median annual income (families and individuals)	$4042	$4597	$5088
Nonwhite median income	$ 936	—	$2520
Median education, years, adults over 25	6.7	10.0	10.6
Unemployment rate	8.3%	3.4%	5.5%
Nonwhite unemployment rate	11.4%	—	8.5%
Percent underemployed (employed, but worked less than 50 weeks)	74.3%	43.2%	46.3%

Source: United States Census of Population, 1960, vol. I, Characteristics of the Population (1960 statistics are a better choice than 1970 data for understanding the social system in which the Chinese have lived).

penditure are markedly lower in Mississippi than in the nation as a whole.

The general distribution of incomes can be more usefully pictured by a Lorenz curve, a graphic technique which plots individuals or groups on a horizontal axis and their incomes on a vertical axis.[5] Figure 2 compares Lorenz curves for annual incomes of Bolivar and Livingston counties. The Gini Index, a measure of inequality which can vary from 0 (complete equality) to 1.0 (complete inequality), is 0.534 for Bolivar County, 0.389 for Livingston. Most contemporary industrialized societies, including the United States, have indices of about 0.4; Bolivar is thus a marked exception, a highly stratified system with an income distribution approaching that of feudal societies.

Figure 3 completes the picture: white incomes are fairly evenly distributed over various income levels, while nonwhite incomes fit a sharply falling curve concentrated at the extreme low end of the continuum.[6] Only 5 percent of all nonwhite households earn more than the white median income. Not only is Bolivar County highly stratified, then, but the stratification is primarily on a racial basis. Its social structure is therefore extremely rigid, since to change racial identification is essentially impossible.

Substantial space has been devoted to carefully delineating the income distribution for Bolivar County because this income structure has important consequences for the position of the Chinese in the system. Three inferences are listed below which will be of great significance to later analyses. First, the level of Negro incomes is so low that black consumption spending must be concentrated in three basic areas — food, rent, and clothing; hence with a 70 percent Negro population the Delta cannot support a large number of commercial transactions except in those spheres. Second, the low black income level means that any occupation which might involve direct competition with Negro workers cannot be remunerative and must be avoided. Finally, although money is not exactly convertible directly into leverage on community decisions, it is obviously highly correlated with such leverage. Negroes have had no power deriving from wealth, since their household incomes are so low that even the small amounts they do have must be spent immediately for current necessities and cannot form a pool for boycott or investment. This means that any

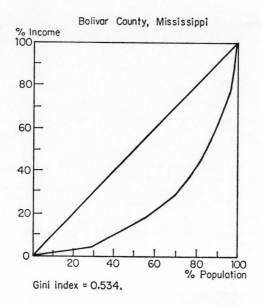

Bolivar County, Mississippi

Gini index = 0.534.

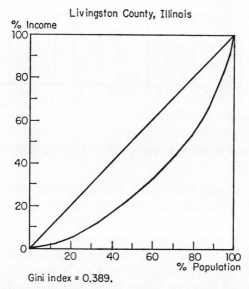

Livingston County, Illinois

Gini index = 0.389.

2. Distribution of annual incomes, Bolivar (Mississippi) and Livingston (Illinois) counties, 1959.

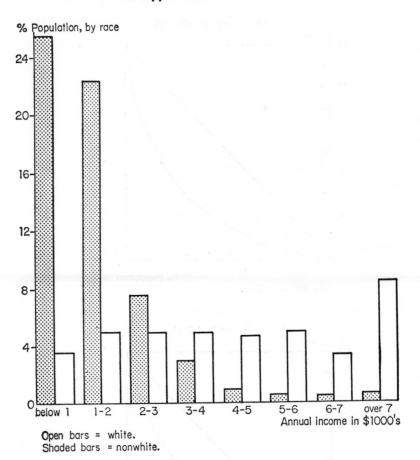

Open bars = white.
Shaded bars = nonwhite.

3. White and nonwhite incomes, Bolivar County, 1959.

accurate analysis of community decision-making and power in the Mississippi Delta must concentrate almost exclusively on the white population; the blacks, although a vast majority numerically, have been almost powerless since 1876.

Within the white population, there is an established decision-making group. Although it may not be true that all areas of the United States or Mississippi possess a fully developed class system, the Delta does indeed have a group of families and individuals who constitute an upper class, in the narrow meaning of the term. That class has been the decisive element with which the Chinese have had to deal. And so it is appropriate to analyze at greater length its resources and consciousness.[7]

In the early days of the Delta's development, the planters comprised the aristocracy. In more recent decades they have been joined by the wealthier businessmen. The planter had to take account of the businessman, for he was essential to plantation operation. Often he was even a creditor, and as he gained more money, he had to be recognized. In some cases, country clubs were formed because of the impetus of businessmen, and gradually the businessman gained entrance to the Delta Council, the elite "civic organization" for the area, while his daughters entered the high-status organizations in high school. Planters still occupied the pinnacle of status, and so many businessmen bought land or married into landholding families to become more identified with them, but even without such maneuvers the businessman gradually began to receive near-equal status. He was even specifically lauded as a community patriot, and by the 1960's all white candidates for public office in the Delta ran as "proven businessman," or "leader in both business and agriculture." [8]

At the same time, however, the planter so completely co-opted the businessman that what was good for the plantation became defined as good for the community. The businessman, looking to the planters as his reference group, from which his own status definition in part derived, said nothing, while his own self-interest was often ignored; for there have been instances where the purely economic interest of businessmen and planters diverged. United States Senator James Eastland, a planter from Sunflower County, has done everything within his power to block or delay the food stamp program, the $1 per hour minimum wage for agricultural laborers, and Head Start and other poverty programs. Even though it is in the direct self-interest of Delta businessmen to work for the implementation of these programs, which directly increase community expenditure on items merchandized locally, they have never voiced a protest. And if something were said, it would be treated as strange talk, "outside" or subversive talk, not within the political rhetoric of the ingroup which the planters and the businessmen comprise.

It is artificial to maintain that the businessman has been "taken in" by the planter and, victimized by false class consciousness, does not pursue his own "rational self-interest"; for although the businessman did not attempt to "beat" the planter, he was at least able to join him, and the status increment he thus gained for himself and his family seemed more important to him than possible economic advantages available otherwise. By becoming one with the planter, the businessman gained more than prestige and a pass to the golf course. He became a part of the power elite.

This local oligarchy is rather freely acknowledged, again setting the Delta apart from other sections of the United States, including hill Mississippi, where it is bad form to admit the existence of a power clique or ruling class. In the Delta, small groups control county and municipal governments, by sitting on the County Board of Supervisors and by influencing, through status superiority, the lesser hangers-on who in American small towns become mayor, police chief, newspaper editor, and sheriff–tax collector. One rarely hears working-class Delta whites speak of "we" in connection with a municipal decision. Delta Negro leaders are of course even more graphic in their analysis of the "power structure," and the elite itself is surprisingly frank in its admission of the existence of a small decision-making group. To explain why his town has enjoyed a greater amount of industrial development than surrounding Delta cities, a newspaper editor told me: "Well, the people who run ——— have been very progressive, on the whole. In the Thirties a bond issue failed, because the planters feared an upheaval of their labor. But then minds changed. Now, Rosedale has been controlled by Walter Sillers and a banker, and they have not been progressive. They want to keep it closed and controlled. But in ———— no one family has dominated. The city government is honest, because it is controlled by men of wealth. And these people, I guess you'd call them the power structure, have been *progressive* people." Such rhetoric, although strikingly different from the talk in the Midwest or in Mississippi hill towns, is typical for the Delta.

In the Delta, the elite of wealth is made up of the same families who form the elites of power and status. On a national scale, some of them would be categorized merely as "upper-middle" in status, though some are multimillionaires, but they determine public and private policy in their home communities; when "upper class" and "power structure" are used later in the book, it is specifically to this group that I refer.

Whites, Negroes, and Chinese Immigration

Even before the first Chinese sojourner entered the state, Chinese were the subject of much speculation by members of the upper class, which had special interest in promoting Chinese immigration. During Reconstruction in Mississippi (1866–1876), there was great need for labor in the Delta to clear and drain the land and build the plantations. During this period, therefore, Negroes were brought into the Delta from surrounding counties. And also at this time a continuous discussion began about the alleged necessity for importing other labor. From 1865 to World War I, but particularly during the Reconstruction decade, immigration schemes and proposals were frequently debated. There was more involved, however, than mere need of working bodies. *Negro* bodies were specifically at issue.

Negroes were voting during those years, of course — voting Republican. Republican rule lasted in Mississippi until the resignation of Governor Adelbert Ames in 1876, and during the decade before that date, Democratic attempts to get political control grew more and more violent. The Negro was clearly a political enemy, although an economic necessity. Furthermore, even his economic availability was less secure than it had been: besides voting, the Negro's primary new freedom was that of motion, and there was indeed considerable moving about from place to place, away from the most odious planters, after every harvest season. This was in fact the most galling thing to the planter, for in order to hold his croppers, the planter now had to take account, in some measure, of their reactions to his policies and accordingly had to mitigate those policies.[9] Having to take account of blacks as persons rather than as things struck particularly hard at the "subhuman" rationale for Southern slavery, so recently ended. The major emphasis, therefore, was on *white* immigration, and the increasing concentration of Negroes in the Delta was viewed highly ambiguously, as economically necessary but possibly suicidal politically.[10]

In 1869 an immigration convention met in Memphis. The problem was baldly stated by William M. Burwell in an article in *De Bow's Review,* the leading journal of commerce in the South, in July of that year: "We will state the problem for consideration. It is: *To retain in the hands of the whites the control and direction of social and political action, without impairing the content of the labor capacity of the colored race.* We assume that the effort to restrain the political influence of the colored race in the South . . . has failed."[11] Planters' associations and others made numerous attempts at obtaining European and Yankee white immigration, and a few groups actually did come to the state,[12] but Southerners seemed to realize that they could not lure many whites in, at least not as sharecroppers on the economic level of Delta Negroes. And so, since white labor could not be found and black labor was proving troublesome, the solution seemed to be Orientals, as specified by the editor of the Vicksburg *Times:* "Emancipation has spoiled the negro [*sic*], and carried him away from fields of agriculture. Our prosperity depends entirely upon the recovery of lost ground, and we therefore say let the Coolies come, and we will take the chance of Christianizing them."[13]

Newspapers printed many editorials and letters, and planters organized several conventions in an effort to secure Chinese immigration to the Mississippi-Arkansas-Louisiana cottonlands, during Reconstruction and again in 1879, during the "exodus" of Negroes from Mississippi to Kansas. Thus, already, before the first Chinese even set foot in the Delta, his position was intricately tied to the continuing and unequal struggle between whites and Negroes in the state.[14] Powell Clayton, Reconstruction Governor of Arkansas, observed this accurately: "Undoubtedly the underlying motive for this effort to bring in Chinese laborers was to punish the negro [*sic*] for having abandoned the control of his old master, and to regulate the conditions of his employment and the scale of wages to be paid him." [15] The Vicksburg *Times,* then a supporter of Oriental labor for the South, was equally frank in the admission that the move was aimed at the Negro. Writing about the anticipated arrival of several hundred Chinese coolies on a Mississippi River steamboat (a false rumor, incidentally), the *Times* had this to say: "Our colored friends who have left the farm for politics and plunder, should go down to the *Great Republic* today and look at the new laborer who is destined to crowd the negro [*sic*] from the American farm." [16] The apolitical noncitizen coolie, it was thought, would be a step back toward the more docile labor conditions of slavery times and would also destroy all arguments about the indispensability of Negro labor to the Southern way of life.[17] Chinese immigration was encouraged as a means of increasing white political power by displacing voting Negroes; for the Chinese, it was expected, would not vote, as he did not in California. And finally, the "Chinaman" would not only himself supply a cheaper and less troublesome work force but in addition his presence as a threatening alternative would intimidate the Negro into resuming his former docile behavior.

It will be apparent throughout this book that the course of Chinese life in Mississippi has been continuously influenced by the fact that the Chinese have lived in the middle of a polarized segregation system. We have seen that the requirements of that system led in the first place to the pressure for their introduction; but more than that — the call for Chinese as replacements for Negro sharecroppers meant that they would be defined as the equals in status of the race they were to displace. Furthermore, the emphasis (in letters, news columns, and editorials) upon the docility and apoliticality of the Chinese points up the fact that the Chinese were expected to shun politics completely and that political rights were not to be extended to them. Their alleged docility and their noncitizen status made them desirable immigrants precisely because it augured that they could be controlled with even greater ease than could the Negro. Their power and status in society, accordingly, would be even lower. It would not be an auspicious beginning.

The propaganda campaign for Chinese immigration, which occupied some newspaper editorial columns for months, produced only a trickle of migrants, however. The first Chinese in the state did apparently come in response to planters' solicitations. On August 12, 1870, the Jackson *Semi-Weekly Clarion* reprinted a *Bolivar Times* report that Chinese coolies were working on a plantation in the southern part of the state: "Messrs. Ferris and Estell, who are cultivating on the Hughs place, near Prentiss, recently imported direct from Hong Kong, a lot of Chinese, sixteen in number, with whom as laborers, they are well pleased." Other planters in Mississippi, Arkansas, and Louisiana were also using Chinese farm laborers. They recruited immigrants directly from Hong Kong or promised employment to Chinese already working in New Orleans.[18] By 1880 the United States census lists fifty-one Chinese in Mississippi, almost all in Washington County, probably a marked underenumeration (see Table 3).

Whether the present Chinese population stems from these first pioneers is not entirely clear. Pao Yun Liao, a Chinese sociology student from Arkansas, has implied that the Chinese in that state are related to the immigrants brought in by planters long ago.[19] Although the present Chinese residents of the Delta have no verbal tradition of descent from recruited plantation laborers, several Chinese sources independently gave to me the same account of the first Chinese residents in Mississippi whom they know to be connected with their

Table 3. Chinese Population, Mississippi Delta, 1880–1970[a]

Year	Total population	Chinese
1880	187,700	51
1900	367,400	183
1920	394,200	322
1940	479,700	743
1960[b]	409,300	1145
1970	341,100	

Source: The *United States Census of Population* for the respective years. Especially in earlier years, the figures are probably somewhat lower than the actual number of Chinese in the Delta. In addition, persons of mixed Chinese-Negro parentage would be classified "Negro" and would not appear in Chinese totals, except in a few cases.

[a] See Table 1 for a definition of the area included in the Mississippi Delta. All Chinese totals include Vicksburg, even though it is not in the Delta, strictly speaking; total population figures include part of Warren County but exclude Vicksburg.

[b] In addition, there were in 1960 about 900 Chinese in counties adjacent to the Delta, as follows: Arkansas (Delta counties only), 578; Louisiana (Delta counties), 48; Shelby County, Tennessee, 282.

group. According to them, several Chinese men were working on sugarcane plantations and "shrimpfarms" in Louisiana after work ended on the transcontinental railroad in 1869. An oversupply of workers prompted eight or nine to book passage on a steamboat to Greenville, to work for a plantation owner near Stoneville in Washington County. The planter did not pay them what they had been promised, so as soon as they could they opened tiny stores, first in Sunflower, Mississippi, and then in Greenville and elsewhere.

I believe this story, but I doubt that these eight or nine

initial settlers antedate the plantation work gangs; other evidence would set the date for their entry at about 1875.[20] But even if the present Chinese inhabitants of the Delta are not related to the first labor recruits, they do trace their settling to other pioneers, also originally sharecroppers, who entered Mississippi in the same decade, and both groups entered the Delta as farm laborers, in competition with Negroes for what were defined as Negro jobs. Despite the repeated efforts to promote Chinese immigration very few Chinese were actually brought in. There were several reasons for this. Chinese labor did not prove superior on the farm to Negro labor, nor was it cheaper, especially when the cost of importation was included. Moreover, the Chinese themselves had no interest in remaining sharecroppers once they perceived that the planters had no intention of treating them fairly.

Finally, in 1876 the major premise of the immigration movement was destroyed by what Kirwan calls the "revolution" of that year,[21] when white-supremacist Democrats ousted, by fraud and violence, the Reconstruction government of Adelbert Ames. In that year the political power of the Negro in Mississippi was effectively destroyed, and Negro social and economic rights went into a steady decline for the next several decades. As a result, planters came to prefer Negro labor to any other kind, since Negroes worked harder, could be fired or disciplined with greater ease, and could be taken advantage of, financially, with little fear of retribution.[22] Except for sporadic importation of Italians in the early years of this century, and infrequent use of Mexican migrant workers in subsequent years, the planters organized no more immigrant schemes, for Chinese or anyone else, after the Reconstruction period.[23]

Origin and Orientation of the Chinese

The early Chinese in Mississippi were not true immigrants, intending to become permanent settlers in a new homeland, but were sojourners, temporary residents in a strange country, planning to return to their homeland when their task was accomplished. Like the overwhelming majority of all Chinese immigrants to the United States, the Mississippi Chinese came from the Sze Yap or Four Counties district southwest of Canton in South China, and they spoke Cantonese Chinese, mostly in rural village dialects. South China, especially Kwangtung and Fukien provinces, developed rather differently from the rest of China over the past two centuries. Commercially it was more complex, with small mercantile enterprises and trading and industrial activities in each village; it had a higher population concentration, greater commercial sophistication, and a history of much more contact with foreign traders — Japanese, European, Arabic, and American — than other parts of China.

Park has stressed that acculturation of newcomers actually begins even before they arrive, in the communities from which they leave, for there they receive letters, visits, money, and an interpretation of the new land from others of the village who have already left. The villages of South China near Canton emphasize the emigration of young male adults as a customary means of adding to family fortunes and success. These communities are clear examples of this process of pre-departure socialization, and as China has increasingly come to confront Western ideas over the past century, South China has often been in the forefront of change. It has been South China, and not the whole of the nation, which for centuries has sent many millions of traders and emigrants out to all areas of the world — to Latin America, South Africa, the United States, and above all to Southeast Asia.

Besides the region, it is also important to ascertain the strata — the occupational and educational background — of the Chinese who emigrated to Mississippi. In an excellent study of these emigrant communities, Ta Chen notes that "the majority of the inhabitants depend for their living in part on remittances that come from members of the family who are abroad," and that such families are substantially better off economically than families or villages without emigrant support.[24] His analysis indicates that the emigrants, even the initial labor recruits, were not from the lowest classes of poor peasantry. That they were not from the landed gentry is evident too, for this class had no need to emigrate and did not do so (until 1948). Furthermore, the Mississippi Chinese admit that in China they were mostly illiterate and could speak no Mandarin. Almost all adults can now read Chinese, but many learned after they left China. Adult Delta Chinese still manifest a marked inferiority complex toward those other Chinese who are more educated, speak Mandarin, or do stem from a higher stratum in China.[25] Finally, their admitted rural origin also indicates a non-gentry background, for the rural-urban split in South China was also partly a peasant-gentry division.[26] Thus the Delta Chinese probably came from peasant and artisan families who because of their earlier emigrant connections were better off than the mass of rural Chinese but who were clearly not in the landlord class. Within these families, the individuals who left were probably those least well off. Most had little business background but were oriented toward independent business as a means of future advancement.

Many came directly to Mississippi, at first as labor recruits and later as relatives of already established merchants; others went first to California, Chicago, or other areas of the United States. Except for the initial group, in the 1870's, the Chinese did not arrive in Mississippi without resources. Some came with enough capital to open a small grocery on their own. More often, a relative or friend already established in the Delta sponsored the newcomer and provided a place for him to work and stay. Such favors implied that the sponsor was well-established and influential in his new home and thus increased his status back in his native country.

Almost all of the incoming Chinese were young male adults. Their families and their orientation remained in China. Their duty in the new country was to make money, send some home to help support the family, and accumulate some so as to start an independent business and make more money. In a few years, the sojourner hoped to save enough to make a journey back to China, remain for a few months, take a bride, and begin a family. Then after returning to Mississippi he would continue to work and send money home, accumulating for subsequent visits. Eventually he planned to return to China, to retire in the bosom of his family and friends, as a rather wealthy man, and to be buried in Chinese soil.[27]

Most Chinese families were reluctant to allow their sons' wives to go abroad. In part, this reluctance stemmed from the hostage value of the wife and children; as long as his family remained in China, the sojourner could probably be counted upon to remain dutiful in his financial obligations and to return eventually to his homeland.[28] In addition, United States immigration regulations made it extremely difficult to bring Chinese females into this country, and in many cases forced a man's family to remain in China. As a result, a sort of international extended family pattern developed. This pattern retarded assimilation, for when a grocer sent for his son, age twelve or fifteen, he received a Chinese boy, far less Americanized than himself. Therefore the usual conflicts between child and parent over the old ways of life were slow to develop, because the child was less acculturated than the adult. A second- or third-generation sojourner might be only a first-generation immigrant.

Thus American immigration regulations, in conjunction with already established Chinese emigration patterns, were major factors causing the sojourning orientation to persevere long after it might otherwise have died away. So were the restrictions, both legal and traditional, which Mississippi placed in the way of full participation by Chinese in the institutional life of their new homeland. And of greatest importance was the negative evaluation of the Chinese by the Mississippi white society in which they lived. From their first entry to the state, Chinese were classified with Negroes. The disgust that a few old-time white residents express even today about the Chinese, disgust regarding their innate racial and human identity, is still a potentially shattering experience. For many decades, therefore, there was good reason, for their own psychological well-being, for the Chinese to look to relatives in China for their status definition.[29] And so the sojourning orientation persisted for a long time among the Mississippi Chinese, continuing with gradually diminishing intensity until World War II.

This attitude of sojourning, rather than of permanent residence, had profound repercussions on the way of life and thought of the Chinese immigrant in the Delta: "He [the sojourner] clings to the culture of his own ethnic group as in contrast to the bicultural complex of the marginal man. Psychologically, he is unwilling to organize himself as a permanent resident in the country of his sojourn." [30] The sojourner had a cultural basis for self-esteem which was independent of the judgment of his Mississippi peers. As long as his occupational choice did not give rise to actual resistance or opposition from whites, he was far less affected by their evaluation of him or his occupation than he was by the evaluation of his family and peers in China. If he fulfilled his familial duties, sent money home regularly, and was successfully establishing his own independent business, he was meeting their requirements for esteem.

Economic success, rather than local social status, was the primary goal of the sojourner. He was therefore interested in enterprises promising rapid monetary return. Plantation sharecropping was not such an enterprise. A sharecropper had difficulty breaking even, let alone accumulating capital and sending money home to China. And Chinese sharecroppers faced particularly intensive handicaps. As we have seen, the planters imported them during Reconstruction to obtain a source of labor which could be exploited even more effectively than Negroes. Note the tone of the following report of one of the first planters to utilize Chinese laborers: "They are . . . easily controlled . . . Captain Ferris thinks that they are par excellence as a laborer, and [can] be made to work without the interference of a bureau or the military." [31]

At least in some instances, the Chinese were so angry at their working conditions that they attempted to revolt. The

Jackson *Clarion,* an advocate of Chinese immigration in 1870, had done an about-face by 1873. Reprinting copy from the New Orleans *Times,* it reported: "Over 200 Chinamen were brought from China to this state . . . we think there are none left on the plantations at the present time." In several cases, the account went on to say, planters shot and killed or wounded workers who had become unruly; in another instance the labor gang was so enraged by the false promises that had been given them that when the Chinese agent who had initiated the transaction visited the plantation, they attempted to lynch him.[32]

Powell Clayton sums up the situation concisely: "The efforts to utilize Chinese labor proved a disastrous failure. Planters soon learned that after all the negroes [*sic*], as laborers in the cotton fields, were better in all respects than the men of any other race, and in a little while the Chinamen sagaciously learned the purposes for which they were introduced. I do not know of a single plantation that is now [1915] worked in whole or in part by Chinese labor." [33] Quite obviously, the plantation system did not allow Chinese or other sharecroppers to succeed economically. Therefore the Chinese moved off the plantation as soon as they could. The occupation they then entered, their extraordinary concentration in it, and their relative success form the focus of the next chapter.

Economic Success   2

The Beginning of the Chinese Grocery

Oriented toward economic success, having left the plantation, the Chinese did not confront a wide range of occupational alternatives. In other regions of the United States, Chinese were becoming launderers or domestic servants, but that
option was closed in Mississippi, for here again Chinese
would be competing against Negro labor on a black wage
scale. Indeed, there could be little possibility of making a living from the spending patterns of the small white population.
Conversely, as the analysis of plantation sharecropping indicates, Negroes had little money to spend for anything, except
perhaps food and clothing. And so, as soon as he could accumulate even a small amount of capital, through extremely
frugal living and eating habits, the Chinese sojourner rented
a tiny store, usually a single room, and sold groceries from it.
In back was an even smaller room in which he ate and slept.

It is impossible to say when the first Chinese grocery was
established in Mississippi, but it was probably in 1872 or
1873. By 1881, Chinese names appear as landowners in tax
records of the business district of Rosedale, in Bolivar
County. The early Chinese store was not self-service but had
either two parallel rows of counters with space for the cus-

tomers between or a single large counter facing the door. In those days, before refrigeration and modern store displays, only a few staple items — "meat, meal, and molasses" — were carried. An initial capital investment of as little as $100 sufficed in early decades; even as recently as 1940 a newcomer could open a grocery store with only $400 in cash. Wholesalers would sometimes stock the store on credit, especially if the merchant had relatives who would vouch for him, and allow him to pay them back a portion per month for the first several months of operation.

The clientele consisted almost entirely of poor Negroes who worked on the nearby plantations or at menial jobs in town. The situation was in some ways quite incredible: Delta Negroes, many of whom had never been farther from home than the nearest town, encountering a visitor of strange appearance and customs, from across the globe, speaking no English. In some stores a pointer stick was positioned at the counter, and the customer could point to the items he wanted, the grocer's English being limited to the price. When the wholesaler came around at month's end, he found that the merchant had without fail saved the last package of each item he sold, so that he could present it to demonstrate to the salesman what he wanted to reorder. Other wholesalers developed a working relationship with their customers such that they restocked the shelves themselves for the merchant, almost without verbal communication; still others learned to understand a bit of Chinese.

In those years, as we have seen, most plantations operated their own commissaries. Negroes from plantations without commissaries, however, were given cash or credit slips instead of commissary "furnish" during the summer months. Furthermore, even on plantations with commissaries, most croppers had some money to spend during the months not on furnish, especially from harvest to Christmas. From these sources, and from town Negroes and workers who were paid cash to clear new land, the clientele of the Chinese was built up. In other words, the rural population was not completely locked in by the furnish system, and enough cash purchasing power existed so that the Chinese merchant could earn a living. And of course, a "living" for the Chinese in those early years did not usually mean much, for they lived behind their stores, kept their families in China, and had almost no living expense beyond the minimal cost of their own food.

Nevertheless, they were engaged in a rugged undertaking. It is important to understand that even today, in the smaller towns, Southern justice operates with equity only for persons who are within the reference group of those who operate it, that is, for the people in the power structure and their status equals.[1] Before World War I and even much later, this group certainly did not include the Chinese. Without legal recourse, the Chinese grocer could be taken advantage of by customers, other businessmen and power structure members, and by common thieves.[2] Furthermore, credit often had to be extended in order for business to be transacted at all during the lean winter and early spring months, when harvest money was long gone and few odd jobs were available to the farm workers. But credit risks were great, because many planters defrauded their tenants. Finally, although by establishing grocery stores the Chinese had, to be sure, evaded the strictures of direct competition for employment within the black wage scale, they were left in the unenviable position of trying to make a living from the spending money of a population with extremely low buying power per capita.

Most merchants were successful, however. They were prosperous enough, in fact, to encourage male relatives to come in from China and from other parts of the United States, because the economic situation in Mississippi was so promising. From time to time some Chinese tried other occupations, including laundering, and other locations, including several Mississippi hill towns, but almost always they drifted back to the Delta and to black-oriented groceries. In 1960, fourteen Delta counties contained 92 percent of all Mississippi Chinese, and the Delta alone had more Chinese than any other area or state of the South, excluding Texas. In some Delta

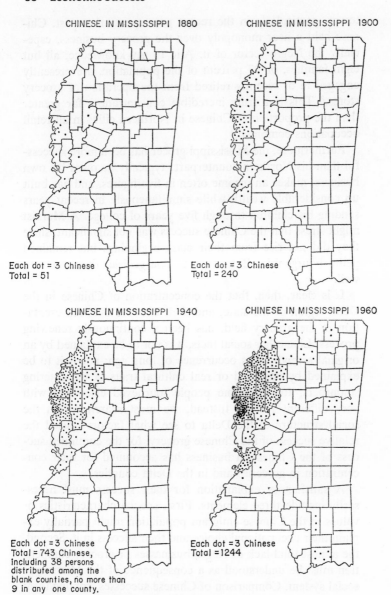

CHINESE IN MISSISSIPPI 1880

CHINESE IN MISSISSIPPI 1900

Each dot = 3 Chinese
Total = 51

Each dot = 3 Chinese
Total = 240

CHINESE IN MISSISSIPPI 1940

CHINESE IN MISSISSIPPI 1960

Each dot = 3 Chinese
Total = 743 Chinese,
including 38 persons
distributed among the
blank counties, no more than
9 in any one county.

Each dot = 3 Chinese
Total = 1244

4. Chinese in Mississippi, 1880–1960.

towns, particularly in the recent pre-supermarket past, Chinese held a near monopoly over the grocery business, especially the Negro sector of it. And to my knowledge, all but eight families, or 97 percent of the population, are presently engaged in or recently retired from the operation of grocery stores.[3] This is a truly incredible concentration, far greater than the proportion of Chinese in Northern cities in all retail occupations combined.[4]

Furthermore, the Mississippi grocer has been more successful than his Northern counterpart: typically he owns his own business, makes an income often in five figures, and has built up considerable wealth while simultaneously in recent years sending his children through five years of college. A Marxist might stress that the Chinese success was not significant, since they did not rise from their class beginnings but remained petite bourgeoisie. But as petite bourgeoisie, they did very well.

It is clear, then, that the concentration of Chinese in the Delta region of the state, and their extreme over-representation in the grocery field, has been a continuously renewing process. Like other social facts, it is not to be explained by an original serendipitous occurrence of long ago; nor is it to be explained by imagined or real cultural traits of the entering sojourners, for the same people journeyed elsewhere with very different results. Instead, we must search within the social structure of the Delta to see what factors caused the relative success of the Chinese grocery, for the continued success of the Chinese in business has accounted for their concentration in groceries and in the Delta counties.

A satisfactory explanation for their success must necessarily include three elements. First, special characteristics or values in the Chinese emigrant population might partially explain their occupational choice and their success in it. Second, the almost total lack of Negro businesses or grocery competition must be understood as a consequence of the Mississippi social system. Comparison of Chinese successes, coming from outside the system, and Negro failures, from within it, should highlight certain effects that the system has upon the people who live in it. And third, the white population in the Delta did not present a formidable adversary to the beginning Chinese merchant in his struggle for business. Segregation seems to have made the dominant caste almost as incapable of real business success as it has the subordinate population. As an ideology, segregation has not operated in any simple way to rationalize and facilitate the efficient exploitation of the oppressed Negroes by the white minority. Instead, it has created a profitable niche for the Chinese which neither blacks nor whites could take advantage of. Here again, then, analyzing the reasons for the success of the Chinese will supply insight into important aspects of the Mississippi segregation system.

Chinese Causes of Chinese Success

We have already taken notice of the particular drive of sojourning Chinese in general toward independently owned retail trade establishments. I found this tradition strongly in evidence among Delta Chinese. Indeed, Ryan's description of it as manifested among the Chinese in Java could be translated to the Mississippi setting without error even in detail: "The crucial requirement . . . is that each adult male should have his own business in which the responsibility for risks of loss and the possibilities for profit are borne by the individual . . . Persons who work for others . . . fall into the lower rungs of the prestige scale and have, in actuality, little voice in community affairs." [5] The Chinese came, then, from a value system that explicitly sanctioned hard work in commercial enterprises as an efficient and honorable means of advancement. Their economic independence allowed a happy mix of personal and business life. Since the family lived in or behind the store, living expenses were very low, and family members formed the store work force without destroying family solidarity. Therefore, although manual and farm labor was also a part of the Chinese experience both in South China and in the United States, we should not be surprised that Chinese immigrants in Mississippi gravitated toward independently owned businesses. And their drive toward business must be accounted a strength partly explaining their business success.[6]

Of greater importance, however, was a much more tangible asset possessed by the Chinese merchant — his tight family structure. After the initial entrance of Chinese in the late 1800's, a new Chinese immigrant usually would have been sent for by a relative already successfully operating a Delta grocery. Upon arrival, he would be taken in and put to work in the relative's store, thus accumulating a priceless legacy of business experience, a legacy unavailable to at least the Negro sector of his potential competition. Then, after he had learned sufficient rudiments of English and store operation, he would be set up in his own business by a combination of savings, a loan from his relatives, and credit from wholesalers, with whom he had become acquainted during his "training period." [7]

White wholesalers and Chinese grocers emphasized in interviews with me, citing many specific examples, the excellent credit rating of Chinese merchants. In the few instances when a storeowner did default on a debt, his relatives made good the loss directly to the wholesalers. The reputation all Chinese thereby gained for financial impeccability was a crucial asset for getting the credit lines needed to open a new store. The business other Chinese groceries transacted with a wholesaler meant that personal ties, bolstered by the implied threat of possible boycott, provided added incentives for the wholesaler to do business with and extend credit to the neophyte. Since more than four-fifths of the Delta Chinese population are included under the headings of only six family names, it is clear that most Chinese had a formidable number of potential family connections to draw upon.

The extended-family organization of the Chinese thus supplied two crucial needs of the new businessman: experience and capital. But it is obvious that these strengths did not specifically presuppose success in the grocery business. The same assets would have been called into play had the Chinese specialized in any other retail undertaking or even in farm operation; therefore they are not directly relevant to an explanation of concentration and success in grocery retailing. The same is true of a final strength, which at first might appear to be a liability: the lack of close personal ties between the Chinese merchant and his prospective black clientele. This is an asset, as will become clear later in the section on Negro liabilities, because in the context of Delta Negro society, with many families always on the edge of immediate want, personal ties mean personal claims. The lack of such ties meant that decisions about credit extension could be made on a purely business basis; unlike many smalltown businesses, therefore, especially those run by Negroes, the Chinese grocery was differentiated, as a business enterprise, from the grocer's networks of personal and familial claims and obligations.

The factors we have delineated — a tradition of independent business operation, a tight and useful extended-family network, and a lack of personal ties to others in the society — clearly represent assets in the operation of Delta grocery stores by the Chinese. However, as a result of their immigrant background the Chinese had to overcome several negative factors. Unfamiliarity with the language and customs of the new land; little understanding of the legal system, coupled with a historic aversion to its use; no political power and very little initial informal influence — these are major handicaps to any prospective businessman. Positive factors associated with the Chinese background thus do not begin to explain the extraordinary concentration of Chinese in groceries and in the Delta. For that explanation, we shall have to look at the situation of the other two races in the system. This is obvious; after all, in other parts of the United States, Chinese immigrants with identical geographic and class origins showed no comparable occupational clustering. It seems almost as if there was a ready-made niche for the Chinese grocer in the Delta, a slot which existed for reasons intrinsic to the social system, and which for similar reasons could not be filled by persons produced by that system.

Causes of Negro Failure and Chinese Success

In most Delta towns, blacks are conspicuously absent from ownership or management of grocery stores. This is not a result but rather a cause of Chinese domination; it is as true where there are few Chinese merchants as where there are many. Yazoo City, for example, a town of about 11,000, has only one Chinese merchant, but it has only two Negro-owned groceries of any consequence. By way of contrast, Greenville boasts five or six fairly substantial Negro-owned groceries, although it has for decades supported about fifty Chinese stores.

Black businesses in the Delta are strikingly confined to three service lines: beauty and barber shops, undertaking, and cafes and beer parlors. These are the service areas which, because they would presuppose intimate physical or social contact between races, are shunned by Mississippi whites. Only in areas of dense Negro population, such as Negro ghettoes in the larger Delta towns, and especially in Mound Bayou, an all-black town in Bolivar County, are there exceptions to this rule. In Mound Bayou three reasonably large and modern Negro-owned groceries do exist, along with service stations and other small businesses. But beyond the narrow areas in which, due to black residential concentration or white occupational avoidance, blacks enjoy a monopoly, their successful business enterprises are incredibly rare.

Delta Caucasians still assert, of course, that blacks are innately and constitutionally incapable of the discipline and skills required for success in business. In fact, however, the reasons for Negro business incompetence — reasons which explain why he has represented no real competitive threat to the Chinese grocer — are quite different.

First, unlike the Chinese, the Negro brings with him no prior history of a "push" toward independent business enterprise and no particular cultural legitimation or sanction for such an occupation. In fact, the opposite is true. Elements in African culture relevant to lines of work or goals within work were destroyed by American slavery, long before Reconstruction. Therefore, to a degree beyond other immigrant groups, the Negro has been influenced by the definition of high-status occupations prevailing in the culture around him and in the social groups above him. That definition has not favored owner-managed retail businesses. Negroes in America have not looked primarily to independent business as a major vehicle for status advancement. Mississippi Delta blacks, in particular, do not aim toward business. They have taken over from Delta whites the notion that neither hard work in business nor "waiting on" or catering to the customer are "honorable" tasks.[8] Like whites, therefore, some black businessmen make every effort to employ help to do the actual work of waiting on customers, stocking, and delivery, while they expand the paperwork and the negotiating with wholesalers far beyond the time required for its efficient execution. The exceptions, the black businessmen who really do put in "Chinese hours," are clearly eccentric. Other Negroes regard them so, and in conversation the businessmen go out of their way to justify their behavior as a preferred personal idiosyncrasy. And in a circular process, since there have been few Negro businessmen, local or national, to achieve great success and fame from the white or black populations, compared to great status heroes in entertainment, sports, music, and politics, there are few models to legitimate the line of work for newer generations.

A second characteristic of black social structure is also the obverse of a Chinese strength: black families over the past century have been less stable than have Chinese. Moreover, the extended family structure of the Chinese provides would-be merchants with crucial business experience. Working under a relative, the neophyte learns the rudiments of store operation, including the subtle nuances of credit-extension decisions, inventory size, and bargaining with wholesalers. And he is put into contact with the wholesale salesmen, who become familiar with him as a reputable grocer. In contrast, the Negro has no avenue open to him in the business world. Segregation practices completely preclude his learning as an apprentice or assistant in a white-owned store.[9] The essence of occupational segregation is the exclusion of blacks from "white" jobs; thus the only positions in most firms open to Negroes are merely custodial and offer no chance for training, advancement, or meaningful experience. Simultaneously, the Negro is locked in the cycle of not having any black-owned stores of importance in which to begin. In a study of the problem done at Fisk University, Paul K. Edwards notes: "Of 35 Negro grocers interviewed in Nashville during 1929, only 12, or 34.3%, had had any experience either as proprietors of groceries, or as employees in grocery stores, prior to the opening of their present establishments . . . The problem of obtaining an adequate background of practical experience prior to the inauguration of his own enterprise is, perhaps, *the most serious of the Negro merchant's difficulties* . . . The limited number of really successful Negro units in all fields of business endeavor makes it impossible in most cases for the prospective Negro merchant to learn adequately the game in enterprises operated by members of the Negro race." [10] And so the rate of failure of the tiny black-owned grocery is even higher than the rate of failure in small business in general. Usually the store stays open until the capital its owner has saved to go into business with is exhausted; then, defeated, he closes up and goes back to the job he left. Even if he does manage to remain in operation, however, lack of capital from any source will keep his business small and his stock meagre. The Negro merchant has no capital available through stores owned by his relatives, and an entire network of potential sources of capital excludes him, including banks, wholesalers, the Small Business Administration, and the black communities themselves.

Banks, until the last ten years, have not often loaned money to prospective Negro merchants. In part, these decisions have been motivated by sound business practices, as even radical civil rights leaders will admit. The problems of beginning businessmen are always great, and the coupling of Negro inexperience and inadequate capital from private sources has meant that bankruptcy was a likely outcome. And if the business failed, quite probably the bank's equity could not be recovered from the ruins of the enterprise. It is also true, however, that bankers, as members of the white upper class, are interested in and influenced by what white businessmen think of their actions, and white businessmen are not likely to show marked enthusiasm for bankers' assistance in capitalizing competitive black enterprises. And so it is not surprising that bank loans to Negro businesses have been concentrated overwhelmingly in those lines of services restricted traditionally to Negroes — beauty, death, and entertainment and food. "Why don't you open a little cafe, sell some beer . . ." says the banker to a Negro applying for a business loan.

The Small Business Administration, nominally an arm of the federal government, is in fact operated by local economic notables. A Clarksdale banker told me that selections for its decision-making boards are biased toward "upper-class white bankers," who "don't want to make S.B.A. loans through their own banks," even though such loans are partially guaranteed by the federal government. The result is that few S.B.A. loans to beginning businessmen are made in the Clarksdale district; the quota of possible loans is simply not filled.

Wholesalers are also reluctant to extend credit to Negro grocers. Again, this reluctance is based partly on a sound financial assessment of the risks of the situation. Thus, black grocers must usually buy on a cash basis. But still greater obstacles face the black grocer in his relations with white wholesalers. First, he is in competition with larger groceries which, because they exceed a required minimum volume level, can buy from a large wholesale house on a substantially lower "cost-plus" basis. The black grocer thus is caught in a vicious cycle: small volume causes high wholesale costs, which in turn cause high prices, which keep his volume of sales small. Furthermore, the purely business requirement of a minimum volume is intermixed with social considerations which turn it into a tool of oppression which discriminates against Negro merchants. There are several black grocers who could qualify for cost-plus, but they are neither solicited nor admitted to the system; at the same time, white grocers have told me that they are carried on a cost-plus basis despite their failure to meet the monthly volume minimum.

It is becoming increasingly impossible for any small grocery to compete successfully with large supermarkets, however. Most supermarkets in the Delta are independently owned but use a standard name and wholesaler for supply. The independent owner relies upon the wholesaler for initial financing, planning of layout and location, and co-signing the lease. Wholesalers select prospective owners primarily from their existing pool of cost-plus affiliates, a pool which includes no blacks.

To be fair, however, a large part of the credit-capital problem must be laid at the door of the merchant and the black community. Even with regard to the wholesale volume problem, pressure has not been organized and persistent. Several Negroes pointed to a timidity about risk-taking in general as a prime source of black business failures and of their smallness. The Negro merchant wants credit to expand but is often unwilling to put up his own home or other collateral to get it. Also, he intermixes personal and business finances with the opposite outcome from the Chinese: business capital slowly gets drained into personal expenses, without an accounting knowledge of it. As a white banker put it, both the black and the Chinese businessmen may be good technicians, in terms of store ownership and customer relations, but the Negro fails in financial management, estimation of overhead, etc. Therefore financial rather than business woes result and bring an end to the enterprise.

The fault is not only the merchant's, however. Black communities do not constitute milieux which can supply the kind of support required by a beginning businessman. Instances of cooperative stores or even partnerships are quite rare, and the consumer will not even buy from the new enterprise to help it get started. In 1929 in Nashville, Edwards found that 99 percent of all black housewives bought from white-operated stores, and 79 percent bought all their groceries there. Only 29.3 percent [sic] bought *any* groceries from Negro stores, and a tiny 13.5 percent of that group, or 4 percent of the entire sample, gave them their entire trade.[11] The situation in the Mississippi Delta today is the same. Black grocers can count on one hand the number of customers they have who buy all their food, or even a well-rounded selection of it, at their stores.

This extraordinary phenomenon is by no means a result of the limited appeal of the Negro store; in fact, it is much more a cause than a result of that store's small stock and floor space. In turn, the causes of Negro avoidance of black-owned groceries are embedded deep in the segregation system. Through a series of causal processes, the segregated social structure has led to what might be called a "white-dominated psyche," a cultural pattern within black society whereby potential Negro solidarity is undercut by the insidious prestige claimed by white society and culture. There is a marked pattern of jealousy in Delta Negro society. The overwhelming number of blacks know that they personally will not get ahead to any significant degree. As a result, the alienation between the poor majority and the few who are making it is very great, and the poor do not support enterprises whose purpose is to help others advance.

Even less does the Negro middle class shop black. Here the explanation is closely tied in with the caste split between Negro and white. When whites define Negroes as subhuman, to be shunned, this has a massive effect upon the Negro. It presents to him a basic self-definition which is incredibly negative. Writing about the similar racism inherent in African colonialism, Fanon called it "a systematic negation of the other person and a furious determination to deny the other person all attributes of humanity." [12] At the same time, by setting whites up as the higher group, segregation defines them as a reference group whose thoughts are automatically important to the subordinate population, far too important to be ignored. And segregation is backed by a codified set of norms which makes the consequence for an aberrant Negro very serious indeed; ignoring the norms is completely out of the question. The Negro therefore takes over the white view of things, the upper-class white view.[13] So the black man feels contempt (along with respect, of course) for the lower-class white, because the upper-class white does. And so the Negro attempts to emulate white standards of respectability, especially if he is in the black middle class.

I very early discovered, through interviews with blacks of various stations, complex and deep reasons for the apparently inconsequential decision of whether to shop at a Negro-, Chinese-, or white-owned grocery. I asked Negro schoolteachers, college administrators, and others on that status level, whether they shopped in Chinese stores, and they were reluctant to admit they did. They want to "do a little better"; they want to shop at Caucasian stores, because they want to prove they can get service from whites, like the white folks do. To be waited on by a white carryout boy is important to them, as is being handed change by a white clerk. But in all, they receive only a pitiable bit of courtesy. I have watched the white grocers. Most are formal and businesslike in their interaction with Negroes, and Negroes cannot claim much payoff for their sellout.

The situation leads to ironic paradoxes. In Cleveland a Chinese merchant who is curt and even nasty to his Negro customers gets more middle-class trade from Negroes than two nearby Chinese stores which are more friendly.[14] I asked a schoolteacher if she got good service from the discourteous store, and she was proud to claim that she did. "*Educated* Negroes get treated nice there," she said. Once again, the key to understanding this attitude is in the rationale underlying segregation, which treats all Negroes alike as inferiors. To treat them all alike as equals misses the point. Some Chinese merchants feel that they can and must be nasty to the lower-class black in order to get business from the middle class. Being rude to "niggers" sets the Chinese up as a surrogate white, so that it is an achievement to gain his courtesy. Thus Negroes may go back to get it, if they are middle class. It is not satisfying to demand and get courtesy from a black merchant. He has to give it. He has to give it also to any white whom he happens to meet. Black courtesy confers no great distinction. White, and now Chinese, does.

Thus the middle class has no sense of solidarity with the black storeowner. As grocer after grocer reported to me: "Most of my trade is welfare people, old people, poor people. The middle-class Negroes hate to see another Negro get ahead." The black population is split by class differentials and by factions within classes. It is still as the proverb says, "The rich hath many friends, but the poor man hates even his own neighbor." [15]

Besides sellouts for caste reasons and in addition to class jealousies, Negro merchants face a simple lack of trust in their competence and honesty. Many blacks believe what white culture tells them — that Negroes are shiftless and will cheat you and lie to you. They feel confident that they are getting better buys in a white store, even when my own comparative shopping did not confirm it. Negro doctors and dentists face the same problem, and Moench has noted that on Tahiti, natives often buy from a Chinese grocer because they trust him over a native Tahitian.[16]

Yet another obstacle stems from what might appear to be a potential strength: ties and friendships which any Negro grocer is likely to have with his black clientele. Andrew Lind makes the same observation about the Chinese and Negroes in Jamaica: "Unlike the black or coloured populations of Jamaica, who were handicapped as tradesmen by the personal claims of relatives and friends, the immigrant Chinese and Syrians found in trade the one field of economic endeavour in which their alienism was an asset rather than a liability." [17] In short, it is a drawback to be a full member of the social community which includes one's customers. The black grocer, even if he tries to be businesslike, must treat his customers diffusely.[18] He must comply with credit requests or face losing a friend as well as a customer; hence he cannot consider them solely in conjunction with their store trade.[19] This is true especially because the black grocery depends upon the good will its proprietor has built up in the community. Unlike white or even Chinese grocers, the black grocer cannot coerce his customers. He does not get the support of the legal apparatus: justices of the peace will not spend time garnisheeing paychecks for a black merchant. Many observers have pointed out that white abstention from legal regulation of disputes and crimes within the black community works to the detriment of that community; with regard to Negro business the rule is clearly borne out.

The persons who might operate black businesses in the Delta are mostly uneducated, since they came of age before 1945, when Negro schooling was poor to nonexistent. Many of the young males have left the society and are in the North. Those who remain are often precisely the individuals who face extraordinary personal and familial claims and who therefore cannot take risks with capital. Finally, economic success has not been the best route to win safety and approval from Delta whites, and they have directly suppressed successful Negro businesses. In 1937 Dollard observed: "Frequently economic success on the part of a Negro will draw aggressive responses from the whites without his having offended white caste principles at any other point. It would seem, as already noted, that the Negro success itself is perceived as a defiance of white people." [20] David Cohn of Greenville stated this bluntly: "There is room in the Delta only for the Negro who 'stays in his place.' " [21] By 1967, repression was more subtle but still existed; a Negro shoe store owner told me, "If I tried to get trade away from white stores, they would tell the wholesaler to cut me off."

The amazing thing, then, is not that there are so few Negro groceries in the Delta, but that there are any.

Causes of Caucasian Failure and Chinese Success

To expect Delta Negroes to be in command of their own economic enterprises, given the system in which they mature, is hardly reasonable. We might on the other hand predict that Delta whites, who almost by definition have been given the advantages blacks lacked, would enjoy extraordinary success in retail business. But this is not so; on the contrary, native whites have left a vacuum in the field into which came the Chinese (and Italians, Lebanese, and Jews). Mississippi whites have been neither attracted toward nor particularly successful in retail business, and their failure has opened concomitant opportunity to the Chinese to replace them. The explanation of this peculiar result lies in the working out of caste and class relations in the Mississippi social system and affords an opportunity to penetrate that system's social structure and ideology.

Class relations within the white population subtly interact with, reinforce, and are reinforced by caste patterns between white and black. This process can be observed in the social situation of those whites who do compete with the Chinese in "niggertown." In Cleveland, for example, whites operate four or five small groceries in the black part of town, with a predominantly Negro clientele. Their status in the white community is disastrously affected by their occupation. More than one member of the white upper class told me they are depraved and spoke of probable sexual or criminal deviance in their private life. The white establishment has little to do with them, as the following conversation with a Cleveland businessman attests.

> "Nobody *condemns* them for it, but we don't invite 'em to our *homes* and our *social* life — the type of people you're talking about . . . Of course, we *all* sell to nigras.
> ["But there's a big difference, isn't there, between selling to white *and* Negro customers, compared to stores oriented primarily to Negro trade?"]
> "That's right!"

The society editor of a Delta weekly put it this way:

> *"Occasionally* you find a white merchant down there, but they're usually either a Dago or a Jew!
> ["They're not very well thought-of, are they, if they have a store down there?"]
> "Oh no, huh-uh!"

In short, operating close to the caste line wrecks one's position in the white class structure and brings down upon one status threats so severe that, as with Negro status itself, one's very identity as an acceptable member of the human species is endangered. Since most men do want to rise in the estimation of their peers, there is a movement away from purely Negro stores. Whites want to run stores in which their friends and status equals can comfortably shop — stores oriented toward white trade only or toward white *and* Negro trade. No white who can help it is willing to identify himself with the black community. The only persons left selling exclusively to Negroes are those who could not make a go of it selling to whites, and even they claim to be oriented toward both white and Negro. Therefore they treat their occasional white customers royally and show marked discourtesy toward blacks in the presence of whites.

The Chinese, on the other hand, were sojourners in the Delta. While sojourning, their basic standards for defining self-worth emanated from outside the Mississippi system. They were thus relatively impervious to the status attacks against businessmen in black neighborhoods which kept whites from competing with them effectively. Moreover, whites have been more tolerant of the Chinese than of their fellow Caucasians. Since they came from outside the system, their violation of its etiquette rules seemed less threatening. They could get away with actions which would subject native whites to "turncoat" or "nigger-lover" attacks. Thus the Chinese have been free to locate stores right in the heart of Negro areas and to live behind them and keep them open fifteen to eighteen hours a day. And they were willing to define their stores as black-oriented — by location, choice of foodstuffs, and most importantly, by courtesy.[22] As a Negro customer said: "They [Chinese grocers] don't worry the hell out of you about saying 'Mr.' or anything." Or as a grocer himself put it: "We have to treat colored and white all alike. The American money, they don't make special for colored, special for whites." The Chinese did not bother anybody, in other words, while in white milieux blacks must always be on the alert to make proper signs of deference. Emmett Till, it might be remembered, was murdered because he was insufficiently courteous to the proprietor of a small white-run grocery in the Delta, may even have whistled at her.

The low prestige of their job may lead whites to give less than their best to selling to Negroes. Merchants hoping for white customers are likely to be rude to the next black one. In some cases, their bitterness at their near-outcaste position hardens into fierce hatred of the race whose proximity "put" them there, and thus in Cleveland one white grocer is alleged by Negroes to attack black customers without provocation and is reputedly a member of the Ku Klux Klan. This atmosphere of potential terror has been generally absent in Chinese stores, where neither the grocer nor other customers are white.

In addition to the effect the white class system exerted upon the personnel and the style of operation of white-owned groceries, the caste-class system generated an ideology which was markedly unfavorable to business enterprise in general. Delta businessmen are essentially pre-capitalist, almost feudal, in ideology. That is, they are primarily oriented not toward profit-maximization, but toward maintaining and remaining in ordered status positions. Thus Hodding Carter notes that most recent immigrant groups to the South have been extraordinarily successful: "Wherever in the South the venturing aliens have come they have generally prospered out of proportion to their investments, their hopes, and even their talents." [23] And he too traces their success back to the ideological assumptions of white Southerners. "They [the immigrants] practiced a thrift which was foreign to too much of the South. They were not restricted by the traditional distinction between what a white man could and could not do without losing caste." [24]

To this day, Delta whites, even those of lower-middle store-owning rank, exhibit a startling aversion to manual labor or repetitive tasks. Soft-drink routemen, for example, usually take along one or even two black helpers, who handle all the cases while the white discusses the transaction with the storeowner; in the North, such salesmen are usually unaccompanied, and if they need help in unloading, the storeowner himself may supply it. Veblen, as usual, supplies an intriguing insight: "During the predatory culture labor comes to be associated in men's thoughts with weakness and subjection to a master. It is therefore a mark of inferiority, and therefore comes to be accounted unworthy of man in his best estate. By virtue of this tradition labor is felt to be debasing, and this tradition has never died out." [25] In Mississippi the tradition is vastly strengthened by the continuing division of nonmanual and manual labor along racial lines, so that manual labor is avoided as "nigger work." The ideal has been to live as a planter off the work of others. To work hard oneself, and to serve others in trade, has not been considered quite honorable. To serve Negroes predominantly is even less honorable.

This pattern of occupational avoidance is repeated in other racially polarized societies. Silin constructs the same argument to explain Chinese dominance in retail trade in Jamaica. Whites were unwilling to demean themselves by serving their former slaves, he points out; consequently: "Within the social system of Jamaica, there was no value that sanctioned the position of shopkeeping, and, in fact, there was a stigma attached to such work." [26] And to Mississippi, as to the Caribbean, the Chinese came in from outside the system with exactly such values as sanctioned hard commercial work. Their present dominance in retailing, along with that of the Jews, Lebanese, and Italians, is therefore not surprising. By their own social and cultural system, native whites were prevented from maximally exploiting the race they had subordinated.

Implications for a General Theory of Segregation

In the entire area of consumer sales to blacks, Mississippi whites have proved ineffective, leaving the field open to the Chinese and to other ethnic groups. Chinese grocers now earn perhaps twice as much, on the average, as the white median income in the Delta. And over the past thirty years, the commissary on the plantation and the plantation store in town have practically vanished. This inability of whites to profit from their dominance to the fullest extent poses a dilemma for any theory of segregation which is simplistic in its economic determinism. For it is segregation itself and the ideology underlying its etiquette code, enforced by the distinctions within the white class system, which prevent whites from so profiting.

Segregation hampers whites in other ways as well. For example, included in the list of commodities which an upper class can unequally co-opt from a lower, according to Marx, is sex; and in Mississippi the pattern of white males cohabiting with Negro females is too familiar to repeat. However, it occasionally happens that a white man really likes his Negro mistress, falls in love with her, and would want to marry or live with her. He cannot, however. In fact, only with difficulty can he establish her merely as his permanent mistress, even if he is single. Such relationships are condemned by the white establishment, while occasional and casual sexual exploitation is condoned. Attempting to live with one particular Negro woman implies taking her seriously as a person, threatens to bring her into the white caste, and goes against the rationale within segregation that Negroes are subhuman, not to be interacted with on an equal social basis. As a result, in every small town, residents can tell of at least one or two tragic cases of "impossible" love. Sometimes the couple makes a painful and permanent separation; they may elect to move to the North together; or the white male may cross over to the Negro community, an extraordinarily difficult feat. The point is that white norms are not merely flexible appendages to provide convenient rationalizations for whatever practices are in white "interests." As codified in the etiquette rules of segregation, they possess a consistency and potency of their own, and they often prohibit or interfere with the exercise of whites' short-run economic self-interest. Whites are clearly on top, yet they cannot take full advantage of their situation, because the system of rationalizations with which they bolster their position and by which they defend their actions interferes. If a different ideology had developed (and alternatives can be imagined), not dependent upon dehumanizing the Negro, then whites might not have been shackled with the corollary denigration of work itself or of avoidance of Negro-oriented trade.

Whites have more effectively maintained their caste and class dominance via the plantation system than in mercantile occupations. But even here one cannot assert that the system has worked at greatest efficiency for their advancement. Although it has kept them on top with a vastly disproportionate share of gross income, when measured against the development of economic enterprises in other sections of the United States, even including some Mississippi hill counties, it seems unimpressive. Whites controlling industrial and commercial enterprises in other regions quickly outstripped the Delta aristocracy in income and power, and the Delta upper class found that it no longer commanded high respect in Memphis, let alone in New York City. Its children are beginning to migrate outside the region in order to enter occupations which do not exist in Mississippi. The planter's success is as limited in its way as the success of the Chinese grocer within the petty bourgeoisie, and the Delta upper class might even be termed a sort of "petty aristocracy."

The occupational success of the Chinese, in concert with these other examples, demonstrates that segregation must be viewed as a complex ideological system which has assumed its present identity in response to impetuses from several sources over many decades. To be sure, the primary push upon it has come from the economic system, from the need to rationalize and defend its inequities. We shall return to the basic causes of segregation in Chapter 5, in connection with an analysis of the anti-Chinese opposition which segregation fostered. For the present, it will suffice to note that the interrelation between economics and ideology has not been a simple one and that segregation does not operate to bolster and enhance the economic position of the dominant group in any "rational" manner.[27]

Ethnic Occupational Concentrations and the Delta Chinese

A final implication can be drawn from the startling occupational concentration of the Mississippi Chinese. As has been demonstrated, it is a mistake to explain their concentration solely by citing factors in their own cultural heritage. "Common-sense" explanations of the occupational concentrations of various ethnic groups have traditionally been of this kind. So it is that the urban sophistication and respect for learning of European Jews "explains" their tendency in America to excel in medical and academic fields. The tradition of commercial independence among the Chinese allegedly is relevant to their ownership of small shops in the North, while more obscure factors in the Irish temperament and heritage can be brought in to explain their overrepresentation in the administrative bureaucracies of our large cities.

If, however, we attempt to use the same arguments to explain ethnic occupational concentrations of more than half a century ago, quite different premises would be required. Before 1900, for example, the Chinese in America were mostly manual laborers, foresters, miners, and farmers. Many Jews were small businessmen, while still more worked in garment factories and other large industries on the East Coast. And in another few decades, the Chinese will be overwhelmingly concentrated in the natural sciences and in medicine, and all explanations of their new concentration based on national character will have to be revised.

It seems almost true, in fact, that we have been guilty of stereotyping backward, of imputing to the cultural backgrounds of ethnic groups whatever values seem to underlie their present behavior. But the Mississippi Chinese case makes clear that, at least in some instances, "pulls" from the American social structure far outweigh possible "pushes" from the value system brought over by the immigrant with his luggage. For the position of grocer, selling largely to Negroes, was not in competition with important or upper-class whites; hence the Chinese faced few acts of repression, even from competing merchants. Established white grocers valued white customers over black for status reasons. Therefore they were ambivalent about losing some of their Negro trade and were usually not willing to make concessions or organize white support to win it back. The only white grocers who were really hurt by Chinese competition were those dependent upon a Negro clientele, and such merchants were without status in the white community. Thus they were unable to influence the white establishment to take anti-Chinese actions.[28] Whites probably would not have tolerated Chinese competition in other fields; the few Chinese businessmen who have attempted to enter other lines of activity have reported rough sledding, especially at first, to get a white clientele.

In other words, different situations have faced ethnic groups as they entered different parts of the country in different time periods. There seems to be a sorting process at work, so that immigrant groups seek or are channeled toward certain occupations. Most often this channeling probably works to put newcomers into occupations which do not offend established native groups. As Park might have put it, there is a sorting away from competitive jobs toward symbiotic ones. Discussing a book on Oriental immigration, he wrote: "The Japanese, the Chinese, they too would be all right in their place, no doubt. That place, if they find it, will be one in which they do not greatly intensify and so embitter the struggle for existence of the white man." [29] A student of Park's, R. D. McKenzie, went further and asserted that in the early decades of this century, anti-Oriental sentiment on the West Coast was largely directed against the Japanese and not the Chinese; this he asserted was because they were still in visibly competitive occupations, while the Chinese were supplying wants which whites could not or did not cater to.[30]

In short, native Americans avoid or prefer certain occupational groupings. An immigrant or sojourning group like the Chinese, oriented primarily toward economic gain, might move toward jobs whites avoid, so that they can establish a profitable monopoly without retribution from groups whose interests have been threatened. As they become more influenced by American views of occupational prestige, they shift toward high-status occupational choices and are more willing to risk competition.[31] Different ethnic groups have to some degree specialized in certain types of occupations, with advancement based on different principles, such as business acumen and thrift, academic distinction, or cultivation of personal friendship ties. In each case, within the ethnic group the occupations were implicitly ranked in worth or impressiveness, and their occupants were accorded corresponding amounts of status. In other words, the amorphous ideas about what constitutes an honorable or excellent job were codified in the status system, and since different ethnic groups had different codes (caused, in turn, by an interaction of their distinctive cultural and social heritage and the objective situations they each faced here), they have sent out their succeeding generations in radically different proportions to the various occupations in American life. In many cases, the most that can be laid at the feet of the "immigrant heritage" is a general push toward income or toward land, status, power, or popularity. This push, then, in combination with forces in the American occupational structure, determines their occupational distribution.

Identification with Negroes

In its everyday operation, segregation consists of a pervasive system of etiquette.[1] Every movement, every point of contact, every interaction, has carefully detailed alternative sets of norms which can be applied to it, depending upon the race of the other party. Biracial segregation forms a complete set of definitions, expressing and codifying the relationship of dominance and subservience. In addition, several related assertions are expressed by American segregation. Some rules are based on the belief that Negroes are subhuman, or at least subwhite, in their innate capacities for learning and "civilization." Others express notions that they are unclean or promiscuous and thus require rigid social and spatial separation. Many of these corollaries are mutually contradictory, but since they are invoked in different situations their contradictions can be ignored.[2] In all cases the prescribed actions do express the basic superior-inferior relation between white and Negro. Whites who become "too familiar" with blacks are subtly corrected,[3] and Negroes who presume too much upon the friendship of Caucasians may be roughly brought up short. There is no provision in such a system for a third racial group. When a Chinese merchant attempts to use a hospital, send his children to school, or get a haircut, or when he happens to encounter white neighbors on a street corner, the whites must decide which set of rules is applicable, implying by their decision that his racial status is "black" or "white." [4]

From their first entry to the state, the Chinese were defined as status equals of Negroes. Their subsequent occupational role — living in the Negro areas and selling groceries almost exclusively to blacks — did little to change that definition in the minds of the white populace. The Greenville planter, William Alexander Percy, included a passage on the Delta Chinese in his autobiographical sketch of Delta society, *Lanterns on the Levee,* published in 1941; in it, through innuendo and false information as well as by direct assessment, he vividly indicates the low esteem in which the white aristocracy held the Chinese before World War II: "Small Chinese storekeepers are almost as ubiquitous as in the South Seas. Barred from social intercourse with the whites, they smuggle through wives from China or, more frequently, breed lawfully or otherwise with the Negro. They are not numerous enough to present a problem — except to the small white storekeeper — but in so far as I can judge, they serve no useful purpose in community life: what wisdom they may inherit from Lao-tse and Confucius they fail to impart. Not infrequently they are indicted for crimes of violence occurring among themselves." [5]

In the same year, Percy's estimation was confirmed by a white sociologist, Robert W. O'Brien, in the only published sociological study of the Delta Chinese: "As the number of Chinese in the Delta increases it will become more difficult to maintain an intermediate position between the Negro on one hand and the whites on the other." [6] O'Brien predicted that the position of the Chinese would eventually merge completely with that of the Negro. Although his prediction was disproved in record time, his evaluation of the status of the Chinese before 1940 was accurate.

Relations with Negroes

Although Chinese were assigned a near-Negro position and had no more legal protection or political influence than Delta blacks, it must be made clear that neither whites nor blacks quite thought of them *as* Negroes. Usually, the Chinese merchant kept somewhat aloof from his black neighbors. In addition to racial, cultural, and linguistic differences, the Chinese were soon in an occupational class higher than that of all but a few Delta Negroes. A certain feeling of fellowship did develop, however. In those early days in the Delta, the Chinese grocery quickly became much more than a business establishment. In front of it usually stood a rude bench on which people could sit and watch the afternoon pass; inside, there were other places to sit and talk. The store became a lunchroom as well. Town laborers, and on Saturday rural sharecroppers, came in to buy and eat sardines, crackers, and soft drinks. Almost all of the Chinese relied on a continuous clientele of regular customers who spent large parts of the day and small sums of money in the grocery. Some grocers sold wieners and rice and other hot dishes, in addition to the usual staple items. And in the small rural service-center towns, where all stores are located on a single main business block, the Chinese grocery became the place to meet friends, drink a beer, or leave children while doing errands.

In some ways the Chinese acted as middlemen between white and black. Their entry into the system coincided with the erosion of the old semifeudal nonmonetary relationship of planter to tenant. And as white-black relations became more commercialized, the Chinese helped Negroes make the transition.[7] They provided essential services to illiterate and commercially unsophisticated rural blacks, such as interpreting and assisting them with Social Security forms and letters; in some cases they posted bond or vouched for long-term customers in minor legal difficulties. Most important, by extending credit more widely and more flexibly than white-owned stores, they gave the Negro wage-earner something of a cushion against the vagaries of the employment markets. Finally, they tailored their store operation to a population with little spending money and scant means of mobility. In small Chinese groceries customers can even today purchase one egg, two cigarettes, a postage stamp, pay their gas bill, and receive a telephone call. That all these services in the long run produce greater profit for the merchant does not lessen their importance.

The Chinese stores became, in fact, the only integrated milieux in the Delta. Negroes and working-class whites could sit around, on separate but equal Coke cases to be sure, and drink beer. In Yazoo City and other towns, Chinese groceries provided the place where whites met and recruited Negro day-labor.

Besides these general relations with the black community as a whole, Chinese grocers got to know a few Negroes more personally. Merchants often hired Negro women to clean the store and help with the customers; these relationships sometimes went beyond formal employer-employee status and became permanent. A Chinese man who married a Negro woman in the 1930's put the situation clearly: "Before 1942, the Chinese had no status in Mississippi whatever. They were considered on the same status as the Negro. If a Chinese man *did* have a woman, it *had* to be a Negro." [8] For until about 1943, United States immigration laws made the importation of Chinese females almost impossible. Furthermore, the pattern of sojourning strongly stressed male immigration; after the males had become successful they were to send money home and eventually return and establish their own family in China. The combination of legal prohibition and cultural sanction resulted in the extraordinary sex ratios shown in Table 4. In some decades there were eight or more males for each female in the Chinese population, both in Mississippi and in the United States as a whole. With such a ratio, the occurrence of occasional conjugal relations between Chinese and Negroes is not hard to explain. And in addition to providing a sexual outlet, taking a wife would be good for business — for she could help operate the grocery, and the mar-

Table 4. Male-Female Ratio for Chinese in Mississippi and in the United States

Year	Mississippi Delta	United States
1880	(51 males; 0 females)	21.06
1900	17.3	18.87
1920	3.74	6.95
1940	2.29	2.95
1960	1.35	2.32

Sources: Ratios for the United States were computed from data in Stanford Morris Lyman, *The Structure of Chinese Society in Nineteenth-Century America*, p. 98, for 1880–1940. Data for 1960 and all Mississippi data from *United States Census of Population* for the respective decades.

riage might also solidify the merchant's standing in the black community, on which he depended for a living. He would also have someone from whom to learn English, and he could start his own family.

In some cases the grocer already had a wife and family in Kwangtung, but taking another in Mississippi was not proscribed. For a man to be faithful to his wife, far away in China, during his stay in Mississippi, would require that he be entirely celibate for perhaps three decades, and such faithfulness was neither expected nor particularly commended. As long as the sojourner remained financially faithful, sending money back regularly, and as long as he still planned and promised eventual return, he was considered a good husband and provider, and what he did sexually in the far-off land was more or less his own business. After all, Chinese morality did not condemn polygamy; until fairly recent times rich men often showed their wealth by affording two or more wives simultaneously, both in the home village. Furthermore, some families reasoned that taking a Mississippi wife or mistress might prevent wild-oat sowing and help a husband remain constant and dutiful. In any event, relatives in China had little power to regulate the sexual behavior of sons or husbands far from home.[9] The pattern of Chinese-native marriages in Mississippi was not unusual for the Chinese. In Java, for example, "once the settlers had secured a livelihood, they formed alliances with indigenous women." [10] In Britain, "at the very least, 60% of the married men are married to English women." [11] Nearly one in three Chinese in Trinidad in 1946 was of mixed (part-Negro) parentage; in Jamaica in the same year the fraction was 44.6 percent.[12]

In fact, what was unusual in Mississippi was the relative rarity of such relationships. In 1946 probably no more than 5 percent of all Delta Chinese were of mixed blood and less than one Chinese male in twenty had a Negro or part-Negro wife. Several factors combined to cause the low Delta rate, all deriving from the Mississippi segregation system. The English are not polarized into two racial groups. The Mississippi polarization, and the low status of the Chinese, meant that white-Chinese marriage was socially improbable. Such marriages were also legally prohibited: "The marriage of a white person and a negro [sic] or mulatto or person who shall have one-eighth or more of negro blood, or with a Mongolian or a person who shall have one-eighth or more of Mongolian blood, shall be unlawful, and such marriage shall be unlawful and void; and any party thereto, on conviction, shall be punished." [13]

Compared to some biracial societies, such as Jamaica and British Guiana, the Mississippi social system is different in a crucial way. In the Caribbean, the "colored" populations — Negroes of lighter skin tone and above-average economic standing — have long enjoyed social and racial status higher than that of impoverished blacks. Although both Jamaica and Guiana contained strong elements of racial discrimination under the British, treatment was partly based on class differences and never coalesced into a pure segregation system. The Mississippi Delta, on the other hand, never produced a classification system at all comparable to the Jamaican hierarchy. In Mississippi, any Negro, of whatever occupational eminence, has always been confronted by a code of etiquette classifying him with all other blacks, a code based on premises which directly deny his worth as an individual. To marry a Negro was to deny those premises, and that leap of faith few Chinese were willing to make, especially as the decades passed and they began to take Mississippi definitions more seriously. Furthermore, the Delta has produced few Negroes of comparable economic position for the Chinese to marry among.[14]

The estimate of mixed marriages in 1946 is substantially lower than the percentage before World War II, and the difference is accounted for by the many extralegal conjugal relationships which existed between Chinese and Negroes before 1940 but ended at about that time. This is the reason why older Negroes still think of the Chinese as close associates and why Negro informants say the Chinese are still viewed "mostly in a friendly light." In effect, then, the Chinese majority profited from the image of fellowship with blacks established by the minority of merchants who did have close ties, including marriage, with members of the Negro community. These ties were therefore not discouraged until they hindered the advancement of the group into white institutions.

The feeling of racial fellowship was furthered by the fact that most Chinese grocers did not require the deferential courtesy forms customarily demanded by whites. And most important of all, the Chinese merchant lived in the black community and was subject to the same discrimination and prejudice from whites. In some towns, not until after World War II did it become clear that the Chinese were attempting to escape Negro status, and as long as they accepted it, relations between proprietor and clientele were cordial, if not close.

Relations with Whites

If most Chinese were rather withdrawn and isolated from close ties with Negroes, their relations with the white community were even more distant. And of all the legal and informal barriers enforcing that distance, most significant to the Chinese was their exclusion from white public schools.

Before World War II, school systems outside the larger towns were rather rudimentary. County and city consolidated schools for whites were built in some cases well before the Depression, but schools for Negroes were almost nonexistent until the mid-1930's. Some planters established one-room schools, usually operating for only three or four months of the year, for their plantation's Negro children. By 1935 public schools for Negroes had been established on an eight-month basis in some areas, but Rosenwald schools, established with aid from a private foundation, were still the most important sources of education for the black population. The Clarksdale system, advanced for its area, was paying its Negro teachers in 1941 just one-fifth the white rate. Bolivar County, in a Depression year, spent $283,161 for the education of 6216 white school-age children, in contrast to a tiny $38,765 for 35,708 Negroes.[15]

Those Negro schools which did exist on a more or less equal financial footing with their white counterparts were staffed by teachers with a bare "normal school" education from the state's public institutions of higher learning for Negroes, none of which were accredited. The only competent black school was a private institution, Tougaloo College, near Jackson,[16] and its graduates were not and are still not hired in much of the Delta. For, as a long-time white county school superintendent told me, "They have too many *ideas* — they give people *ideas*." Up to 1970, as a result of white dominance, the black schools remained far inferior. In some areas they let out weeks before white sessions ended. Run by teachers who were products of the disastrous earlier periods, they were and still are further weakened by the absence of any state compulsory education law, so students come and go haphazardly during the course of the school year. Throughout the entire Delta, only the private Catholic schools for Negroes in Greenville and Clarksdale produced students without serious educational deficiencies.

By the mid-1920's, several merchants who had managed to bring over their families from China faced the problem of providing their children with an education. Rejection from white schools was tantamount to complete exclusion from public education, as we have seen. Furthermore, many Chinese by this time were already trying to evade their "black" classification and did not want to utilize even the existing Negro schools. Chinese men with families were particularly likely to feel this pressure, since they had already begun the transition from sojourner to immigrant. They made desperate attempts to avoid discrimination against their children. A few smalltown school systems, including Rosedale, Louise, and one or two communities in Coahoma County, had admitted one or two Chinese children. Typically only one or two Chinese families lived in these districts. Other families then attempted to send their children, by boarding them with a Chinese family or by moving in themselves. The white community then found itself faced with two, three, or more families, with five to ten children; and in most cases school officials and leading citizens grew sufficiently alarmed to exclude all Chinese.

When this occurred in Rosedale, in the autumn of 1924, the grocer whose daughter was rejected responded in a fashion rare for the Chinese — he went to court. The resulting legal battle went to the United States Supreme Court and became a famous case in the series of post-Plessy decisions upholding segregation. Gong Lum, a Chinese merchant with considerable standing in the white community in Rosedale, had two daughters. Both were born in Bolivar County and attended white Sunday School. Martha, the older, "had been admitted to the public school for whites along with others of her race." [17] But, "at the noon recess [of opening day in October, 1924], she was notified by the superintendent that she would not be allowed to return." [18]

Her father hired an established Clarksdale law firm, Brewer, Brewer, and McGhehee, and filed suit on October 28, 1924, against the trustees of the Rosedale Consolidated

High School. His lawyers pointed out: "She is not a member of the colored race nor is she of mixed blood, but that she is pure Chinese . . . [Furthermore,] there is no school maintained in the District for the education of children of Chinese descent." [19] Therefore they argued that separate and equal facilities were not provided for her, nor was she allowed to utilize white facilities. Their arguments were persuasive, and the Mississippi Circuit Court for the First Judicial District of Bolivar County decided in her favor, whereupon the school officials appealed to the Mississippi Supreme Court.

The state Supreme Court reversed the decision, citing the 1890 Mississippi Constitution, "separate schools shall be maintained for children of the white and colored races," and asserting that Chinese are not "white" and must fall under the heading, "colored races." Lum and his attorneys, now joined by a second firm, J. N. Flowers, appealed to the United States Supreme Court. Brewer and Flowers constructed a hard-hitting argument. They boldly asserted that it was a known fact that the white race was "the law-making race" in Mississippi and that it created special schools for itself to avoid mixing with Negroes: "If there is danger in the association [with Negroes], it is a danger from which one race is entitled to protection just the same as another . . . The white race creates for itself a privilege that it denies to other races; exposes the children of other races to risks and dangers to which it would not expose its own children. This is discrimination." [20] Their reasoning was explicitly equalitarian; although good use was made of the white racist rationale for segregated schools, this assumption was never accepted by them but merely used as a basis for argument.

The Supreme Court, at its lowest ebb in racial decision-making, accepted that rationale, agreeing with the Mississippi Supreme Court: "It has been at all times the policy of the lawmakers of Mississippi to preserve the white schools for members of the Caucasian race alone." [21] Although this reasoning explicitly contravened the Fourteenth Amendment to the United States Constitution ("nor deny to any person within its jurisdiction the equal protection of the laws"), the majority decision, delivered by Chief Justice Taft, tortuously attempted to harmonize the two: "A child of Chinese blood, born in, and a citizen of, the United States, is not denied the equal protection of the laws by being classed by the State among the colored races who are assigned to public school separate from those provided for the whites, when equal facilities for education are afforded to both classes." [22] Taft went on to cite *Plessy v. Ferguson* and noted that no argument had been presented that Rosedale public schools for Negroes did not exist or were inferior. [23]

The decision was a harsh setback to the Chinese throughout the Delta. [24] The Lum family moved to Elaine, Arkansas, to secure educational facilities, [25] and other families with children went to Memphis or left the South entirely. Delta Chinese sent their children to live with relatives in other states so that they could obtain an education, and other families employed private tutors at home. In general, however, the children who came of age in the Delta before 1936 received little formal schooling of any kind. In a few cases, they did attend the Negro schools, especially the parochial grade school and high school for Negroes in Greenville. And a few families in two or three small towns were able to continue sending their children to the white schools, although the practice was now explicitly against state law. But the vast majority of Delta white school systems were closed to the Chinese until well into the 1940's. In Rosedale itself, a separate school for Chinese operated for a time in 1933, and the Chinese were not admitted to the white public schools until about 1950.

The Gong Lum decision also confirmed the Chinese in their pessimistic view of their chances before the Mississippi legal system. Even in China the average citizen held a cynical view of law and its administration, a feeling fostered by the rigid and corrupt bureaucracy, with little local discretion, stressing suspicion and control, and "as a result, the inhabitants often came to regard anything that involved the government with indifference, suspicion, or fear." [26] A Delta lawyer with a number of Chinese clients pointed out another factor reinforcing their distrust: "The Chinese were also afraid of the law, even though they themselves had little contact with it, because they saw the way it operated with the Negro." According to a Chinese informant, "in the early '20's, only one or two Chinese out of ten had the guts enough to register to vote."

Even now the Chinese are reluctant to deal with the law and the governmental bureaucracy. They prefer to put their faith in one or two key whites whom they feel they can trust. The lawyer quoted above, for example, was once given title to a Delta grocery while its proprietor vacationed in China. He said, "One reason I had title was because the Chinese didn't think they'd be treated fairly in court." As the lawyer admitted, the Chinese view of the situation was far from unwarranted; in the first three decades of this century a Chinese grocer in most towns had small chance of legal redress if robbed or defrauded by white customers or even by blacks. At times he was directly intimidated by white merchants or plantation commissary managers. In Dundee, a small town in Tunica County, a Chinese merchant was driven out of town, after severe threats not to go into business there, by whites who shot into and burned his store. Incidents of direct oppression were rare, though, for as shown in the last chapter, the Chinese occupational niche was irrelevant to the white establishment and offended only those white competitors who themselves were without adequate status or power to muster the establishment.

To the larger white community, the Chinese merchant before 1940 remained nearly invisible. His linguistic and cultural differences worked against close contact, and his lower-caste status increased the distance between the groups. The cleavage was not total, however. In smaller towns, Chinese were becoming known by their white customers, who occasionally bought from them if their usual supplier was out of stock or high in price. Throughout the Delta, other whites, especially wholesalers and some religious leaders, were developing more extensive contacts between the races.[27] And more basic forces were already at work, both within and outside the Chinese group itself, forces which were to transform their position and confute O'Brien's prediction that they would sink completely to the Negro status level.

Segregation and Sojourning

The first process which was to change the status level of the Delta Chinese stemmed from the impact of segregation itself, upon the immigrants. As long as the Chinese remained sojourners in orientation, with their families still in China and their self-evaluation rooted in the value-system of the homeland, they were not likely to move toward escaping Negro status and joining white society. But the sojourning tradition was gradually losing its force, as it so often does. According to Paul Siu, the emigrant leaves to accomplish something — the job — and intends to return home, but, "in due time, the sojourner becomes vague and uncertain about the termination of his sojourn, because . . . he has already made some adjustments to his new environment." [28] The contradiction is built into the task itself: success to the sojourner means the establishment of an independent business, but, as he gradually accumulates property and a clientele, he automatically becomes more committed to them. He begins to think about events and idea-systems in the new land as they affect his business, and he works to make that business more secure for the future. The prospective future in China begins to take second place.

Also over the decades some Chinese grocers were able to bring their families in from China. By visiting China, one could father children, who were then American citizens if the father had been naturalized. They could be brought in, and their mother could sometimes be imported to care for the children or with another excuse. Some Chinese males married Chinese women from other areas of the United States. Gradually, a number of Delta grocers acquired Chinese families in Mississippi. This meant that the most important continuing element of the sojourning orientation — the desire to rejoin one's family — no longer existed for them. The orientation was further undermined by the extraneous fact that protracted war in Asia (civil strife, the battle against Japan, and the Communist takeover) made the homeland less alluring and emigration more desirable.

But there is more to this transition from sojourner to immigrant than has yet been discussed. What is involved is not only a geographic shift of thought but also a change in the values which form a basis for defining status and self-esteem. Schumpeter has commented that the stratification system in America is the most important single socializing agent affecting new immigrants. The immigrant and particularly his child face a crisis when they realize that many of their personal characteristics which were valued and honored by the society which they left are denigrated or at least disregarded by the new society to which they came. This conflict is the major cause of generational discord within immigrant families. And if the class system can do this to immigrants in the North and East, the caste system of Mississippi must have had much stronger effects, for it goes beyond the assertion that one is low class and unimportant, to label one low caste, not even fully human. As Chinese merchants began to shift even slightly in their orientation, as Mississippi began to grow in their minds as a possible permanent residence, they became increasingly conscious of and bothered by their lowly place.[29]

In Southeast Asia, the Chinese have maintained more of a sojourning orientation than in Mississippi, even though in many cases they have been away from China much longer and have built up a greater economic stake in the foreign land. By 1920, Delta Chinese were far less involved with political developments in mainland China than were Chinese in Malaya or Thailand. There was never a "self-government movement" in Mississippi, as there was in Malaya, for example, in imitation of mainland students.[30]

There were too few Chinese, spread too thinly throughout the Delta's sprawling area, to warrant a "Chinatown" or cultural center for the group. If the Chinese community had been larger or more concentrated, its members could have reassured each other of their worth and dignity according to Chinese standards. As it was, the internalized values of the emigrants were not reinforced, and they found it hard to resist the challenges offered by the value system of white Mississippi. After a while it became crucially important to them that the whites with whom they often dealt, who after all defined and ran Delta society, classed them with the blacks. All their virtuous life, virtuous by Chinese standards — their economic success, continued support of families in China, visits home — counted for naught with the white population. As a Chinese merchant in Greenville put it: "Before World War II we had no chance to prove ourselves. We couldn't bring our families over; they wouldn't let my wife come in even to take care of my two little children . . . They shut us out of society, and then they said we didn't count."

The white man's evaluation had to be taken seriously, because he controlled the distribution of such valued commodities as public accommodations, legal treatment, and public education. The Mississippi system, codified in the etiquette of segregation, is by its very nature inclusive, and cannot merely ignore a group but is required to evaluate and place every individual. Moreover, its assessments are couched in terms of innate self-worth and human dignity. Newcomers cannot live for long, especially for more than a generation, among people who label them so negatively, without changing their old evaluative standards to be more like those of the new reference group. The Chinese did gradually change from sojourner to immigrant, as a consequence, and began to take seriously white Mississippi's low placement of them. They then worked systematically to eliminate the causes of that treatment, in order to rise from Negro to white status.

Transition 4

Social Control and Image Change

In the last chapter we saw that a biracial system of etiquette has no provision for a third race. Such a race tends to be assigned subordinate or near-subordinate status or gains admission, at least formally, to the dominant caste. This line of reasoning led O'Brien to predict in 1941 that the Chinese were moving toward Negro status.[1] He gathered no historical data on their previous relations with whites and blacks, however, and thus he could not know that in fact they were about to make a leap upward on the social hierarchy. Their transition was a racial one. That is, the Chinese entered white society as a group, a racial group; individuals were not accepted separately. This was as it had to be, for quite clearly, especially in the larger towns, segregationists could not allow some Chinese to enter white institutions while most of the race was identified with Negroes.

Closely involved with the transition was a change of image. Few whites had a material interest in maintaining the low social status of the Chinese.[2] Most felt an ideological interest, however, in keeping them out if their own "racial integrity" and "way of life" would be threatened. Thus it is to the social structure of the Delta, and not to any specific characteristics of the Chinese, that we should look for an explanation of the difficulty of their transition from black to white. Other Delta minorities, including Italians, Mexicans, Lebanese, and of course Negroes, have had to fight similar discrimination, although their characteristics are very different from each other and from the Delta Chinese. It seems clear, then, that to begin by looking toward the group discriminated against, rather than at white society, would be a backward procedure.

The objections whites raised to each group, however, have had specific content, and when the Chinese attempted to enter the public schools and other institutions, whites did not hesitate to inform them of the exact nature of their reservations, which centered around the identification of Chinese with Negroes. Living in segregation meant that the Chinese were held back, because whites had options regarding their placement; having assigned them Negro status, whites were now worried about reversing themselves and making exceptions. Aren't Chinese colored? they asked. If we let them in, won't Negroes want to integrate? In fact, might not these Chinese themselves have Negro blood in them?

Social association between some Chinese and Negroes was in fact the critical irritant which whites seized upon to justify their exclusion. As a Chinese businessman told me: "Those two or three instances [of Chinese-Negro marriage] brand the whole Chinese community. At least, this is the excuse that they use. In Mississippi, it's thumbs down whenever you do something like that." Before 1940, the percentage of all Chinese men who cohabited with or took legal wives from the Negro population amounted to perhaps 20 percent at its peak. It is difficult to assess with certainty the feelings within the Chinese community of that time regarding intermarriage with blacks. Certainly Chinese men had never chosen Negro wives in preference to Chinese.[3] However, at least one Chinese merchant who had established a common-law marriage with a Negro retained enough respect from his Chinese peers that he was considered a primary leader of the group in the large Delta town where he lived. In addition, informants from all three categories — Chinese, Chinese married to Negroes, and Negroes married to Chinese — confirmed to me that there used to be considerably more interaction and acceptance between Chinese and "Chinese-Negro" families than in the more recent past.

Since 1940, no new Chinese-Negro marriage has been contracted, and only about a dozen such relationships, involving less than 5 percent of all Chinese men, still exist in the Delta. Many Chinese men who married or lived with Negroes in Mississippi had already established families in China before emigrating. When legal restrictions were relaxed during World War II, allowing Chinese women to come into the country with much greater ease, many of these men brought their families to Mississippi and severed relations with their Negro wives and mistresses. Young Chinese bachelors no longer looked for Negro mates but instead anticipated returning to Canton or Hong Kong, selecting a Chinese wife, and bringing her back. The revision of immigration regulations during World War II was thus a major factor in the abrupt cessation of new Chinese-Negro relationships.

Of much greater importance, though, was coercion from the Mississippi system itself. Even in earlier decades in some of the smaller towns, pressure had been put on the Chinese to avoid formal or stable marriages with Negro women. A Chinese grocer in a small south Delta town lived with a Negro woman for a year or two, near the end of World War II. She helped him in the store, and they became formally engaged and entered a stable common-law relationship. After a child was born to the couple, however, whites in the community, alarmed by the partial violation of Mississippi segregation mores, threatened the father with loss of business and the mother with physical harm. So the merchant did not marry his mistress, and she moved within a year to nearby Greenville.[4] In larger towns, pressure against mixed relationships did not come directly from the white community, but through other Chinese. To eliminate all Chinese-Negro relationships was clearly in the interest of the larger Chinese community.

In several towns, school officials stated explicitly to Chinese leaders that no consideration regarding the overriding issue of school exclusion would be shown them unless social associations between Chinese and Negroes in the community were ended.

In other districts, whites did not lay down the line so openly, but the Chinese were made aware that their progress toward acceptance in white society was greatly impeded by those among them who continued to live with Negroes. In a large Delta town during this period a Chinese grocer had been admitted to the town's only real hospital, a private institution. Its staff did not know of his Negro wife, but they became aware of her when she tried to visit him in his room. She was stopped; he was thrown out; and the hospital has barred all Chinese ever since.

Chinese leaders knew that since whites categorized them as a group, rejection of Negro relationships by Chinese would have to be nearly unanimous to produce an effective image change. They therefore set out to eradicate the Chinese-Negro minority, by influencing Chinese males to end Negro relationships and throw out their Chinese-Negro kin, or by forcing the families to leave the community. Several weapons were at their command in this campaign. First, they socially ostracized stubborn individuals. This was a powerful tool, since few members of other races associated with mixed families either. The leadership could also ensure, simply by informing the power structure of the questionable racial ancestry of associations of a given individual, that no privileges extended by white society to the Chinese as a whole would be granted to him.

In about 1947, a child of a Chinese father and Chinese-Negro mother, in appearance indistinguishable from pure Chinese, attended the white Catholic school in Greenville until expelled for misconduct. The parents then attempted to enroll him in the white public school, but by agreement between officials and the Chinese leadership, such a step required a guarantee that the child be pure Chinese. This the leaders refused to sign, and the family later left the state. More direct tools of coercion were also available to the Chinese. Since Chinese groceries are often informally associated with each other through extended family ties, the store nearest an unwanted citizen could undercut his prices and accept financial loss, reimbursed by other members of the family, until the man was driven out of business. This drastic step was only rarely utilized, however, since it proved cumbersome and unprofitable, and since Chinese family and business ties were not always strong enough to stand up under such an arrangement. It was easier simply to tell the various wholesale houses not to do business with the offending merchant. The wholesaler would usually go along, since dropping one customer was much less distasteful to him than losing all other Chinese groceries on his route.

With no one to talk to, no one to lend money or help, and almost no one to buy from, unwanted merchants usually decided to leave the community. And so it happened that Cleveland, Mississippi, for example, has not a single Chinese-Negro marriage, formal or informal, even though it has a large Chinese population (110 Chinese in 1967) and a history of some earlier Negro associations. The final irony is supplied by a Chinese man in Coahoma County who did remain married to his Negro wife. "You don't dictate to the human heart," he said, explaining how he arrived at his present lonely position. But of course, as the majority of his counterparts proved, "you" do precisely that.[5]

In at least one instance, the Chinese community also moved to end nonmarital friendships with Negroes. After a school for Chinese was established in a large Delta town, one girl, although pure Chinese, was felt to be closely tied to the Negro community. A white woman, formerly her teacher in the school, told me the story:

> I was told that any time I had a problem with any Chinese, I should see a certain Chinese leader. One time I had a well-developed Chinese girl, large for her age,

which was unusual, and she was always seen around with older Negro girls, never with Caucasians. So I called the man I had been told to call, and he was a complete gentleman; he came to see me with another Chinaman, and said he understood and you'll have no further problem with her . . .

I didn't know what they intended, but it turned out that they put her on the train that very night and sent her to her parents in San Francisco.

This discussion should not be concluded without a qualification. In the foregoing paragraphs perhaps too much emphasis has been placed on direct coercion. Instances of immediate Chinese or white pressure against Chinese-Negro families have been rather infrequent, and a few such families have continued to exist, without much harassment, to the present. The basic point is that after the wane of the sojourning orientation, conversion from a Chinese-Negro to an all-Chinese community was inevitable, given the racial definitions within the white caste. Thus other Chinese or Caucasians did not often have to apply direct coercion against Chinese-Negro families. Rather, the families segregated themselves. Knowing they were not fully welcome among pure Chinese, they seldom accepted social invitations, which could then continue to be extended, *pro forma*. And they made few attempts to enter white institutions either, remaining peripheral members of the Negro community, so unobtrusive as to be nearly invisible.

The pure Chinese were quick to let whites know that they had taken action regarding their "poor" brethren.[6] A white businessman from a large Delta town, probably Clarksdale, was quoted by George Rummel on the subject: "The rich Chinese won't have much to do with the poor Chinese, and even less with the nigger. Oh, they'll take his money just like any of us will, but they won't have anything to do with him socially. We have some good Chinese in our church and they give to the church . . . , but they don't let their poor relatives in, and they keep them under control." [7] As the businessman indicates, the Chinese went further and denied that they engaged in relations of sociability or courtesy with Negro customers. In the presence of whites, the grocer would joke about blacks, telling whites of the Cantonese derogatory term for "nigger" and relating amusing requests of illiterate share-croppers. The final step was for the Chinese to convince Caucasians that they too believed in racial integrity and had no intention of mixing with anyone. And they succeeded, as a remark from an ultra-right Delta editor attests: "They don't believe in mixing. They have nothing to do with the Negroes socially. I think all the races are like that . . ."

This last step was doubly significant, for by it the Chinese simultaneously denied that they married Negroes and explicitly vowed that they would never marry whites in the future. This was perhaps the most important thing they could do for themselves, for in a way it made a positive virtue out of their racial distinctiveness. Whites were much more easily persuaded to let Chinese into schools or other institutions after they realized that the Chinese represented no threat of this kind. The Chinese know this and are still reluctant to countenance any behavior which might appear to bridge the sexual distance.[8] One very Americanized businessman put it clearly: "Maybe we're holding up our own progress [by reluctance to push ahead in all areas], but then again, we don't want to lose anything we've gained by being too familiar, by having Chinese young people become too familiar with white young people or anything like that."

Control over younger Chinese for image-change purposes went beyond sexual proscriptions. The Chinese took pains to stress differences between their family structure and that of Negroes. Although the stability and close control within the Chinese family were not caused by white pressure, they were, and still are, reinforced by it: "I tell my boy not to get in trouble or foul up, or they won't say 'that boy,' they'll say 'that *Chinese* boy!' " This family influence is backed by the rest of the community: "If some Chinese starts getting out of line, the others of us would talk to him, straighten him out."

The resulting low delinquency rate is a source of pride to the Chinese and was stressed by many whites in interviews. Whites cite it not only in "defense" of the Chinese but also in defense of themselves and their own racial segregationism.

In addition to sexual equality with whites, another potential demand the Chinese gave up was equality in etiquette. Even today most Chinese adults interact with Caucasians from a position of deference. This is another of the "nonessential" slights the Chinese have been willing to accept in order to secure their more essential goals — economic security and an education for their children. They "joke" with whites. Whites call them by their first name or say "Hey, Jue!," but get "Mr." in return. Many Chinese abet the practice by giving their store only their first name (e.g., "John's Market"), using it so exclusively that their last name may be genuinely unknown to many customers.

Whites like this. I listened to a Greenville lawyer talking to a Chinese grocer on the phone. The grocer mentioned that he was going to enroll in a public-speaking course, as part of a self-improvement regimen. The lawyer pooh-poohed the notion: "Public speaking's no damn good for you! The grocery's how to make good money — you stick to that. You keep your mouth *shut* in public!" he bellowed jokingly, all the while grinning over toward me and winking. The similarity to white behavior toward "silly nigger notions" is very close.

Acceptance of this subordination removes from the upperclass mind the idea that they are being asked to ratify that Chinese are as good as they are. Therefore, they could easily justify dispensing such favors as school admission — as long as it was also clear that no precedent was set for possible Negro requests. And so, in addition to ending Negro relationships, the Chinese adjusted in other ways to present an image different from Negroes and acceptable to Caucasians. In Cleveland, an influential white gave them specific instructions:

I was approached some twenty years ago by some of my

Chinese friends and asked, "What about getting our children into the [white] schools?" They had oversubscribed their quota in a United States War Bond drive for me earlier . . .

[But] they had married Negro women; their children ran around on the streets not in full clothes; and so forth. So I said, "you've gone part of the way [Negro associations had been ended.]; now paint up your stores, get your children dressed, and so forth, and we'll see what can be done."

A major white reservation about the Chinese was their life style. Most families lived in a few rooms behind or above their store. These quarters were in the Negro section of town, and they did not appear to whites to be part of an acceptable way of life. The congruence of home and business was traditional to the Chinese, however, and greatly strengthened both business and family. A Chinese girl in a small town outside of Cleveland pointed out the sacrifice involved in giving up this way of life: "It is much easier to live next to the store, as we do. The Cleveland Chinese have a rough time keeping the house clean, keeping the family together, and so on — especially the women. Most of them can't drive, and they have to depend on others for their transportation back and forth." Establishing separate home residences, which the Chinese in Cleveland and most other towns proceeded to do, was a concession to Mississippi demands. So were the brick facades and painted storefronts, for these investments were nonremunerative and hence seemed nonessential to the Chinese.

In most towns, these changes in Chinese life style were instituted by individual families more or less without community coercion. Probably after some socialization to American standards, it became a matter of keeping up with the Wongs. But the model is in every case white. Chinese patterns are being pushed to one side, but there is no patterning from Negro characteristics among the young people. The way they dance, sing, the argot they use, their gestures and mannerisms

— all are incredibly free of black influence, when it is remembered that most Chinese children live in Negro neighborhoods, wait on blacks in the stores, and have more contacts with Negroes than with Caucasians of their age groups.

The accents of a few Chinese, mostly adults, are heavily Negro, and perhaps as a reaction, correct grammar and enunciation have become nearly a fetish with many younger Chinese. Another fetish is clean food, individually served. The custom of eating soups and other dishes from a communal bowl is distasteful to the younger generation. And so, at every large banquet there are two arrays of food: Chinese dishes on the tables in traditional service, and a buffet line, with fried chicken and potato chips, for the children and students.

Direct borrowing of white patterns is strikingly visible in the first names Mississippi Chinese have given themselves and their children. They are usually traditional Southern white names, such as "Coleman" or "Patricia" — not "Beulah" or "Ernestine." In at least one case the merchant named his son after a planter who had befriended him; two Chinese girls in Bolivar County were named after leaders of the local chapter of the Daughters of the American Revolution; in Greenville there is Frank Smith Chow, named after the former Delta Congressman.

In a variety of ways, then, the Delta Chinese have altered aspects of their lives and patterns of their thoughts. They changed as individual families, under their own volition, and as a group, with community pressure, but in any event the changes were based on white standards and were in part due to a desire to transform their image in white minds. In short, there has been rather complete acculturation, even in the face of opposing factors, in those areas which were important to whites. Chinese children were excluded from the public schools and thus were deprived of its socializing influence. Moreover, they were in close contact with their parents, in home and store, almost twenty-four hours each day. Much of the impetus for acculturation therefore had to come from the parents themselves, in contrast to our stereotype of rigid adult immigrants who inhibit the adaptation of their children.[9]

The characteristics of individual Chinese were not the true source of the discriminatory actions by whites against them, however, and the Chinese knew this. They therefore began to alter the institutional structure of the Chinese community and to establish concrete ties with the white upper class. Their efforts will be the focus of the next two sections.

Parallel Institutions

For decades the Chinese were barred from white institutions, and they are still excluded from many social and recreational organizations, fraternal groups, and country clubs. Furthermore, their incredible store hours preclude extensive socializing. Nevertheless, they developed a number of organizations and activities of their own. Two tongs operated for a while in Greenville, and one maintained a clubhouse there until sometime in the late thirties or early forties. There is still a family association with a clubhouse in Memphis, though it is not particularly relevant to the Delta Chinese. Almost every Sunday a number of Chinese men can be seen driving from all over the Delta to Greenwood, Rosedale, or other towns to participate in an all-night mah jongg session, and the tradition of large wedding banquets and other observances has continued to be strong in Mississippi.

Because of the thinly distributed Chinese population, however, with no Chinatown or other cultural center, and because of status pressure from white culture, Chinese organizations never attained real vitality. The tongs were never powerful, and by 1930 they were but shadows. In part this was because by that date the Chinese, with some white help, were beginning to establish institutions parallel to Delta white organizations. Most important of these is the independent Chinese Baptist Church of Cleveland, Mississippi. There are also Chinese missions in Greenville, Clarksdale, Hollandale, and Vicksburg; Chinese dances for college and high school students; separate Chinese schools in past years; and sporadic other institutions, such as summer schools and social clubs.

Most of these Chinese organizations were consciously structured to replicate their white counterparts. They are similar even in unimportant details; in their early years, whites were often invited to tour them and see the acculturation that had come to pass. They should therefore be considered parallel institutions, and they have played a major role in Chinese social life in the Delta. In Cleveland, for example, the church has become a center for wedding banquets, funerals, and other social events. Announcements can be transmitted to other Chinese throughout Bolivar and Sunflower counties by means of its formal and informal structure. Community projects, such as a Thanksgiving Day fund-raising dinner, have been organized around it. It provides, in short, both the physical and the institutional setting for socializing, contacts, and organization. That an American rather than a Chinese form was chosen indicates that the group was already perhaps beginning to believe that American ways are better.

But these parallel institutions had purposes more direct than mere reaffirmation of Chinese solidarity. Their larger goals can be seen by surveying the founding and growth of the Cleveland church. This congregation developed from a much older mission, established at First Baptist Church of Cleveland in about 1930 by Reverend Ira Eavenson, who had been a missionary in China for several years. He began with a Sunday School for the Chinese on Sunday afternoon. At first he had difficulty; by the end of the first summer only two adults and six or eight children had enrolled. Gradually, however, the Chinese realized that the mission offered them crucial aid in their drive toward full participation in white society, for it provided a way to show whites that Chinese were not heathen but had an acceptable and distinctly non-Negro Christian religion. Mr. Eavenson credited the mission for greatly changing the Chinese image, thus raising their status.

More specifically, the mission offered hope for a solution of the most pressing problem, schooling of their children. In about 1936, under the aegis of the Cleveland mission and with the aid of the white connections it provided, a drive was launched to get about $25,000 for a "Chinese Mission School." The steering committee for the venture included: "members appointed from the Rotary Club, Firemen's Club, American Legion, and the Chinese community, all of which organizations have endorsed the school." [10] Wholesalers agreed to return 1 percent of their gross sales to Chinese food stores for the project, and other white donations were solicited. The Mississippi Baptist Convention gave a substantial amount, as did out-of-town churches. Land was purchased in a strategic location: at the edge of town, not near any white area, yet far from the Negro ghetto (an earlier parcel was vetoed for being too close to Delta State College and the white neighborhoods around it). A two-story structure of concrete block was erected, with classrooms, meeting rooms, and dormitory accommodations for out-of-town students. Bolivar County supplied and paid two white teachers, and the Chinese paid for the services of a native of China, who drilled the children in their parents' language after regular hours. The regular program paralleled the white curriculum as closely as possible, considering that only two teachers confronted ten grades. It was not equal to the white schools, but far superior to no school or to the rudimentary Negro makeshift institutions. It was also better than the Chinese schools which operated sporadically in Ruleville, Rosedale, and Greenville, where one white teacher had to cope with the entire grade-span. A Greenville alumnus gave a negative but probably fair evaluation of that school's academic preparation: "The Chinese school was really mostly just play. I don't think too much of it, though it was better than nothing."

However, the Chinese schools had a larger role than mere preparation of pupils. They offered important possibilities for further advance. At the time of their establishment, they represented the greatest upward step the Chinese could achieve, and in fact the whites who taught at the Cleveland school received substantial criticism from other whites for doing so. But like the missions, the schools gave the Chinese sites for demonstrating to whites that they possess a cultural heritage and "innate" capabilities different from Negroes. The schools presented plays and Christmas parties for white audiences and engaged their Caucasian counterparts in spelling bees and other contests. Their students' reputation for academic excellence grew even beyond the facts, and their quiet, trouble-free operation gave the Chinese a talking-point in their continued pleading for admission to the white systems.

Image change in white minds was in fact a paramount purpose of the Chinese schools and missions, and also of the more recent youth organizations. In the Greenville mission, this motive is clear. The mission pastor is the Caucasian assistant of the First Church; whites teach the Sunday school classes; and the pastor's wife plays the piano, although a Chinese could do this job. Until recently, the Sunday school chairman was a Caucasian, and white ministers and lay leaders are often invited to speak before the group. The service, like all Delta Chinese church services, is bilingual, but only nominally so; the sermon and even many of the hymns are solely in English. This is true even though most of the adults are more at home in Chinese, and some of the older women speak no English at all. But the Chinese want the continued white involvement. At least in part this is because they want to maintain the institution on an integrated basis and want influential whites to be able to vouch that Chinese religious and social life is very similar to their own.[11]

During the transition period whites tended to deal with the mission leaders as representatives of all Chinese in the community, even though many Chinese did not participate in mission activities. Thus the missions and school directly solidified the power of certain Chinese leaders to coerce their communities with regard to white standards. In Cleveland, this power was graphically demonstrated by the following story of the treatment of the last merchant in town who still lived with a Negro woman: "When the mission got under way, the leaders of the mission instructed the man that he had to straighten up his way of living; and he put the Negro out, straightened up the store, and later left Cleveland." [12] In Greenville, four Chinese men, leaders of the mission, were assigned by whites the responsibility of vouching for the racial purity of each child before he was admitted to the Chinese school and later to the white system.

An additional reason for parallel institutions has been their acculturating influence. The schools and missions and the youth organizations and activities played a key role in socializing the Chinese into American patterns. It is difficult and frightening to step in and join an ongoing white congregation, for example, if one knows nothing about Christianity. In the mission, one is among friends, who like oneself are taking unsteady first steps toward learning new practices and beliefs. A second avenue of acculturation is through the children. They attended the Chinese schools and later the white public institutions; furthermore, many families sent their children to Sunday school with awesome regularity, even if the parents themselves did not go. Their attendance familiarized them — and through them their families — with the skills and rituals necessary for full participation in white society. In Vacation Bible School in Cleveland, the young children today learn and recite for their parents the "Pledge of Allegiance" to the United States and Christian flags and to the Bible. They recite no Chinese.

Some parallel institutions were set up as direct responses to exclusion from the white prototypes. This is most obvious in the Chinese Cemetery in Greenville. Chinese were barred from the white cemetery; it is not clear if they can yet use this facility. But the Negro burying ground is overgrown with weeds, and in addition, Chinese did not want to identify themselves with Negroes even in death, lest they be so classified in life. Therefore, quite separate from both white and black cemeteries, there is a small, neatly kept Chinese graveyard, with a high fence around it. The tombstones within are inscribed in both Chinese and English. In imitation of Southern white custom, there is even a separate tiny "Slumberland," with three or four stones bearing lambs and insipid inscriptions, marking the final resting places of infants and young children. Chinese from all over the Delta were buried in it at one time, but most Chinese families outside Greenville now bury their dead in the white cemeteries in their home communities.

The Chinese church and missions and participation in Chinese and Caucasian schools point to contradictory processes in the relation of segregation to acculturation. Segregation led first to the social isolation of the minority, shutting them out from participation in white activities and organizations; hence it retarded their acculturation. At the same time, its extremely negative evaluation of them as a race led to efforts to escape their lowly position. And so they have acculturated very rapidly since 1930 or 1940, when the opportunity first opened to them. Thus it is that the percentage of Chinese in the Delta who are Christians is far higher than the small portion of Christian Chinese in the country as a whole.[13] Nor is it by chance that most Chinese Christians in Mississippi are Southern Baptists, like most Caucasians.

The Delta Chinese have also set up a rather comprehensive set of youth activities, again based on white templates. Chinese students at Mississippi State University and the University of Mississippi form informal clubs which hold dances several times each year. After major banquets there may be a party for the young people. The Cleveland church has an extensive youth program, including Chinese Baptist youth conferences and retreats, choir, Baptist Training Union, and recreational events. Especially interesting are the dances: in compensating for the Caucasian affairs, at which Chinese, especially in larger towns, are still not fully welcome, they become exact replicas of them. They are totally non-Negro in style; white bands are usually hired; and the Chinese dance "white."[14]

In all, the Chinese have developed a wide range of institutions and activities — from birthday parties to funerals — rather closely approximating Mississippi white prototypes. They constitute sites for interaction and solidarity, where contacts and projects can be initiated. Their Caucasian atmosphere and structure proves to whites that Chinese are not like Negroes. In continuing and furthering acculturation of individual members, they prepare them for full participation in white society. They provide a substitute for those activities Chinese are shut out of in the larger community. Finally, the institutions have strengthened the control apparatus of the Chinese community by supplying a commodity — membership — which can be dispersed or withheld according to how one measures up to white standards. Thus they made official certain Chinese as mission or school leaders, solidifying their power to coerce their constituencies.

Interlinking Individuals

Concomitant with the development of Chinese leaders, and also facilitated by the parallel institutions, was the cultivation of specific interlinking individuals in the white establishment. Chinese came to feel that certain Caucasians were their friends and could be trusted, and they approached these few whenever they had business with the white community. Caucasians, for their part, would ask these "friends of the Chinese" whom to contact within the Chinese group when the cooperation of the Chinese was desired. Such occasional informal "negotiation" between Chinese and Caucasian leaders has led many Mississippians, black and white, to stereotype the Chinese as a unified group under powerful leadership. In Cleveland, several whites directed me to see one man whom they assured me was the "boss" of the whole Cleveland Chinese population. And an otherwise astute Negro political leader in Greenville informed me that: "the Chinese have a tight organization with a dictator-like leader . . . Their stores are all tied together financially, and the whole operation is out of Hong Kong. It's an international cartel, with international financing." Students of overseas Chinese in other areas or of China itself will be amused at such conceptions, for the Chinese have a well-known inability to cooperate with each other on long-term endeavors. They tend to relate to leaders ambivalently, usually following them only when their own short-term interests demand it. As Latourette put it: "[the Chinese are] rather unsuccessful at cooperation. They point out that much of existing concerted action is under the pressure of strong necessity . . . , that reciprocal distrust exists, that most Chinese find it impossible to believe that the organizer is acting from sincere public spirit." [15]

In Mississippi I found considerable evidence for Latourette's view. The Chinese show very little continuing cooperation, even when it would be to the advantage of all parties. Different families think of each other mostly as competitors first and are prone to backbiting and gossip. They have organized no way to deal with customers who are chronic credit risks; in Cleveland they do not even participate fully in the bad-check warning system. No cooperatives for buying from wholesalers have been established, and the Chinese have not organized as a group to counter residential discrimination or solve other group problems. They are ambivalent toward the leaders they do have, distrusting and following them at the same time. Thus when interviewing a Caucasian, I usually felt free to say that another white had recommended I see him, for it is infrequent that two whites, chosen from a number of possible associates, feel long-term animosity toward each other. But when meeting a Chinese, unless I could cite a reference with the same last name, and sometimes even then, I was apt to elicit only a scowl for my recommendation. It was safer to announce my purpose unreferenced, or to cite a Caucasian. The Delta Chinese are deeply split, with rivalries between families; between subgroups leaning more toward white, black, and Chinese identities; between towns; and idiosyncratically, on the basis of past slights or feuds.

However, Latourette noted that "under the pressure of strong necessity," concerted action is possible. A long-term Caucasian friend of the Mississippi Chinese made the same point: "There isn't much interconnection between the Chinese now. Some are friends with each other; some aren't. They would probably get together and organize to take care of a threat to their standing, however, such as a Chinese-Negro relationship." As we have seen repeatedly, living in a biracial society has led to many "threats to their standing," and so the Delta Chinese have maintained more permanent, unified, and significant leadership than have most overseas Chinese populations. They fall somewhere between scholars' traditional picture of a population riven by splits and jealousies and Mississippians' conception of a united monolithic group.

Indeed, the Chinese leadership was partly *caused* by the white stereotype of it. If Chamber of Commerce leaders in Cleveland want to mobilize the business community to advance a civic venture, they see one or two Chinese men, who are mandated to recruit the rest of the Chinese stores. This greatly enhances their standing, whether other Chinese like it or not, for they have been privileged with information and interconnections with the white establishment. When a "local color" feature on the Delta Chinese is desired by news editors in Jackson or Memphis, one man in Greenwood seems inevitably to be contacted. Similarly, one person in Greenville is the contact for the United Fund and is supposed to solicit from all other Chinese in the area. This ascription by whites of strong leadership positions where they do not really exist leads to bitternss and irritation among other Chinese, but it has proved a natural and perhaps necessary concomitant of their troublesome position between two races. For in their attempts to rise in racial status, the Chinese have relied upon their traditional practice of relating to other groups through trusted intermediaries. In each community, there were a few benefactors whom the Chinese had come to know intimately, through their assistance with Chinese institutions or through wholesaling or other business transactions. Their friendships were cemented by profuse gift-giving by Chinese grocers to white individuals and institutions. From them in turn the Chinese learned details of the problems and received advice about strategies to best achieve their aims. Their friends could also be counted on to spread knowledge of Chinese cultural life, exemplified in the parallel institutions, and thus further the process of image change. Finally, these Caucasians became their actual links with the white establishment and in many towns negotiated with the power structure on the Chinese behalf. An upper-class businessman told me: "Later I discussed with certain members of the School Board about the reasonableness of their request, and after one especially obstinate member retired, it was accepted." That pattern led inevitably to the elevation, within the Chinese population, of the one or two Chinese most closely acquainted with the white links.

In short, the special interests of the Chinese as a race, deriving from Mississippi's racial categorization of them, had to be represented systematically by a racial leadership which could negotiate with white leaders. White stereotypy was not the sole cause of the strength of Chinese leadership. When, for example, Caucasians proved willing to admit Chinese children to the public schools, on condition that they be pure Chinese, in the nature of the case someone had to assume a leadership position and make such a guarantee. The missions provided handy places to develop interracial contacts and leaders, but in fact the situation itself called forth the leadership. In turn, the Chinese leaders now had at their command privileged access to whites. Their prestige and power were thereby considerably enhanced within the Chinese community, and the leadership group remained strong during the transition period.

The Chinese style of operation, through influence rather than through power, with persuasion behind the scene rather than by open confrontation with whites, has perhaps been a key to their progress. In the last fifteen years, the leaders in some towns have become rather timid, and some Chinese argue that more direct pressure should have been applied to counter job and residential discrimination, but after the Rosedale decision went against them in 1926, the Chinese had little reason to feel that legal battles could achieve their objectives. Nor, with their small total number, could they hope to prevail at the ballot box. And their indirect way has, on the whole, served them fairly well.

Steps in the Transition

By persuasion, negotiation, and pleading, through trusted Caucasian intermediaries and on their own, the Chinese began to make progress. More and more white institutions opened their doors to Chinese Mississippians. Small-town churches and some congregations in larger towns had already recruited Chinese to full membership. In Greenville and Clarksdale, public accommodations, especially transportation and restaurants, were the next to break. Barber shops came later.

Different school systems admitted Chinese children at rather different times. A few small-town districts had never barred them; others had kept them out for only a few years. Greenwood was perhaps the first large system to admit Chinese, in the late 1930's. Clarksdale changed its policy in 1941, while Greenville followed suit in the fall of 1945. Schools in most of the small towns in Bolivar County integrated in the mid-1940's. Cleveland, the location of the Chinese Mission School, came a little later, probably because the school itself, though central to the process, allowed whites the temporary excuse that adequate instruction was already being provided. On the whole, small systems let in the Chinese earlier than did larger ones, although Leland and Merigold, both small, held out until 1952 or 1953.

The students faced ostracism and frequent fights as they made their way into some white schools. One of Greenville High School's first Chinese graduates, now an established businessman, told me: "We more or less were set aside. We had a *few* people who would associate with us — maybe one half of one percent." Ten years ago, if a Chinese student won an academic prize or was slated for a commencement post, the honor might be abolished or given to another candidate. Since then, their situation has slowly improved. But in the large schools, they are still not fully accepted.

Mississippi high schools, like those in other parts of the nation, surround their curricula with a wide range of social and athletic organizations. In smaller towns these activities are the major events in the social calendar, and just as the planter-business aristocracy has dominated civic life in the Delta, so its sons and daughters have dominated high school activities. Not only the Chinese have been excluded; for example, the large Italian minority in Shaw has broken into the major organizations and leadership positions only in the last five or six years. From yearbooks, I was able to compute actual organizational memberships for recent Chinese graduates of Clarksdale High School and for a random selection of Caucasian students. The results confirm interview data from white teachers and Chinese parents: Chinese seniors belong to an average of 4.0 organizations, Caucasians 7.6.[16]

Even more important is the nature of the organizations in which Chinese do participate, for there are quite different kinds of groups in Delta high schools, signifying different social positions. Chinese memberships are concentrated in the school band, occupational clubs such as Future Teachers, and academic organizations, such as honor societies and science clubs. The high-prestige posts — cheerleader, "hall of fame" member, class officer — are largely held by whites, and in many communities, including all of the large towns, Chinese are mostly ignored in the round of private parties given graduating seniors.

Discrimination is not the only factor at work, to be sure. The Chinese have not always pushed to enter areas that might admit them. Chinese children, much more than Caucasians, must work in the store after school. Additionally, their parents sometimes prohibit their participation in athletics and other activities because they are afraid the children will be physically injured or socially rebuffed. Wider participation in Caucasian activities is in fact an area of continual muted conflict between children and parents within Chinese families. But exclusion is also a factor, as the Chinese attest and their teachers admit, and in all but the very small towns, few close friendships are formed between white and Chinese. The two groups go separate ways after graduation, partly because most Chinese still live in Negro neighborhoods. A 1962 Greenville High School graduate described his interaction with white peers bitterly: "When we were all in high school, everything was just fine. But after we got out, they wouldn't have nothin' to do with me."

Almost all Chinese high school graduates go on to college, and although some have attended Northern schools, most end up at Mississippi State University or the University of Mississippi ("Ole Miss"). There again they are largely off to one side, partly because of discrimination or a feeling of not being wholly wanted and partly because they are not very assertive. They tend to room together and to cluster near each other. At Mississippi State, the fourteen Delta Chinese boys are concentrated in seven of the seventeen dormitories, with nine in two adjacent buildings. At Ole Miss, eleven male students are spread out over only seven of twenty-three dormitories, and five are in one dormitory entry. The girls too are nonrandomly placed: eight of the ten coeds live in just two of the eight female dormitories on campus.[17]

At Ole Miss, still dominated by the Delta aristocracy, Chinese have been barred from all fraternities and sororities. Three or four Chinese have joined fraternities at Mississippi State, in the hills, or social clubs at nearby Mississippi State College for Women. Usually they are chosen by new and less prestigious organizations. Groups below the high school level in Delta towns have accepted Chinese fairly freely in the last few years. A Chinese youngster is the star catcher of a Cleveland Little League team, and Chinese are in the Boy Scouts, Girl Scouts, YWCA, and YMCA in most areas where these exist.

The record is less encouraging with regard to adult activities. Although the Chinese have been in some white churches since at least 1920, few are in the larger elite congregations; those who are participate only nominally for the most part, limiting their activities to financial contributions and to attendance by their children. The church secretary of a large Greenwood congregation told me why: "The minister did everything he could to make them feel welcome. But they never became members. There were always some members who treat them like the nigras, don't make them feel welcome." In Marks the Junior Chamber of Commerce has a Chinese member, as do one or two small-town Rotary Clubs, but country clubs are generally closed, and most civic clubs exclude them. Probably Jonestown has gone furthest in demonstrating acceptance: in 1965 it elected John Wing, owner of its largest grocery store, mayor.

Although they still do not enjoy full equality, the Chinese are definitely accorded white status, affirmed for example by the "W" in the appropriate blank on their driver's licenses. "Whites talk about civil rights in front of us, so they must think of us just as if we were whites," a college student told me. And in the final irony, Chinese merchants have been actively recruited by the [white] Citizens Councils, the Greenwood-based bastion of "States' Rights and Racial Integrity."

Ecological and Economic Factors

Throughout the last two sections, it has been hinted that the Chinese are now much better accepted in the small Delta towns than in larger ones, such as Greenwood or Clarksdale. This is exactly the case. Jonestown, which has a Chinese mayor, had a population of 889 in 1960. Itta Bena, whose Chinese grocer was elevated to a position of leadership in the Rotary Club, has 1914 inhabitants. In small towns the length of the Delta — Lula, Louise, Glen Allan, and others of up to about 2500 population — the Chinese have become members of the white establishment in some important respects. Interracial dating, almost invariably between females on the Chinese side and Caucasian males, has occurred without much friction in towns of this size. In larger communities, there is a sharp difference. There, Chinese are still sometimes mentioned in the same breath with Negroes and their status is still ambiguous. At the end of the population continuum, Greenville treats its Chinese minority distinctly worse than does any other Delta town save Greenwood, which is also a large town and which has a history of violent intransigence toward blacks.[18]

Two explanations for the general progress of small-town Chinese can be drawn from the demography of the situation. In these towns, there are usually only one or two Chinese families, not more than four. This makes a full social life within the group impossible, and ties to Chinese in other towns cannot make up the difference completely. An eight-year-old, for example, may be the only Chinese boy in his cohort. He is therefore forced to make friends outside his race, persevering even in the face of slights. Second, the demography of small towns leads to differences in the interaction of whites with Chinese. These towns have only a single "downtown" business area, patronized by both races. Thus the Chinese grocer is located centrally, and gradually he receives some white business. Sometimes he caters to white trade, and the identification of Chinese with Negroes begins to erode.[19] Furthermore, the merchant's residence above or behind his store is less of a liability in a small town, for the store is in a nonresidential area, not in the Negro ghetto. And the small-town business interaction between Chinese and white furthered the development of nonbusiness contacts and a non-Negro image. Thus the social position of a town's Chinese citizens today can be predicted almost without error from two parameters: the number of Chinese in the town, and its total population.

Ecological or demographic patterns have been a major factor behind Chinese progress. A second condition underlying their social mobility has been their economic success, for their business achievement made possible the changes they effected in life style, their gifts and favors to white friends, and the development of white contacts in general. And the fact of their affluence itself constituted the most far-reaching difference in image that could be imagined, contrasted to the destitute black population. This difference was impressed upon the white establishment by conspicuous consumption (the Chinese Church parking lot is filled on Sunday with recent-model Buicks and Oldsmobiles) and by what might be called "conspicuous contributions" (individual grocers in Cleveland have subscribed to $10,000 or more in Caucasian church building bonds). I would rank economic success the most important basic cause of the upward racial mobility of the Chinese. But wealth in itself was not the means of solution. Their situation was transformed only as a result of the process of image change, parallel institutions, and behind-the-scene negotiation outlined in the earlier sections of this chapter.

Image change was in fact the key to the process. The white upper class had no economic "self-interest" at stake in keeping the Chinese down. Their economic and even their social rise was irrelevant to whites, except the small grocers, who in turn were irrelevant to the upper class. There were no objections to the Chinese based on economic interest, therefore, but there were serious ideological objections. The identification of Chinese with Negroes meant, first of all, that Chinese were thought to possess objectionable characteristics. These the image-change efforts spoke to directly. In a news interview explaining the admission of Chinese by Greenville public schools in 1945, School Board President Henry Starling made the importance of the new Chinese image vividly apparent: "It is purely a matter of democracy," he said. "The children of native Chinese strain are pupils of high scholastic and character standards." [20] The Chinese-Negro identification also meant that whites did not want to go on record with a principled policy reversal that might set precedent for equal treatment of all races. Chinese efforts to distinguish themselves from blacks spoke to this objection also, as did the cultivation of interceding white benefactors, who could argue for admitting the Chinese as an exception or favor.[21]

That opposition to the Chinese was ideological is also shown by the comment of several Caucasians that China's position as a wartime ally affected their thinking about the Delta Chinese, for such a point could bear on no interest-generated feelings. One by one, the objections whites had to the race were rebutted, and the points of similarity between them and blacks were altered. In the end, as a white Delta minister put it: "When you finally run out of rationalizations and have to face the truth, then there is change."

Only a few wholesalers and businessmen stood to profit personally from accommodating the Chinese requests, but few whites could anticipate personal loss from acceding. There was, however, an ideological profit to be had. That is why ninety white members of the First Baptist Church in Clarksdale signed a letter requesting of the school board "whatever honest consideration you might make in there [*sic*] desire and hope to have access to the facilities of the Clarksdale Public Schools." [22] Once whites had been convinced that Chinese were non-Negro, fully human, and should be full citizens, it became, as the school board president in Greenville said, "purely a matter of democracy." Admitting the Chinese thus functioned to lessen the contradiction between equalitarianism and discrimination which Myrdal labeled "an American dilemma." Upper-class Mississippians could now reassure themselves that they were good Americans and good Christians and that their oppression of Negroes was called forth by that race's particular and peculiar lack of capacity.

It would be splendid if behind the dramatic rise in racial status of the Chinese lay an easily mastered artifice, equally available to all races. It would be splendid if I or another sociologist could confer upon the Delta black population the strategy they need in order to emulate the Chinese transformation. In an interview with me, a Negro political leader expressed this hope: "Many of us look at it [the Chinese advancement] as a kind of wedge *we* might use, someday. We don't begrudge it to them." But any positive connection between Chinese and Negro progress must unfortunately be very tenuous, for there are two overwhelming differences between the groups. First, Negroes, unlike Chinese, grew up within the Delta's social and ideological system. They have almost no cultural roots outside it. Therefore, the kinds of assertions about oneself inherent in the Chinese denial of Negro status are undermined. Blacks cannot easily attempt an image shift similar to that completed by the Chinese, because their family structure, level of education, and occupational stature really are debilitated by the system in which they have matured.

Second, Negroes cannot emulate the cultivation by Chinese of intermediaries in the white aristocracy, since such connections can be used only for persuasion, not for open confrontation or the mobilization of political power. Time after time, whites who were interviewed pointed to the quiet rise of the Chinese and complained of the open abrasive demands of Negroes. But persuasion will never accomplish very much for the Negro. Michels said why, long ago: "Attempts at persuasion fail miserably when they are addressed to the privileged classes, in order to induce these to abandon, to their own disadvantage, as a class and as individuals, the leading positions they occupy in society. A class considered as a whole never spontaneously surrenders its position of advantage. It never recognizes any moral reason sufficiently powerful to compel it to abidate in favor of its 'poorer brethren.' Such action is prevented, if by nothing else, by class egoism." [23] And much more than "egoism" is involved. In the first chapter, we noted that plantation owners in 1936 typically realized a profit of $550 from each working family they employed, more than the entire cash and noncash income of the family. The Chinese grocers, an insignificant percentage of the total population, were not in an exploited position; their economic and social rise ended no one's special profit, but Negroes are in a 70 percent majority in the population, and no basic change in their status has been possible without contravening the interests of the planter class which employs and exploits them.[24]

A more general conclusion can be drawn. The Chinese have fared better where they were so few as to be isolated families, in small towns; where they numbered in the scores or hundreds, in Greenville and other cities, they have done less spectacularly. Similarly, Montana Negroes do not suffer the privations of Delta sharecroppers, and their per-capita income is undoubtedly far higher and far closer to the white average.

If the Chinese case, then, offers little hope for Negro replication, at least by similar means, it does offer insight into workings of the segregation system itself. In the next chapter, analysis of that system will be continued, with emphasis on the nature and causes of the opposition against the Chinese which segregation generated.

Opposition

The Myth of Lower-Class Opposition

Each new step taken by the Chinese — school integration, moving into white neighborhoods, or attempting to gain membership or employment in white-dominated organizations — met with resistance. In some instances the hostility flared briefly and died out; in others, whites successfully worked to delay Chinese advancement for years or even decades. White opposition to the Chinese is especially interesting for the light it sheds on their more general resistance to black advancement in the Delta. Since the Chinese have progressed far beyond any acceptance yet granted to Negroes, they provide good test cases for analyzing general white responses to efforts by any minority toward integration.[1] Of even greater value is the fact that certain characteristics of the Chinese — their economic position, family structure, and above all their far smaller percentage of the total population — undermine the premises of various explanations of white intransigence toward the Negro. Nevertheless, the Chinese faced white opposition. In exploring the sources of white opposition to the progress of the Chinese and, more widely, of all minority groups, we shall see that, for the most part, opposition to the

Chinese was generated by the internal dynamics of the white class structure.

In sociological literature the question, "who — what class — is most prejudiced against the Negro," or against other minority groups, has become a monotonous litany. It is the lower class which indulges in acts of violence, some claim; thus it is this group which, fearing direct economic competition if discrimination barriers tumble, feels the most virulent prejudice. Some argue, on the other hand, that upper-class Americans have merely learned, as a consequence of their wider educational experience, to respond with sophisticated equalitarianism to questionnaire items, while behind the scene they are more discriminatory than any other group. Still other theorists construct arcane hypotheses blaming "strivers" or "skidders" — persons whose position in the class structure is improving or deteriorating.

The parties to this debate are attempting to get at some "gut level" of prejudice. For example, by controlling for education and then comparing levels of prejudice among different groups and strata, survey analysts are implicitly assuming that deep in one's heart of hearts there lies a "true" feeling about the minority in question. A similar approach has been to search for item wordings that are extremely subtle and manage to slip by the educated respondent's sophisticated verbal defenses to tap the reservoir of prejudice beneath. Freudian and other genetic theories of prejudice — popular at least since the 1950 publication of *The Authoritarian Personality* — reinforce this style of thought, but in fact any psychological or sociological theory which holds that prejudice antedates and causes discrimination should be included in the same category.

There is a certain spuriousness in the entire enterprise, however. The analyst who partials upper- and lower-class respondents by education is looking at rather artificially-constructed subsamples. The set of upper-class respondents having only an eighth-grade education, for example, is not only nearly empty; those few individuals it does contain are far from typical aristocrats. The same is true, conversely, for manual laborers with Ph.D's. Education is very close to constituting a part of that syndrome of ascriptions which we label "upper," and to devise ways of "removing" it can never be wholly satisfactory.

Equally unsound are the parallel attempts, often painfully complex, to ferret out prejudice from erudite answerers by asking questions which only obliquely and with great subtlety approach their true target. For the process of education is not purely a cognitive or learning experience in people's lives; it is much more coercive than that. Educated individuals often do appear less prejudiced on questionnaires. But to say that they "learned how to answer" is an inadequate way of framing the process that has taken place. During their educational careers, individuals are confronted with new reference groups — students, faculty members, even authors — who demand new kinds of responses before bestowing approval. Students gradually "learn" what is expected of them. They learn, for instance, that it is inappropriate, even "camp," to state that one is an unreflective believer in old-style Christianity. And they learn not to state outright that they are prejudiced against ethnic groups. In a sense they have developed an ideological interest in expressing themselves in a certain way. That is, they are aware that their own image is tarnished if they respond with prejudice on a questionnaire, just as it is hurt by bad grammar.

They continue to demonstrate this new "knowledge" to the research interviewer. Indeed, it is not surprising that this ideological interest is particularly tapped by ideological queries (such as attitude items). So it is that in important areas of action, including perhaps the greater portion of all verbal or written speech, many Americans refuse to show prejudice and chastise those who do. However, we know that in different circumstances, with other reference groups or with other norms seen as applicable, these same individuals respond quite differently. For example, they may strain to join an exclusive club and may then support its discriminatory policies against Jews and Negroes.

It is not correct to assume that such persons are basically prejudiced and that their questionnaire responses are merely a gloss. Nor is the opposite likely; they are not equalitarians who happen to be a party to racial discrimination. Instead, in both cases, their actions are oriented toward demonstrating things about themselves and toward realizing certain ends. In fact, the contradiction between equalitarian questionnaire response and overt discriminatory act is not all that great; both actions reflect positively, given American values, upon the actor. His questionnaire responses make him appear educated and genteel and upper-class; his exclusive neighborhood and club make him appear exactly the same.

In other words, neither prejudiced nor nonprejudiced replies to attitude items should be viewed as atomistic attributes of the respondent. Such an analysis is rarely applied to instances of actual discrimination in society, because those actions obviously involve more than one actor and take place with tight reference to the social structure of the situation. Neither should a prejudiced nor an equalitarian response be analyzed as a private, personally held opinion of the individual. It is a public opinion — that is, an act made with a reference group clearly or vaguely in mind, to whom the respondent wishes to prove something, if only to prove it to himself. Thus it is not a constant or even a varying characteristic of the individual, but a response to be comprehended only with knowledge of its intended audience and situation — a structural act.[2]

The routine way of phrasing the issue, that is, by asking which group is most prejudiced, can partly be explained by its resonance with individualistic explanations of human action, whether these theories derive from Freud (as in the familiar displaced-hostility argument), are based on other psychological schools of thought, or are sociological in origin. But there is an additional and quite different reason for social scientists to put the matter in their traditional way. Most social scientists are white. Few black sociologists have in fact spent much time discussing which white stratum is at heart most prejudiced, but have concentrated on more structural analyses of actual discrimination by whites and its effects on the black community. White sociologists, on the other hand, are very much interested in "explaining" prejudice as an aberration, thus explaining it away. They have a narcissistic longing to demonstrate that prejudice is not a universal element of the white condition, but results from those "other" whites — the lower class, the upper, or perhaps the pathetic authoritarians, bereft of a warm and sturdy upbringing.[3]

In reality, however, both classes are prejudiced, in different ways and in response to different things they want to prove. The upper class is surely less violent in its prejudice and in its discriminatory actions toward minorities, but that is partly because violence is less its style in any endeavor. It is at the same time much less likely to accept minority groups, because exclusion, even of those whites whom it ranks as status and economic inferiors, is part of what being "upper" is all about. Thus upper-class individuals may feel less concerned, less threatened, and may be more sophisticated regarding verbal answers, while the working class does interact more with minorities and does accept such interaction socially to a greater extent. Returning to the Chinese, then, we shall concentrate on explaining the acts of discrimination they faced, rather than on searching after "true" levels of anti-Chinese prejudice among upper- and lower-class whites.

My first information on this subject, as on so many others, came from the white upper class and the public and semi-public officials. I have argued in Chapter 1 for the existence of a self-conscious and coherent upper class in the Delta. Historically this group has been dominant in the dissemination of written and spoken material about the social system of which it is a part. From Greenville, in particular, this stratum has produced a number of authors and books, of which two — *Lanterns on the Levee,* William Alexander Percy's autobiography, and *God Shakes Creation,* by David Cohn — have been particularly popular and influential outside the Delta. Of more immediate importance is the influence of the newspaper editor in each Delta town. His status and position, like that of the mayor and school superintendent, is a function of his usefulness to the power structure. Therefore, the rhetoric and point of view in much of the Delta press is the rhetoric and viewpoint of the upper class; the same can be said of D.A.R. and W.P.A. chroniclers. In turn, this point of view, overwhelmingly overrepresented in the printed record of the era, pervasively influences the later writing of history.

But most important of all, the outside visitor — businessman, government official, or sociologist — does not easily meet persons who cannot take time off from occupational or familial responsibilities. He meets and interviews those whose positions include, as a duty of office, transacting business with outsiders, or whose power over the daily texture of their own lives is sufficient that they can take time off at their discretion. School officials, librarians, editors, some businessmen, bankers, lawyers, and ministers fall into the first classification, while planters and other businessmen are in the second. In other words, the people whom significant white outsiders usually contact are of upper-middle status, attempting to enter the upper class, or are members of the upper class itself or its sycophants, the public officials.

And so it is that in my own work I count 72 upper-class or "establishment" businessmen, 10 newspaper editors, and 46 public officials among my 163 white interviewees.[4] In part this disproportionate representation is due to my own deliberate decision: since I was gathering data on encounters Chinese have had in various spheres of activity, I chose to interview many individuals connected with or in command of different white institutions. However, to a considerable degree I was influenced, like any other visitor to the Delta, by the channels that were most open: "establishment" persons who by the nature of their jobs and past experience with outsiders were much more available for interview.

Most interviews included substantial discussion of the respondent's general evaluation of the Chinese as a group, and all but a handful of these establishment individuals had high praise for them. Their perseverance and thrift were noted with approval; their strong family ties and low delinquency rates were lauded; and most of all, their unobtrusiveness and quiescence were commended, in explicit contrast to the "other" group, Delta Negroes.

There was considerably more diversity in response to questions about the sources of opposition to Chinese progress. Often the respondent offered an ideological principle — usually citing past relations between Chinese and Negroes — rather than pointing to any one group or individual. Such "explanations" were usually coupled with vague references to "the community" as the responsible actor or to a general consensus, implied by passive verbs. Sometimes, however, specific groups were blamed: Italians, Negroes, or most often, working-class whites. A long-time Bolivar County resident informed me that the objectors to Chinese school attendance in Boyle, where a Chinese boy had attended a white school for a year or so and was then forced to withdraw owing to white complaints, were "low-caliber" whites. The (white) postmaster of another small Bolivar County town told me that Chinese children had been accepted in the local public schools for several years in the twenties, until they were forced out by pressure from Mexican and Negro farm workers, who envied their preferential treatment.

A Chinese merchant who owns a rather large supermarket was not allowed to buy a lot or home in the corporate limits of a small Delta town a few years ago but was forced to buy a lot and build just outside of town. Recently I was assured by a planter's wife that he could now buy anywhere in town, "anywhere he would *want* to live" — that no neighborhood would be closed to him except perhaps those inhabited by the "peckerwoods," the lower-class whites, who might make trouble. Repeatedly, then, the white upper class blamed the resistance to Chinese upon working-class whites or other lower-status groups. The Chinese, however, analyze the situation quite differently, and their view is confirmed by detailed information from some members of the white establishment.

Actual Sources of Resistance

It is instructive, first of all, simply to observe the locations of homes belonging to Chinese grocers. The Chinese have come up with three solutions to their housing problems. Many still live behind, beside, or above their stores, in Negro neighborhoods. But this is not a strategic answer to the problem of presenting a distinctively non-Negro image to the white community, and so two alternatives have been developed. The merchant may build a home in an area formerly not residential at all, and hence not defined black or white. This has been done by families in several small towns, who live outside the corporate limits, and in Cleveland, where a complete Chinese neighborhood has grown up. It is only an interim solution, though, and even in Cleveland it is being superseded by purchases in white neighborhoods, for in buying a house in a white neighborhood, the Chinese grocer takes a major step toward defining himself and his family as full members of the white community.

The areas into which Chinese have successfully moved, whether in Cleveland, Clarksdale, Greenwood, Greenville, or Rosedale, are almost invariably working class. In all Delta towns with which I am familiar, only two instances, both very recent, can be cited of Chinese entrance into neighborhoods of prime or near-prime status.[5] In many more than two cases, whites refused to let Chinese purchase or move into homes in such areas. As a result, the Chinese family typically buys a modest home, not new, in a working class neighborhood, and then improves it, adding a room, carport, or perhaps a brick facade. Thus it becomes an above-average home for the area.

When Chinese integrate residentially, then, they almost always do so in working-class neighborhoods. That should not be surprising, however, for whenever integration occurs in America, wherever Negroes and whites live adjacently in

Northern or Southern towns, the working class is almost always the white stratum involved. In part, this is due to its lesser influence in the community. Realtors are or would like to be members of the upper or upper-middle class, and they are therefore quite interested to avoid affronting those groups. Via actual or potential status grants the upper class can co-opt and control their actions. This is exactly what has happened in Mississippi, as a white businessman made clear in an interview with George Rummel: "There are some real estate agents in this town that make sure the Chinese stay in their place because they won't let them buy any property in our section of town. Mind you, I'm not prejudiced against those people, but I think that they should stay in their place, the nigger in his place, and we'll stay in ours." [6] The opinions of working-class families, on the other hand, may not matter to realtors, especially if the transactions look lucrative.

Thus patterns of residential land ownership by Mississippi Chinese may merely demonstrate that both upper- and lower-class whites share a similar distaste for Chinese neighbors, while only the upper class has the social resources to translate that attitude into effective action. Even this finding, however, strongly contradicts the upper-class assertion that the prime sources of opposition to Chinese advancement lie in the working class; for though both groups may be hostile to the Chinese, the effective opposition — discrimination, compared to mere prejudice — is mobilized only by the upper class.

And the postmaster's story about Mexican-Negro pressure against the Chinese, recounted above, is preposterous, because it alleges that indigent Negroes and Mexicans in the early thirties were in a position to force the white school board to make decisions relating to their operation of the white schools. The record was set straight by a retired county school administrator, who told me that Negro "pressure" was in no way involved, and probably had never existed, but that three members of the white upper class — two planters and a lawyer — had complained to the school board.

In one Bolivar County town, I talked with a wealthy planter who himself, he admitted, had been one of a group of upper-class citizens who had systematically bought up lots or talked to property owners to make it impossible for a Chinese family to buy or build a home within the city limits. The grocer was forced to build outside of town, on the highway, and proceeded to construct a beautiful modern brick dwelling. Nevertheless, although his own ideas might have changed in the interim, the planter suspected that most of his friends who had shared in the discriminatory action would do so again. In other words, the upper class, not the lower, was responsible for the discrimination. Time after time this pattern repeated itself, as I was to learn from interview after interview. The Chinese indicated to me who opposed them, sometimes with specific details, and their reports were corroborated by interviews like that reported above. A former resident of Louise, Mississippi, for example, told me that: "The Chinese were always in school there. They had a vote on it once; and only two people voted against us, we later found out — both planters with money." And in Cleveland, a retired school board member said that it was the upper class that influenced opposition to school integration there too; "they were the only group that took an interest in the schools anyway." Finally, in Leland, which might otherwise have followed the small-town pattern of early and easy integration, one important planter influenced the school board to deny entrance to the Chinese until 1952, making Leland perhaps the last school system in the Delta to admit them.

Discrimination can be localized in the upper class. What evidence is there, then, that lower white strata are equally prejudiced? Although not able to block or even to learn about a move in advance, they have on occasion reacted with hostility to new Chinese neighbors. In Greenville they dumped garbage on their new neighbors' lawn, and in Clarksdale they made threatening phone calls to dissuade the Chinese family from taking occupancy. However, these instances have been fairly rare and the opposition has proved to be rather ephemeral.

The occasional initial flare-ups can perhaps be understood with more information. The lower class faces a very real threat of Negro integration. (Why this is a "threat" will be discussed later.) In Greenville, Clarksdale, and other Delta towns, Negroes and working-class whites share some neighborhoods. This has long been an accepted pattern. As civil rights rhetoric and progress continue, however, the Negro gradually becomes perceived as a possible social threat, even if only an imagined one, and geographic distance becomes important as a way to restore social distance, remain in all-white schools, and so forth. So it is that new housing developments in Greenville and other towns are completely white or completely black. And older integrated areas, especially those districts under court order to define school populations geographically rather than by utilizing "freedom of choice" loopholes, are rapidly segregating themselves. In such a context, working-class residents feel threatened by Negro integration, and the Chinese newcomer may be viewed as a possible first hole in the dike. Specifically, he may have to face the rumor that he in turn intends to sell the house to a Negro. Once he has moved in and shows signs of permanent residence, such as property improvement, this rumor apparently dissipates, as does the hostility it engendered.

Besides residential neighborhoods, the Delta supports a multitude of voluntary associations of various types, oriented toward different groups within the population. Chinese residents have attempted to participate in many white organizations, with varying degrees of success. On the whole, their active membership has been limited to the American Legion, the Veterans of Foreign Wars, and some churches and church groups. The Legion and the Veterans are oriented primarily toward the lower-middle and working-class white. They have been remarkably friendly to the Chinese, opening their halls for all-Chinese dances and banquets and electing Chinese to positions of leadership. The churches to which Chinese belong vary more widely. Most are Baptist, but a few are Methodist or Presbyterian congregations. Socially, Baptist churches in turn vary widely, from "First" church, in most communities the oldest and most prestigious, to smaller and more working-class institutions in neighborhoods and rural areas. On the whole, the smaller Baptist churches have rather actively sought Chinese membership; the large Baptist churches have handled the problem by establishing separate missions for the Chinese; and the even more upper-class congregations, including Presbyterians and Episcopalians, have almost no Chinese members. Therefore, one must conclude that working-class organizations, for the most part, have admitted the Chinese to membership and in some cases have actually sought their participation.

In contrast, Rotary, Kiwanis, the Delta Council, and the country clubs have in almost all cases excluded the Chinese. Even Chambers of Commerce have been highly reluctant. In Greenwood, no Chinese grocer has been accepted, even though several own rather large stores and at least one has asked. The Greenville chamber has admitted Chinese to membership, but their reception is at best *pro forma*. One highly respected Chinese leader described it as follows: "Some people welcome us in private, but then they feel uneasy when I sit next to them in public . . . I went for a while, but the guy next to me at dinner would get up and get another seat. How do you suppose *I* feel? After a while I quit going." The only YMCA in the Delta, in Greenville, under the dominance of a long-time resident and businessman, refused to admit Chinese until 1966.

Other minority groups report the same experience as the Chinese. In Shaw and Shelby, towns with sizable Italian minorities: "the Italians aren't even allowed to *date* the aristocracy. The ————'s, among others, put their foot down. They sent their daughter away to school so she'd stop dating a Jew." [7] Similarly, a businessman of Lebanese descent in

Vicksburg told me, "We have *fine* relations with the other minority groups [Chinese, Jew, Negro]. The problem here has been with the *majority!*"

Conversely, Chinese merchants report little difficulty in getting along with other ethnic groups. "The Jews are the best friends we ever had," according to a Greenville grocer, while in Vicksburg a Lebanese banker was the first to express willingness to loan money for a Chinese merchant to buy a home in an exclusive white suburb. And in Shaw, a Chinese merchant told me: "The Italians accept Chinese better than the old-line families do. I *know* that." Nor was this an isolated opinion; most Chinese whom I asked agreed with it.

Hodding Carter, publisher of the Greenville *Delta Democrat-Times,* the largest daily in the Delta, agreed that not only is the upper class more able to discriminate but it is also more willing to do so: "Integrating the Chinese antagonized the old Greenville first families, which I couldn't understand, because they should have been the last to be upset about it. The ordinary people didn't care, because they had come to know the Chinese merchant in his store. Almost complete social barriers [against the Chinese] still exist among the people of consequence."

Acts of anti-Chinese discrimination do not originate solely from the ranks of the upper class, however. Occasionally, competing white grocers have organized against Chinese merchants, carrying along a few of their petty-bourgeois friends. The best example, documented by petitions, letters, and school-board minutes, concerned the proposed admission of a Chinese girl to the public school system of Clarksdale in 1941.

On February 21, 1941, the Clarksdale school board received a letter on the letterhead of the Clarksdale Baptist Church, signed by its pastor and eighty-eight other individuals, asking "whatever honest consideration you might make in their [the Chinese] desire and hope to have access to the [white] facilities of the Clarksdale Public Schools." Previously, on November 11, 1940, the board had denied the request. On September 3, 1941, however, in reply to the Baptist letter and the Chinese request, the board unanimously voted to admit the child. Shortly thereafter, on October 8, E. C. Cagle presented to the board a petition signed by him and twenty-nine others requesting "that no person or child or children of the Chinese or Mongolian race be permitted to attend the Clarksdale City Schools," and citing the Mississippi Supreme Court decision of 1925 in the case of *Rice v. Gong Lum*.[8] Of the twenty-six signers whose occupation could be determined, twelve were grocers or grocers' wives. Nine others were small businessmen, including four barbers, two mechanics, a cafe operator, and a drycleaner and his wife.[9] At least five of the thirty were of Lebanese descent, and Italian and Jewish names were also listed. By working to keep Chinese children out of the only acceptable school system, they perhaps hoped to persuade Chinese merchants to leave Clarksdale. More importantly, they were attempting to deny to themselves and to the Chinese that the latter, their equals or superiors economically, were equally high in status and self-worth.[10] The other small businessmen perhaps went along because of this latter consideration, although it is more likely that they happened to be friends and peers of the grocers who organized the effort.

It is still true that competitive grocers sometimes slur the Chinese on racial grounds. Direct economic interest, then, plus the implied status threat coming from sharing an occupation with a racial minority, definitely motivate the behavior of some working- and lower-middle-class whites. With the exception of the competing merchants, however, the working class accepts the Chinese. A final bit of evidence is that the seven marriages which I am aware of between Chinese and Caucasian in Mississippi have without exception involved lower-class white girls.[11] Once again, to those familiar with actual facts of integration and acceptance in other parts of America, this pattern of lower-class integration and upper-class intransigence is not surprising. For example, in a detailed study of cultural minorities in Burlington, Vermont, Elin Anderson observed: "The old Americans, more than any [other] group, emphasized their ethnic origin or expressed race-consciousness." [12] In Mississippi, however, and perhaps also in Vermont, the position of the aristocracy has been assured and could certainly not be shaken by such trivial adjustments as the school or residential integration of a few Chinese citizens. The Chinese represented neither an economic nor a social threat to the white "first families." Why, then, were these families so hostile?

A planter's wife in Shelby told me the story of a friend of hers, who said to her daughter in 1966: "Now you be sure to talk to and be nice to the little colored child in your classroom." The little daughter, only in the first or second grade, replied, "Mommy, why do that? Why start something you know you will have to stop?" And the mother said to me, "You know, I think she's smarter than *we* are!" The story amuses because of the precociousness of the little girl. It is also a key to the upper-class mind. School organization, especially in high school, after the children have grown old enough to have a "social" life, mirrors in microcosm the larger social divisions of the adult world in Mississippi.

After Negroes desegregated the white high school in Hollandale, almost all social activities were eliminated. The dances and homecoming activities were the first to be cut, of course, but the school even dropped its yearbook rather than integrate it. The students were the ones hurt by these decisions, and it was not they who decided them but, as they told me, their parents.

Sex seems somehow to be behind it all. A white teacher described the situation of the Chinese students in Rosedale in these terms: "The Chinese children are completely accepted through about the sixth grade there, but they begin to drop out of social groups when these are formed in the seventh or eighth grades. For the first few years, the parents don't bother with who the children play with at school." She went on to point out: "You know, this exclusion and discrimination is not just a racial thing. The upper crust acts this way towards *anybody*. It's really more class than caste." The upper-class woman who told me the story of the little girl went on to defend her point of view. "It's only natural," she said, "that parents would want their children to marry and live with members of their own group. Every group feels that way. And once the line is drawn at marriage, if you're prudent you want to draw it a little *before* marriage." In short, this way of thinking leads to residential segregation, institutional segregation on both class and caste lines, and at the logical extreme, apartheid.

A major factor in the partial escape of the Chinese from this treatment has been their outspoken emphasis on endogamy, discussed in the preceding chapter. Furthermore, the Chinese merchant usually enjoys a financial advantage over his working-class neighbor; thus he has economic position to offset caste inferiority. Typically he improves his house until it stands as a significant credit to the neighborhood, and his white neighbors can defend it as such to their status equals. An upper-class white resident, who would be called upon to defend having a new Chinese neighbor in myriad subtle ways, would not have this recourse. He could only rely on straight ideology — "open housing" — which of course is out of the question in Mississippi. To put this another way, an upper-class citizen would have to assert that the Chinese, and by implication anyone else, have a perfect right to move next to him, or else he would be forced to admit that although he did not condone the Chinese presence, he was powerless to prevent it. Such an admission of impotence and inadequate status no upper-class individual would willingly make. But a worker's peers would rarely even raise such an issue, because working-class whites in the Delta do not and realistically cannot have such a proprietary feeling about their neighborhoods. The Chinese presence would be taken more as an act of God, something that happened to the neighborhood, but nothing the worker could have known about or controlled.[13] He would not be called upon to defend it, since it would be known that he was not responsible. Even if he was asked, admitting ignorance and impotence would not be regarded a startling weakness, since the questioner would also probably be in a similar position vis-à-vis the power structure.

The upper class, then, views any attempt at residential or institutional integration as a possible threat to their racial and economic in-group and specifically to their endogamy. Only an elite class is likely to feel such an argument strongly, since by definition only it stands at the top of society as an exclusive group. Working-class whites, on the other hand, occasionally even marry Chinese and feel less strongly in general about whom their children play with.

A minister who has worked for many years among the Delta Chinese pushed the argument still further by observing: "The Chinese tried at first to get accepted through the church. That didn't work too well. Church people are somewhat hypocritical: they want the Chinese to be Christian, but they don't want to sit next to them. Then the Chinese tried mingling on a business level . . . and that led to much better acceptance. They get along better with such people as mayors, police chief, business leaders, than in church." Businessmen have excuses and incentives to be more liberal in accepting the Chinese on an equal basis. The Chinese are merchants, too, and it is often in the interest of the business community to get their cooperation in civic ventures. More generally, whites traded at Chinese stores, especially in the smaller towns, before Chinese were welcomed into church, and long before they were admitted to white schools or other organizations. Again, the purchasers had valid and defensible reasons to shop in Chinese stores, such as lower prices or proximity. Church members, on the other hand, have no particular reason to admit or seek out Chinese members, especially since there are so few Chinese that it is unlikely that they could ever be a major financial bulwark of the congregation. Their motivation must be more purely ideological, and of course the ideology for Chinese inclusion runs dangerously near to the rationales for the general inclusion of all minority groups, including Negroes. Hence Christian congregations could be convinced by their pastors that it was a good thing to Christianize the Chinese, especially if it could be done in a separate mission, but they were not ready to extend complete social acceptance to them. As a Chinese businessman said, "Liberal church people can't go too far for the Chinese, because they could be accused of having the position of going all the way with everybody." And so, he continued, "Chinese put on a false front when they go to Caucasian church, because they know that acceptance is one thing *in* church, and another thing outside."

There is also an element of pure ignorance in the upper-class attitude. The working white, as Carter says, does get to know the Chinese and to know him as an approximate social equal. The upper class has less information to go on and therefore is more apt to stereotype.[14] But the causes of hostility toward Chinese, from both upper and lower classes, are more complex than has yet been shown. A full explanation of white resistance requires a more extensive analysis of relations within the white class system and also involves consideration of white-black caste relations. In the next section, therefore, anti-Chinese prejudice and discrimination will be analyzed in the context of anti-Negro actions and feelings. By contrasting the reaction against the two groups, more knowledge of the causes of hostility toward each can be gained.

Anti-Chinese and Anti-Negro Opposition

Lower-class whites, we have seen, commit rather few acts of hostility or oppression against the Chinese. Their reaction to "uppity" Negroes, on the other hand, is less restrained; there are many acts of racial antipathy between the two groups. It is not enough, however, merely to prove that working-class individuals participate in such actions. Historically, this is the way the Delta upper class has phrased the issue — a matter of their own quiescence, with actual opposition to minority progress stemming from lower-class whites. Lynchings were usually attributed to lower-class whites; allegedly the oligarchy looked on benignly. Even after the 1964 civil rights summer, in his introduction to a book detailing acts of brutal repression visited upon civil rights workers mostly by the official law enforcement structure of the state, Hodding Carter III could still repeat the old cliche: "All that is necessary for the triumph of evil is for good men to do nothing." [15] And because of the establishment's unequal influence on the news and history-making media, its view has generally prevailed.

This view is easy to understand. People naturally like to believe good things about themselves and about the circles in which they move. In many instances they do not consciously attempt to deceive the outsider but have no personal knowledge of the incident under discussion and easily assume that lower white strata, for whom they have only contempt anyway, were responsible. For example, I described above an interview with a long-time Bolivar County resident during which she informed me that "low caliber" whites forced the withdrawal of a Chinese boy from school in Boyle. Later in the interview I told her the confirmed facts, which indicated that a rich planter had been largely responsible. She then candidly admitted, "I don't know *who* it was, to tell you the truth." To be sure, the oligarchy has little reason to publicize this kind of action to outsiders, and in many other cases the deception its members practiced in interviews with me, regarding their treatment of the Chinese, was quite deliberate. And equally deliberate has been their myth, carefully nurtured over the years, of kindness and fair play toward Delta blacks.[16]

But this traditional vision — of evil deeds committed by the working class while the aristocracy, though not righteous or powerful enough to intervene, nevertheless consists of "good men doing nothing" — greatly distorts the facts. The fact that most of the violent acts of repression recorded in the very book for which Carter wrote the introduction were initiated by local elected and appointed public officials is sufficient proof of the error of his view, for no other individuals are so dependent upon the good graces of the upper class.[17] Additional evidence that the working class is not the prime mover of racial antagonism is provided by John Dollard. In his famous study of Delta society published in 1937, he concluded that the white establishment, which he termed the "middle class," was the source of the most virulent anti-Negro feeling and action.[18] Sketchy data indicate that the authors of *Deep South*, writing about Natchez, concur.[19] An added bit of evidence is that in the years after the Civil War there were a few Negro lynchings *by other Negroes*. Wharton states that the black perpetrators were "usually urged on by whites," in a system in which "lynching was recognized as one of the methods of control which were to be used by the dominant race." [20] In these instances it is clear that whites did not merely look on benignly, while Negroes, motivated by some natural animosity, lynched others of their race. The parallel to working-class white behavior may be a close one.

In general, in a stratified society with a powerful elite, ideas and actions are to a great degree controlled from above, and even if specific violent incidents are not directed by the establishment, they can nevertheless be traced to evaluative principles stemming from that class and codified in the class-caste hierarchy. Before 1900, Veblen had formulated this idea clearly: "Each class envies and emulates the class next above it in the social scale . . . That is to say, our standard of decency . . . is set by the usage of those next above us in reputability; until in this way, . . . all canons of reputability and decency . . . are traced back by insensible gradations to the usages and habits of thought of the highest social and pecuniary class — the wealthy leisure class." [21] Thus it is not clear that poor whites, who usually act under the influence of rich whites, for some reason act on their own when they move against Negroes, for the upper class controls the moral standards as well as the bases of power in the Mississippi Delta.[22]

We must conclude that the prejudice and discrimination shown by working-class whites is related to their position in the white class structure and cannot be understood in isolation of that structure. Negro political leaders know this; for example, a Delta doctor, active in civil rights, told me: "Ne-groes and poor whites would get along if they were left alone. The problem is with the upper class. They're public liberals, but private demons." In *Caste, Class, and Race,* the major Marxist analyst of the social structure of the South, Oliver C. Cox, presents a similar argument: "It seems clear that in de-veloping a theory of race relations in the South one must look to the economic policies of ruling class . . . Opposition [by the working class] to social equality has no meaning unless we can see its function in the service of the exploitative purpose of this [upper] class." [23] Lillian Smith puts the case even more vividly in her famous parable, "Two Men and a Bar-gain," [24] in which "Mr. Rich White" says to "Mr. Poor White": I'll let you dominate the Negro in order to keep you from thinking about my own domination of you, and that way I'll keep both from making common cause against me.

Neither Cox nor Smith quite make the process believable, however. First of all, they place too much credence in the upper-class assertion that anti-Negro sentiment derives from lower-class whites. Indeed, both of them accept this assertion in toto and then construct their theories in order to explain lower-class oppression, as though it were an observed fact. Smith even blames segregation in specifically upper-class in-stitutions on lower-class pressure: [Mr. Rich White is speak-ing] "And you can make rules about restaurants and hotels too if it'll make you feel better. And I reckon it will, though you aren't likely ever to go into one of the hotels or restau-rants you put your Jim Crow rule on." [25] But as example after example of anti-Chinese opposition has documented, lower-class whites do not even have control over those institutions — such as the public schools — of which they *are* members. It is frivolous to assert that they control or significantly influ-ence organizations that are upper class alone. Moreover, Cox and Smith do not adequately delineate the way in which the upper class is said to influence the lower. In her parable, Smith slides into the assumption that lower-class whites "nat-urally" are anti-Negro and that Mr. Rich White cannot do anything for the Negro lest he offend his friend, Mr. Poor White.[26] Cox is more realistic and notes that there might exist "natural" pressures toward interracial solidarity: "Now, we may ask, why should competition be more natural than consolidation in the struggle for wealth and position? Why should insecurity lead more naturally to division than to a closing of ranks?" [27]

There have, in fact, been a few striking exceptions to the usual hostility between white and black. Since 1865 there have always been instances of serious integration on a plane of social equality between Negroes and lower-class whites, usually arising from similarities in life style and from proximity in residence or work. In a work of great historical erudition, Michael Schwartz chronicles some examples during the last decade of the nineteenth century.[28]

Davis, Gardner, and Gardner describe such patterns as a general rule for Natchez in 1936: "Lower-class whites living in Negro [mixed] neighborhoods treated their Negro neighbors in much the same way as they did their white neighbors. There were the usual gossiping, exchange of services, and even visiting." [29] I took notice of other examples during my fieldwork in the Delta in 1967:

> Three white students attend Coahoma Junior College, an otherwise all-black institution just outside Clarksdale, part-time. They are all from the lower class. No upper-class Delta white attends any Negro college in the state, even though one institution — Tougaloo College near Jackson — is clearly the equal of most Mississippi white schools.
>
> On Poplar Street in Greenville, a working-class neighborhood, white and Negro children from near-infants up to high-school age can be seen playing together. What is significant about this, in contrast to the analysis presented above regarding upper-class high-schoolers, is that the white parents do not stop it.
>
> Working-class whites do not derogate those few whites

who operate groceries in Negro neighborhoods in Cleveland. In fact, I could not draw unfavorable comments from them. This is in dramatic contrast to the spontaneous expressions of disgust from upper-class businessmen and public officials (see Chapters 2 and 3). The grocers live in working-class white residential areas and are accepted by their neighbors.

All Negro doctors report that they have a handful of white patients, invariably from the lower class.

Head Start Programs all over Mississippi report cases of successfully integrated programs. Under certain conditions, to be outlined below, white families do voluntarily send their children to predominantly Negro attendance centers.

It appears, therefore, that working- and lower-class whites may not be unalterably hostile to blacks, but since the failure of the Populist movement in the 1890's, instances of cooperation between working-class whites and Negroes have been extremely rare. Cox's question, "Why should insecurity lead more naturally to division than to a closing of ranks," seems to be the crucial question to ask. Cox poses it more or less rhetorically, but it does allow answer.

The lower-class white cannot step back, take stock of his situation, and elect to make an alliance with his economic peer, the lower-class black. He cannot for two reasons. First, chances of quick success are slim. If a long-term concerted effort could be mounted, the combination of Negroes and whites would surely constitute an effective electoral majority, and with political power, major revisions in the educational and economic systems could be undertaken. But forging, maintaining, and utilizing the alliance would take at least several years, perhaps decades. In the meantime, the second factor would come into play: whites who cooperate with Negroes are subject to overwhelming status pressures.[30] This is what the term "nigger-lover" is used for. Repeatedly it has been observed in this study that the white view of Negroes, crystallized in the etiquette forms of segregation, constitutes a devastating attack on the self-esteem of the minority. Consequently it comes as no surprise that lower-class whites do not want to be classed with Negroes.

One of my best informants, a teacher, who clearly delineated the main dynamics of class and caste relations, unwittingly revealed her own part in their maintenance: "I had one child who would come to school with her face *so* dirty. I would say, 'you don't want to get mistaken for a nigger! — better clean your face, it's pretty dirty,' and send her home to wash up. And boy, that would get her momma *going!*" To repeat, then, the lower-class white really works to avoid being classed with Negroes. And who might so classify him? Only his status superiors, of course. As Veblen pointed out, what his status inferiors, such as the black populace itself, might think of him makes little difference. What is relevant to him, to his self-definition, and to all his endeavors, is evaluation from those immediately above him in the social hierarchy.[31] Mississippi residents know this. The public rhetoric, especially in the newspapers, sometimes conceals the endemic relations of upper-class sentiment to the maintenance of segregation, but this rhetoric is like the cloud of verbiage which surrounds most public and private decision-making in America. When it comes down to actual events, upper-class Mississippians do not admit that activities go on in the community in spite of or without their control, and they give detailed evidence of that control.

It is important to recognize that the system of minority oppression is a structural system and an etiquette system. This means that its maintenance has been a matter of repeated opposition to the small transgressions which occur almost daily. Systematized coercion is required; the very rarity of instances of white-black cooperation on an equal level seems to demonstrate that reluctance or hostility on the part of individuals is not the only factor involved. A parallel will help make the point. In the early 1960's Negro leaders and liberal whites pointed with anger to many all-white communities surrounding Northern metropolises. In Edina, Minnesota, for example, one of the largest suburbs of Minneapolis-St. Paul, not a single Negro family resided. Such complete exclusion must be exactly that — exclusion, maintained by the public and private policies of the town's power structure. It cannot be seriously asserted that of the thousands of Negro families in greater Minneapolis-St. Paul, *none* possessed the money and the wish to live in Edina. And of course, no one did so argue in private — all knew that organized exclusion was responsible.

Similarly, in Mississippi, the fact that until 1966 not one Mississippi white attended Coahoma Junior College or any other Negro institution of higher learning is an unnatural statistic. It could not exist without an aura of coercion, an informal public policy against such breaches of the caste line, enforceable only by those who customarily influence the legal and quasilegal structures — the white upper class. That a few lower-class whites now dare to attend Coahoma Junior College is not due to any substantial revolution in the attitudes of the lower-class whites of Coahoma County, for among those many individuals a few eccentrics could always have been found who might take such a step if not impeded. It is due rather to a deterioration in the ease with which the aristocracy can block all such transgressions, and to a deterioration of upper-class unanimity on the necessity for so acting, partly resulting from a liberalization of attitudes of some members of the group, more attuned to national rhetoric and reference groups.

Therefore, Mississippi whites and blacks who attempt to change the system or to work within it often direct substantial effort toward splitting or weakening the upper class's support of violent attacks or status threats against whites who deviate. For example, Mississippi Action for Progress, Inc., is a federally funded agency operating child development programs in some two dozen Mississippi counties. It organized an entire administrative division to deal with public relations and "community development"; a large part of the new division's responsibilities related specifically to this problem. Its director, Bruce Nicholas, told me that if a few upper-echelon supporters can be found for a Head Start Center, then lower-class whites can be recruited to work in and send their children to it, even if its attendance roll is predominantly black. Otherwise, a familiar pattern recurs: white children come, but are withdrawn after a short time. In the interim an upper-class white has learned of the situation, and sometimes even without direct effort to break it up, accomplishes exactly that, by casually making a remark such as, "You mean to say you've got your kid in that *nigger* Head Start?" The parent at this point has no choice but to reply, "I didn't know it's a *nigger* Head Start!" and then to withdraw his child. He cannot let the other white think he has "cast his lot" with the Negroes, because the implication follows that he is of Negro status and self-worth. In many cases the dissuasion attempt is deliberate and might be followed by direct economic reprisal.

That status threats are most frequently utilized, rather than economic or physical coercion, is indicated by the fact that the few whites who persist in sending their children, or who participate in other ways in predominantly Negro programs or activities, are usually those at the absolute bottom of white society. Often they are exactly the individuals most subject to economic reprisal, but the white aristocracy is so remote from them, their chance of reaching it so slim, that the immediate benefits of the program outweigh any possible further status slights from a group which has already had nothing good to say about them[32] — and so they are not deterred.

In one small town I talked with a white sewage-hauler, with a large family, who lived in a pitiably run-down house and wanted to move into a new federally financed housing project nearby. The white woman who handled applications, although ostensibly more liberal than most whites, who would not even connect themselves with such an enterprise, refused to accept him, telling him that it was a Negro-only project. He objected and continued his attempts to enter, explicitly accepting that his neighbors would be Negro, and defending his action with the equalitarian rationale that, "I've known a lot of them, and a lot of them are better than a lot of white people, a whole lot." By occupation he was of detestable status in the Delta (although not in the North, as noted in Chapter 2), and he admitted as much, saying, "I don't know six white men in town!"

In the face of upper-class unanimity, however, this white sewage-hauler is a marked exception. The difference between white and black status, backed by crucial differences in economic and political rights, is so overwhelming that the vast majority of lower-class whites will do almost anything to avoid being classed with the minority race by power-structure whites. Thus the presence of a large Negro population, despite the arguments of many social scientists over the years, does *not* make whites secure in their status by giving them a race to look down upon. On the contrary, it radically increases their status anxiety and multiplies the ways in which they can be pressured. This fact is crucial to understanding the repeated failure of Mississippi laborers to achieve anything like the labor organization, political influence, and economic position of their Northern counterparts. It is also central to an explanation of their anti-Negro sentiments and actions.

If the observer appears to be in a position of dominance, even his briefest encounter with lower-class Delta whites brings out their most single characteristic — their extreme pliability. Time after time, as I met men in Chinese groceries or picked up hitchhikers, I was amazed by their docile external willingness to agree with me. An individual might begin the conversation by advocating the candidacy of George Wallace, but after learning of my reaction he might conclude by agreeing that a better chance for the Negro wouldn't hurt the white man and that Wallace's thinking was a matter of the past. Of course, this agreement was facile and represented no serious idea reversal. No doubt it occurred in many cases just because I was supplying the ride and was thus in a position of advantage. But then, the Delta aristocracy has been taking the lower-class white for a ride for at least seven decades. Much more than in other sections of the United States, the lower- or working-class white in the Delta is without power, status, and occupational security, and is dependent upon his social superiors for myriad small favors — emergency loans, medical care, interpretation of legal points and influence before the law, temporary employment, and so forth. He therefore must remain "attractive" to his superiors and cannot really contemplate deviation.

It should by now be apparent that workers and poor whites are not the sole seat of antiminority prejudice in the Delta, nor the basic cause of most oppressive measures. But neither should the matter be put the other way: upper-class whites are not the source or cause of Mississippi's racial antagonism either. Given the ongoing system and ideology, both upper and lower white status groups have interests in opposing blacks and, to a lesser extent, Chinese. Mr. Rich White and Mr. Poor White react in their varied ways because of their different social positions. The upper class is more exclusive and more defensive about its position and considers endogamy essential to its continued dominance. Furthermore, its members cannot admit to powerlessness and must occasionally demonstrate their influence when incidents which threaten the etiquette code arise. Hence the upper class is far more discriminatory. The lower class is more status-threatened, especially by the upper class, and to differentiate itself from Negroes and assert that it is above blacks, it therefore performs occasional acts of extreme violence which even the police do not often undertake.[33] The public officials, including police and sheriffs, are (with noble exceptions) responsive to the will of those who influence public policy — the local oligarchies — and can be relied upon for the constant small decisions and daily harassments needed to maintain segregation etiquette.[34]

In all strata, there are a few ideological liberals. Most have been liberal only in private, so they are irrelevant to the analysis of Delta social structure, since they behave publicly like their illiberal peers. Dollard apparently contacted two or three such persons, definitely from the upper class,[35] as did I; the *Deep South* authors interviewed several from lower strata.[36] For example, a Greenville writer and long-term resident said to me with great intensity: "Remember, when you tell this story [of the Chinese], that there have been a few of us who have been and are trying to do the right thing." But as she indicated, with the white majority and an ongoing system against them, they have been ineffectual in the past.

It should not be facilely assumed that this white majority is acting in its own "rational self-interest" when it enforces segregation. Cox assumes it is. He believes their moves can be traced to a conscious rationale that lower-class white and black must be kept separate. He further holds that, given the capitalist system, in the short run the white worker does face a threat of Negro competition, should discrimination bars suddenly come down. Cox therefore can only hope for a radical overthrow of the existing profit system in order to solve the problem of racial segregation and discrimination: "There will be no more 'crackers' or 'niggers' after a socialist revolution because the social necessity for these types will have been removed. But the vision which the capitalist theorist dreads most is this: that there will be no more capitalists and capitalist exploitation. If we attempt to see race relations realistically, the meaning of the capitalist function is inescapable . . . The purpose of revolution . . . is to overthrow the entire system, to overthrow a ruling class." [37] But the upper class is not reacting "rationally" to a perceived and real threat to their hegemony. Carter's statement regarding their opposition to the Chinese is instructive: "Integrating the Chinese antagonized the Old Greenville first families, *which I couldn't understand, because they should have been the last to be upset about it* [my italics]." In other words, the Greenville aristocracy was in truth impervious to any assault which might ever be mounted by a few Chinese grocers, and if the upper class felt that Chinese advances would be only a prelude to a push for equal rights by blacks, they were reasoning without foundation, as subsequent events easily demonstrated.

Their actions against the Chinese, as argued earlier in this chapter, were partly based on their exclusiveness, their endogamy, and their social distinctions. They have "an ideology of contempt," as Carter put it. But many of their actions bear no effective relationship even to this broader and vaguer aim. Since many of the transgressions they suppress have nothing to do with simple economic or political cooperation, their oppression against whites who break the color line can be understood, according to this type of thinking, only as part of a conscious effort to keep all whites and all blacks apart in all endeavors, lest they learn they can get along together. Or their repression must be explained on another basis.

It can be. The interracial activities *offend* the whites. The white reaction is no calculated reply to a rationally perceived threat. It is an emotional answer, an attempt to end an offensive practice, offensive in that it contravenes the rationale of segregation. If Negroes are subhuman, not capable of full citizenship, unclean, probably sexual offenders, barbarians, then social intercourse with them is not only out of the question but is obscene, perverted, and those who engage in it must themselves be abnormal.[38] So we are driven to ask the final question: What is the cause of the *rationale* of segregation? Why was this incredible and horrifying series of assertions put forth and accepted? It was already observed (in Chapter 2) that in many ways segregation gets in the way of rational economic exploitation of the subordinate race. Why then does it exist?

Only two arguments appear plausible. The first is the now traditional theory put forth by Elkins,[39] Myrdal,[40] and others, that existing treatment of blacks in slavery times, coupled with the strong ethic of individual responsibility and equal opportunity which comprised the public American version of the Protestant Ethic, required rationalization. According to Myrdal: "It should be observed that in the pro-slavery thinking of the *ante-bellum* South, the Southerners stuck to the

American Creed *as far as whites were concerned;* in fact, they argued that slavery was necessary in order to establish equality and liberty for the whites. In the precarious ideological situation, where the South wanted to defend a political and civic institution of inequality which showed increasingly great prospects for new land exploitation and commercial profit, but where they also wanted to retain the democratic creed of the nation — *the race doctrine of biological inequality between whites and Negroes offered the most convenient solution.*" [41] By thus defining blacks as subhuman and therefore not subject to the ideology nor the rights of American citizenship, *any* practice, even the breeding for sale, literacy denials, and other customs of American slavery, could be countenanced.

After Reconstruction, Myrdal points out: "the race dogma was retained in the South as necessary to justify the caste system which succeeded slavery as the social organization of Negro-white relations . . . The fact that the same rationalizations are used to defend slavery and caste is one of the connecting links between the two social institutions . . . Even today the average white Southerner really uses the race dogma to defend not only the present caste situation but also *ante-bellum* slavery and, consequently, the rightousness of the Southern cause in the Civil War." [42] In sum, then, this line of analysis is sociological and historical; it ascribes the rationale of segregation to a "need" in the idea system (and in the psyches of those who lived with that system) caused by a development of the social structure.

A second explanation concentrates on what the segregation rationale does. This is a functionalist approach: social institutions can sometimes be explained by what they do. It is also one Marxist approach: if an institution is exploiting the poor, it probably was established to do so and is being maintained because of the interests it serves. The rationale of segregation has a pervasive effect on a subordinate group. Dollard put this argument cogently: "This type of aggression [attacks on the self-esteem of the minority individual] is a chronic policy of the white caste in the South; its aim seems to be to humiliate the Negro, to put him on another and lower scale of humanity, and thereby to paralyze his aggressive tendencies by making them seem hopeless." [43] Perhaps this is the most painless way to retain dominance — by destroying the self-confidence of the subordinate race, so that submission results. Myrdal states this argument himself: "Plantation owners and employers, who use Negro labor as cheaper and more docile, have at times been observed to tolerate, or even cooperate in, the periodic aggressions of poor whites against Negroes. It is a plausible thesis that they do so in the interest of upholding the caste system which is so effective in keeping the Negro docile." [44]

And not only in the South, under segregation, but also in Northern cities, with a less rigid *class* system, the same process takes place. Writing about Burlington, Vermont, a city with several cultural minorities, Anderson put the case strongly: "The small Old American group has been helped to maintain its predominant position by the strength of its traditional feeling of the racial superiority of the Anglo-Saxon. Interestingly enough, the newer peoples on the whole accept the Old Americans at their own valuation, perhaps partly because the premium placed on conformity to standards already set has not permitted them to value their own standards and interpretations of America." [45]

Katrin Norris observed the same process at work on behalf of the aristocracy in Jamaica: "How is this halo of worthiness round the upper class maintained? Mainly by the old psychological confidence trick played by an upper class on a traditionally humble class, of simply adopting an attitude of natural superiority and expecting an attitude of inferiority in return." [46] But the system of segregation, and the assumptions it contains, are surely not a consciously enacted solution to the problem of maintaining racial hierarchy. I find, therefore, the Myrdal-Elkins-et al. explanation more congenial on the whole, especially when explaining the obviously irrational white opposition to the Chinese. However, there are many moments at which upper-class whites do in a way "step back" and ask themselves what might happen if this etiquette breach were allowed and then come in to suppress it. The use of the term "uppity nigger" is indicative of this suppression. So the effect of segregation etiquette is known and does provide further reason for its maintenance.

The exact mix of the two causes is perhaps not an important question. In any event, examining the opposition generated by the segregation system to the advancement of the Chinese can supply us with no further data with which to decide the matter. The weight of my evidence, however, does argue against the traditional prejudice-to-discrimination view. Both explanations we are left with begin from the social structure and only then move to the level of ideas. This is as it must be. The Chinese case — the continuing opposition to Chinese integration — cannot be explained by any current psychological theory of scapegoating, aggression, or prejudice in general. For all individualistic theories in some way invoke as their motive force an innate or socially generated pool of hostility. But there is already a scapegoat in the Mississippi system — the blacks — who receive more hostility than *any* group in most systems. By these theories, therefore, the Delta Chinese should never have faced as much opposition as Chinese did in, say, the state of Washington, and now that they have escaped Negro classification, their path should be especially free of opposition. But it is not. There is more prejudice and more discrimination directed against them in Mississippi than in Washington, just as there is more hostility aimed even at working-class *whites* in Mississippi than in Washington. The presence of a large oppressed population seems to increase rather than release the pressure in the system. It seems clear, then, that in addition to discrimination, levels of prejudice and their causes derive from social structure, not from individual psychology, though prejudice itself is, to be sure, a product of the mind.

Interracial Families 6

Exclusion of Chinese-Negroes by Chinese

As the Mississippi Chinese increasingly made their way into white society and began to be defined as "whites" during the 1940's, one group was left behind: those who had married or were still associated in common law with Negro women. Their position became more and more anomalous as the Chinese group as a whole completed the transition from near-black to near-white. The pure Chinese found it in their interest to exclude them; indeed, such a policy was in some instances explicitly required of them by the white establishment. At the same time, whites did not know exactly how to deal either with Chinese-Negroes or with their Chinese fathers. This ambiguity was taken over from the whites by the black community, so the Chinese-Negro families could not easily feel a part of that group either.

Before 1940, the number of Chinese men who cohabited with or married women from the Negro population is impossible to determine accurately but amounted to perhaps 20 to 30 percent at its peak. Only about a dozen such relationships — less than 5 percent of the total — now remain in the Delta.[1] This group provides yet another twist to the complex tangle of definitional problems engendered by the Chinese in

Mississippi. Rejection of Chinese-Negroes after 1940 by the "pure" Chinese, after essential acceptance before that date, demonstrates that white ideology lay behind the opposition of the Chinese and, as will be seen, of the black community. The concessions whites made to light-skinned Chinese-Negro offspring indicate a similar origin for the color distinctions still prevalent among Delta blacks. The effect of these concessions upon the Chinese-Negroes themselves shows the intrinsic connection between small points of interactional etiquette and assertions about innate self-worth. Finally, the frequency of interracial marriage between Chinese and Negroes and Chinese and Caucasians raises intriguing questions about hypergamy, the tendency for males to marry "down," females "up," in a social system. In this chapter we will be operating close to the color line, dealing with actual crosses of it, and investigating the ways in which mixed marriages and children pose problems for the biracial norms upon which segregation depends.

Particularly because of pressure from within the Chinese group, fewer and fewer Chinese men took Negro wives during the 1930's and 1940's. In earlier times, the grocers who associated with Negroes were by no means at the bottom of the status hierarchy within the Chinese community. Some were leaders of the group or of their extended family before the change. In one north Delta town, for example, a grocer who formerly lived with a Negro woman brought his Chinese wife to Mississippi well before World War II and had a daughter by her. He was a prosperous and respected merchant, and having ended his social connections with Negroes, he eventually succeeded in enrolling his daughter in the white public schools, the first Chinese in the locale to be admitted.

A vastly different fate befell those Chinese who refused to give up their Negro wives, usually because they had had children by them. Even though some of them in past years were eminent in the Chinese community, their position is now extremely marginal. They do not participate to any substantial extent in the social life of any of the racial groups around them. Typically these families have no social life whatever, beyond the nuclear family itself: "If the other Chinese have a social gathering and extend an invitation to me, I very seldom go. I'm not interested in social life at all." [2] This lack of interest stems from a feeling of intrusion, of being out of place, reinforced by the knowledge that the Chinese community would surely exclude the Chinese male's black family and would like to exclude him as well. One very successful "pure" Chinese merchant put it this way: "We didn't associate at all with those Chinese. Well, we *did* associate with them, but just as little as we could."

In particular, those Chinese who came to Mississippi or came of age after World War II reject them. They do not understand how members of their race could jeopardize the image and social standing of the entire group by forming such relationships. Nor do they know that these relations were widespread before the war, that no "jeopardy" was then involved, that on the contrary forming them was good for business, and they do not see that only when entrance into white society came to be viewed as the overriding concern was there any "threat," and that only then was the action morally condemned.

There is still some contact between the two groups. Occasionally two grocers will consult on an immigration or business problem even though one has a black family. If they happen to meet on the street, both will nod and perhaps ask about each other. The Chinese member of the mixed marriage will be invited to the funeral of a former friend or close relative and will occasionally attend. If he dies, he can expect that some of his relatives and former associates will attend his funeral, although they would not attend his wife's.

The amount of contact is exaggerated somewhat by the Chinese members of Chinese-Negro families, indicating that they do not wish to be cut off. Note the ambiguity in the following sentence: "I still have several Chinese as close friends, and they're very polite and still have a certain amount of respect for me." The actual extent of the contact is more accurately indicated by the comments of the "pure" Chinese community, confirmed by the black wives and children of the merchants in question. Especially in the last few years, years of explicit and continuing civil rights discussion, contact between the larger Chinese community and the Negro-related minority has been cut to the vanishing point, as the Chinese attempt to ensure their position on the white side of the white-black dichotomy.

There is resentment in the hearts of the Chinese who have been thus cut off. They claim that the greatest difference between them and other Chinese in the past was that the others lived with Negroes more surreptitiously, and didn't have or didn't acknowledge mixed offspring. Some of them also maintain that the Delta Chinese, by attempting at times so pathetically to enter white society fully, are selling out their cultural identity. And they know that the Chinese, in cutting them off from social association, are basically responding to white-derived pressure.

Ambivalent Rejection of Chinese-Negroes by Whites

When Chinese families began to be allowed some participation in the institutions of the white community, these privileges were not usually extended to mixed couples or their offspring. However, whites do not treat these mixed families in exactly the same way they treat "pure" Negro families, and the differences are instructive to a general understanding of the etiquette of segregation. Lower-class whites, perhaps befriended by a Chinese grocer's act of consideration, sometimes reciprocate with actual friendship, even though the grocer's family is black. Certainly it is true that whites will shop at the store of such a merchant; working-class whites shop even at Negro-owned groceries in some towns. But a more personal relationship, a sort of social visit in the store, may also develop. Again, such friendships even exist occasionally between blacks and whites; between Chinese-Negroes and whites they are more widespread.

Chinese-Negroes sometimes "pass" as pure Chinese among

the working-class whites in whose neighborhood they may live. In one city, for example, a woman who is three-quarters Chinese, one-quarter Negro, is more or less "passing" in this way. The larger Chinese community knows her racial ancestry, and the white upper class knows it or would soon be apprised of it if she attempted to gain entrance to a white institution or neighborhood. The area in which she now lives is racially mixed, as are many older working-class neighborhoods in Mississippi towns, and she sends her children to the Negro parochial school. Negroes in the neighborhood also know that she is part-Negro, and she is in fact fairly cordial with them. The whites whose friend she is do know that she is not "pure" Chinese. But this fact is not salient to the larger white community, and if it did become important, her white friends could claim that they did not know she was not Chinese. In short, they are willing to accept her self-definition as essentially Chinese, thus essentially white. Once again, if this analysis is correct, the Chinese example indicates the interconnection of caste distinctions and white class divisions. When upper class-lower class status pressure within the white community is not involved, lower white strata do not generate anti-Chinese sentiment or action.

Upper-class whites also have something of a special relationship with some Chinese merchants with Negro families and particularly with Chinese-Negro offspring. Here, however, the association is quite different from the occasional actual friendship, on a level of equality, between lower-class whites and Chinese-Negroes. The upper-class white relates to the Chinese-Negro much as he does to an extremely light-skinned middle-class Negro. There is no question of violating caste lines, no notion that Chinese-Negroes might be admitted to white schools, neighborhoods, or other institutions. But there is, nevertheless, a strange sort of regard, based on nagging feeling that the lower-caste individual is "like me," in his basic human stock and hence in feeling — that he is not one of those "niggers," but has by some irony of fate been miscaste. Thus, when the white encounters a Chinese-Negro in the course of business, he will interact with him in a personal way, with a cordiality which he would not extend to most blacks. He will inquire about the man's family, congratulate him for his children's school progress, and so forth. A Negro woman married to a Chinese or Chinese-Negro grocer may receive much more courtesy from a store clerk when the clerk learns her last name. Chinese males with Negro families occasionally have been allowed to use public accommodations, such as drive-in movies and restaurants, which until recently were barred to all-Negro groups. One Chinese-Negro male even reported to me: "Whenever I went for a job, I got an easier job — people sort of felt sorry for me." [3]

When considered in a larger context, compared to actions which would really be significant in changing the life situation of the people involved, these tiny violations of the etiquette code are inconsequential. They are nevertheless highly important to their recipients. The Chinese-Negro is very aware of and oriented toward Mississippi's definition of things; indeed, these merchants, who have in some cases specifically renounced families in China and have chosen to live with Afro-Americans, speak English better and are much more Americanized than the average "pure" Chinese grocer. The concessions of etiquette are therefore touchingly important to him and to his children, as they are to light-skinned professional-class Negroes. The etiquette of segregation expresses the premise that Negroes are qualitatively inferior beings, so potentially debasing that whites cannot even take the chance of interacting with them socially. This code thus represents one of the most powerful attacks on the self-esteem of a "minority" individual which could possibly be devised. By interacting socially with the Chinese-Negro both in a personal way and on a level of semi-equality, by taking account of him and his family as persons, individuals, the white is making evident his feeling that the awful premise behind segregation etiquette does not apply, at least not fully, to the Chinese-Negro. In view of the pervasive effect of segregation etiquette upon the self-esteem of the black population, perhaps no single concession could be more important to the Chinese-Negro, even though to the outside observer it seems insignificant to the point of near-invisibility.

This insight makes intelligible the otherwise frequently inexplicable sellouts of Negro demands by middle-class Negro leaders in Southern towns. It has repeatedly been observed that these leaders may be fairly capable of uniting blacks in a boycott or demonstration, only to come out with empty or farcical agreements from the interracial bargaining table. Their acceptance of the empty settlements is by no means easy to explain; often the bargain weakens their own position as leaders, sometimes beyond repair, and contains so little substance that it cannot even be said that they were "bought off" by personally advantageous concessions from the white community. It seems to be simply not in their interest to accept the package; yet they often rationalize about the agreement, talking themselves into accepting nonenforceable guarantees and inventing reasons why delay seems reasonable.[4]

The same phenomenon, a subtly different interaction pattern for the light-skinned Negro, central to his self-definition and esteem and replicated even in the absence of whites by middle-class Negro teachers, is the factor most crucial to explaining observed correlations between ability and "brightness" of skin within the black population. In other words, whites — and surrogate whites — are communicating to the light-skinned child that he is "brighter" both in color and in intelligence. Over the years the child tends to meet these expectations, just as many of his darker playmates are meeting expectations that they will be slow or unambitious.[5]

The Caucasian, for his part, perhaps expiates some of his guilt about segregation by his actions toward Chinese-Negroes and light-skinned middle-class Negroes. The white acts partly so that he can tell himself that he does recognize individual worth in the "other race." He will also speak well of the Chinese-Negro in conversation with other whites. It is, of course, less threatening to the basic rationale for segregation if one picks mulattoes among whom to recognize individual worth, and it handles the problem of guilt resulting from the sense that the individual has been misassigned.

Beyond these patterns, there is no social contact between Chinese-Negro and Caucasian other than the usual black-white interaction in the Delta. Outside of Mississippi another alternative is available and has been chosen by a large percentage of mixed Chinese-Negro offspring, especially by those who are more Chinese than Negro in constitution and appearance. When they leave their home town, where they are "known" to be Negro, they are usually defined as Chinese. Several served in the army as Chinese-Americans, in white units, during World War II. Others who are darker can still pass as "Polynesian." Most of this generation did not chose to remain Mississippi Negroes when they could pass elsewhere, and all but a handful have left the state.

Partial Acceptance of Chinese-Negroes by Blacks

The Chinese-Negroes who remain are classified with the Negro population, of course, and they therefore live, work, and attend school with blacks. They do not relate exactly as Negroes to the Negro community, however, and that community does not extend full membership to them, not even to their "pure" Negro wives. As one woman, married to a Chinese merchant for more than twenty years, put it: "I'm prejudiced against by *three* races!" In that statement, she summed up the general position of these families in Mississippi society, and as her comment implies, their contacts with the black community are neither extensive nor wholly harmonious.

To be sure, different families have worked out different accommodations. There are instances in which the wife and children are fully accepted by other Negroes, and the grocer himself is popular in the community, if not quite a full member of it. In most cases, however, the Chinese grocer rarely entertains Negroes socially or visits in their homes. It is not exactly that he is reluctant to participate because he feels racially superior; on the other hand, blacks report that the

Chinese merchant does not really want to or try to enter the life of the Negro community on an equal basis. Part of the problem has been that in the Negro community the Chinese grocer can find few peers. There are few black merchants in the Delta; the entire black middle class makes up only a small percentage of the population. Therefore only a few Negroes have the possibility of sharing with the grocer the bonds of common occupational problems and goals. In addition, it is well to remember that his store hours preclude many kinds of extensive social interaction with anyone.

There is much more to the problem, however. "Many people have met us more than half-way, but my husband has held back," one grocer's wife told me. The grocer is unwilling to define himself as Negro. That is the central point. It is not that he considers himself so much "above" the Negro but that he has a deep desire to preserve his own racial and cultural identity. He also may define his wife as "special" — middle class, educated, different from those other Negroes — and he exaggerates her skin brightness. This is his coming to terms with Mississippi's definition system; if blacks are inferior beings, then it is nice to have a rationale to exclude one's wife from that stigma. Such a line of thinking, expressed openly at times and subtly more often, cannot be endearing to the rest of the Negro group.

Several Chinese complained to me, however, that they have not been well received by blacks when they have tried to be friendly. The grocer's wife is also scorned: "My wife is a teacher. But she's *cut* in a lot of places, by people [Negroes], because of her name [Chinese]. They *know* my wife, they grew up with her, but because of the name, they ostracize her. We can't even hire a babysitter!" The shunning begins with the marriage itself, before any other action by the couple could be its cause. For a Negro to marry a Chinese is not accepted by the black community: "All of my friends who lived here dropped me like a hot potato. They resented me getting *married*. The *relationship* would have been O.K. — Negroes have lived with *that* through the years — but the name change, the honorable part of it, offended them." In other words, to sleep with a Chinese (or a Caucasian) is acceptable within the pattern of dominant-subordinate relationships that govern life in Mississippi, but to actually marry a Chinese is "above yourself," and implies a desire to escape being black: "Some Negroes resented it [my marriage]. They think you think you're *better* than they are. They would go to my *husband* to buy things in the store, not to me, even if he was in the back — especially just after the marriage."

This view among blacks is exactly identical to that of the white community, which is its point of origin. It is an expression of the ideology of white supremacy and "racial integrity." And, just as in the white community, racial integrity is not really the issue; illegitimate children would be acceptable; what is offensive is the racial equality implied by the actual marriage. White ideas have subtly been transferred to black culture, so that blacks actually are offended when a Negro by her marriage to a Chinese acts "uppity."

There may also be envy in the black community, along with the realization that this avenue of partial escape from segregation and poverty is not relevant to most Negroes. The Chinese-Negroes are oriented first toward individual advancement, rarely toward community involvement. The Chinese grocer first sends his mixed children to the parochial schools because they are better than black public schools, then supports them through college, like his counterpart in the "pure" Chinese community. They usually avoid Mississippi schools (except for Tougaloo), and they attend such institutions as U.C.L.A., Xavier, and Brown, and usually get a better education than pure Chinese children.

In interaction with their Negro peers, Chinese-Negro mulattoes occupy a better position than Negroes with Caucasian fathers. Other Negroes can often tell at a glance that they are a distinctive racial mixture. That, plus their last names and something in their thinking as well, identifies them as part Chinese. In their early years, they receive resentment and hostility from peers of the same sex. In some cases they overcome the bad feeling and become quite popular. More often, especially with dark-skinned Negroes, they never form close friendships. Again, part of the hostility they receive is understandable. Not only do they come from a more stable and wealthy family than most blacks but they are clearly on a path of ambition and are likely to escape the fate of poverty which awaits most of their contemporaries. Moreover, many Chinese-Negro children are taught by their parents and by teachers and other middle-class adults that they *are* superior to the average dark Negro: "I've always been conscious of who I am . . . Here [Jackson State College], everyone knows you're not a full Negro. Heads turn. You have to not let it go to your head. The teacher [in earlier schooling] calls on you more often, expecting more from you. So you study harder." This "special" status understandably irritates those thereby considered "common," and it also leads to a feeling within one that one *is* special, subtly expressed in the following remark by a recent high school graduate: "My older sister considers herself more Chinese than I do. I've tried to lean more to the Negro side, in order to make friends, but that hasn't worked." This girl feels she can make a *decision* whether to be fully Negro, and this option, this ability to escape one's fate, whether or not it is really possible, angers those who, being darker, cannot consider it.

On the other hand, she and other Chinese-Negroes are unusually popular with their opposite-sex peers and make attractive dating or marriage candidates. Their popularity is still another ironic consequence of the segregation code of etiquette. By dating a Chinese-Negro girl, a Negro male can say to himself that he is special, that she chooses to go out with him when she has the implied alternative, however remote, of going out with whites. This is her advantage; other blacks "have to" date Negroes. Again it is apparent that segregation depersonalizes the subordinate race and debases its sense of self-esteem, so that even this convoluted means of expressing one's individual worth, this faintly symbolic way of "competing" with whites, becomes important in Delta black society.

This same white-derived cultural pressure underlies distinctions between lighter- and darker-skinned Negroes. Indeed, if Chinese-Negro families have close friends, besides other Chinese-Negro families in the community or nearby towns, they will most likely be middle-class Negroes of very light skin. In the Catholic schools which Chinese-Negro children usually attend, the other pupils are from lighter-skinned, more affluent families. There they do form friendships: "As a boy, I took a lot of insults from Negroes — from "pure" Negroes. The lighter-skinned Negroes were closer to me. There was a bond between us — something in common."

The relation between color and status within the black community has been broken down somewhat by the civil rights and black power movements; and, although light-skinned Negroes are thereby losing some of their special status, Chinese-Negro families have been aided. For segregation as an ideology is crumbling, and it was this ideology, held in part also in the black community, that lay behind the criticism such couples received. One woman stated this succinctly: "The civil-rights discussion has helped us a bit. Among Negroes it used to be, 'Oh, *she's* married to a Chinaman!' Now it's, 'Oh, *we* have interracial marriage in ——; look at the ——'s, for example!' "

On the whole, however, relations are not close; as one man expressed it, "We are a group of people without a race, off to ourselves." Although in some cases they do not even know each other, the Chinese with Negro families share a distinctive outlook in many respects. I was first impressed by the fact that they were easy to interview. Not so inhibited by the Chinese norm of secrecy, more Americanized, and with a good command of English, they talked freely with me about their lives and aspirations. And because they are rather alienated from the Chinese group as a whole, they do not feel constrained to be silent in order to "protect" the group against a possible intrusion or threat.

Also striking, compared to that of other Delta Chinese, is

their viewpoint regarding Communist China and the Far East. The main Chinese community is first of all concerned lest Mississippi whites, with their strong anti-Communist set, connect them with Mao and Asian Communism. Moreover, nearly every family went to considerable expense and trial attempting to get relatives out of China in 1948 and 1949, and they still have something of a "refugee philosophy." Their strongly expressed anti-Communism, then, even including defense of Chiang Kai-Shek, is by no means purely a put-on for Mississippi white consumption. The Chinese with Negro associations are almost alone in making positive statements about Communist China. They volunteer that China under Mao has at last taken a major place among the nations and has made its own borders secure against foreign powers; even this admission must be nearly forced out of some "pure" Chinese informants. But the Chinese-Negroes go further: "Red China is getting the job done, a tremendous job, and all by herself. The leaders are doing a tremendous job. People are no longer hungry . . . China today has recovered her dignity." And they argue for a reevaluation of American thinking in the Far East: "China has never attacked anybody and it doesn't want to now. Our policy there is just so wrong, so wrong. I don't even see how we can even undo what we have already done." Several of them therefore criticized the Vietnam war, which other Chinese defended even against my own opposition.

It is not quite clear to me why these different points of view should go so closely in hand with racial marital status. Perhaps the Chinese married to blacks, alienated from the majority, express this alienation by capriciously taking opposite sides from the Chinese community on any question of importance, but I doubt it. Or perhaps, being culturally oppressed themselves, they have more sympathy for Maoist thinking, especially since they do note that Communism is explicitly equalitarian racially. More likely, their views, which after all are not left-wing except by white Mississippi standards, indicate that the position of their "pure" counterparts has been influenced over the years by interaction with the white community and by holding that community up as a reference group and a goal for future full membership.

Not surprisingly, among Chinese with mixed families there is also more willingness to question the basic racial classification system itself. In China, social classification was based on the economic situation of the male parent. But this is not so with their own children in Mississippi, not even if they are only one-quarter Negro. Yet they correctly observe that a daughter (though not a son) of a Chinese grocer and his *Caucasian* wife, if she is pretty, is classed and accepted as a white! And more basically, they reject the whole idea of classification and treatment based on race: "In China we didn't *have* racial prejudice. The only distinction would be poor and rich. That is a more democratic society. But we here in Mississippi are so narrow-minded. People should marry who they want to marry. It's nobody else's business but the two of them and God. The way the Chinese treat the ———'s [Chinese-Negro couple] is wrong; the Chinese learned that from the white Mississippian."

Whites refer to them as "low-class" Chinese or "those Chinese down by the river," and I even heard a member of the Chinese community call them "poor Chinese trash." Yet these men, with their families, own substantial houses in middle-class black areas and send their children to fine schools at great personal expense. It seems clear that they are "low class" only by virtue of their racial connection.

Chinese-Caucasian Families and Hypergamy

Also in anomalous positions during the past two decades have been the seven Chinese-Caucasian marriages I was able to discover. Although the Mississippi Constitution forbade such unions, friction within them has been due not to legal interference but to difficulties regarding the racial status of the wife and children. At least two of these seven matches have ended in divorce; in others there is constant strain within the marriage because the wife feels she is not to be dominated by her lower-caste husband.

It has been commonly observed that when cross-caste marriages occur, the male is from the higher group, his bride from the lower. This is "hypergamy," and has been observed most consistently in India.[6] In Hawaii, Adams has shown that the several racial groups (Caucasian, Caucasian-Hawaiian, Hawaiian, Portuguese, Chinese, Japanese, Negro, and others) are first of all endogamous but conform to a hypergamous pattern when they outmarry.[7] Noncaste hypergamy is also common: within white (and black) American populations, for example, if a college student dates or marries a high school student, almost always the college student is the male. Data on intraracial interclass marriages are less clear, but I suspect that a majority of such unions would prove to be hypergamous. In the Delta, Frank Smith has discussed class patterns of dating: "None of the town girls ever danced with the sharecropper, or 'poor white' or 'resettlement farm' folks, but many a Sidon boy took advantage of the opportunity to strike up an acquaintanceship with some of the poor white daughters."[8]

Sociologists and anthropologists have not supplied much insight into the causes of this phenomenon, and in fact there is little serious work in sociology on intermarriage in general. This sad situation led F. G. Bailey to remark in 1964: "The institution of hypergamy has given rise to a number of speculations and explanations, but no coherent and authoritative theory has emerged."[9] None will emerge here, either, but some facts about the intermarriages and social relations of the Mississippi Chinese do deserve further comment.

The Delta Chinese have definitely been hypergamous. I have verified at least thirty instances of cohabitation, usually including legal marriage, between Chinese males and Negro females. Conversely, I could not discover a single instance of cohabitation or marriage between Negro males and Chinese females. By itself, these figures, though striking, prove little, for, as Table 3 indicates, there were two, three, or even more males per female within the Chinese population in these decades. But there are other pieces of evidence to confirm the pattern.

That the seven Chinese males who married Caucasians during this period, constitute a number smaller than the number marrying blacks is not in itself tremendously significant, because there were stronger legal and informal restrictions against whites intermarrying than against blacks doing so. However, the final piece of the pattern is supplied by the fact that the Negroes who married Chinese were almost without exception from the small Negro middle class, while the white brides were from the lowest white stratum.

Hypergamy is continued in the present: Delta Chinese girls, far more than boys, are dating and beginning to marry Caucasians. Chinese males are not dating Negroes in Mississippi, but in Tahiti and Jamaica, where lines are not so rigid, they are indeed dating individuals in the "native" population, while girls do not.[10] Females date "up," males "down." The most extensive attempts at explaining these patterns, to my knowledge, have been articles by Davis,[11] Merton,[12] and Wirth.[13] Davis notes that a wife customarily takes on the social position of her husband, rather than the other way around. Interclass marriages can therefore be made between upper-class male and lower-class female without loss of status for anyone, for the wife can acquire the social graces required by her husband's position. In some intercaste marriages in India, the couple even goes so far as to falsify the premarital background of the female. But as Davis points out, "any discussion of caste endogamy and hypergamy must distinguish racial from non-racial caste systems." [14] For the wife (or husband) from a lower *racial* caste cannot change so as to make her background no longer knowable.

Davis supplies, then, a major reason *against* the contracting of interracial or interclass marriages involving women from the higher group, at least in patriarchal societies. Such a woman would have to give up her high position and descend to her husband's level; this neither she nor her family would usually countenance. Merton, on the other hand, provides a reason *for* interracial marriages. At least in the United States, such marriages tend to be between persons of diverse occupational status as well as different races. Most unions between black males and white females involve men of the middle class and women from the lower, according to the best evidence.[15] Thus they violate two strong norms at once — class and racial endogamy. But there is a logic to this pattern: the partner from the "higher" race is in a sense compensated for the racial drop by a corresponding increase in economic status. When Chinese grocers married Delta whites, they selected lower-class white women, who could look "up" to their husbands as small businessmen while looking "down" upon them racially; the grocer who married a Negro usually selected a mate at least his equal in occupational class (many were teachers) and usually his superior in education. In some Indian intercaste marriages this exchange is open and direct, in the form of a high bride-price or dowry. In America, this "reason" for intermarriage is not strong. We have no custom of bride-price or dowry. Furthermore, most interracial couples are extremely neolocal; they maintain little contact with either partner's family, partly because usually neither set of parents approves of the marriage.[16] Thus there is no "push" toward making the marriage in order to take advantage of the race, or conversely the money, of the other's family.

There is, however, an entire array of reasons for interracial marriage which have barely been mentioned in the literature. The upper-race initiator of the match receives a major compensation for his decline of racial status: he gets dominance in the courtship and in the marriage. This is clearly visible in the pattern of college-high school dating: the college lad has social grace by ascription, and can choose and win a prettier, more personable, or more popular girl than he could while in high school or within his own age group. Furthermore, he can feel confident that he is in charge of the situation and the relationship. Similarly, the Chinese in Mississippi who have married Negroes, and the two who have married Mexican-Americans, do have dominance in their own households. The patterns of authority within their families are typically "Chinese," and in the case of the Chinese-Mexican couples, the children are being raised to consider themselves Chinese. However, in the Chinese-Caucasian matches, authority does not rest clearly with the husband, and the wife may be unwilling to raise the children as Chinese.

These twin factors — personal attributes which may partly compensate for ascribed racial inferiority, and dominance and confidence accruing to the upper-race individual — provide a "pull" for interracial marriage, a pull which is theoretically necessary, in view of the strong negative sanctions which our racist society applies to such unions. Also, it may be possible to derive from this line of thought some explanations of the major exception to the pattern of American hypergamy: the fact that Negro-white intermarriages in the northern United States involve black males, rather than females, in a ratio of about four to one.[17] No amount of personal charm can counterbalance, to many whites, the fact of Negritude; a beautiful black woman is in many white eyes black first, beautiful second. Conversely, a black man can make considerable psychological capital out of dating and marrying a white woman.[18]

In any event, no satisfactory explanation of hypergamy has yet been devised which will account for this major exception.[19] Furthermore, past theorizing has usually been too limited in scope: interage and interclass unions have largely been ignored, yet the same principles may be operative in such cases, too, and perhaps with greater visibility.

Two other avenues are also suggested for future research. First, it is of interest who initiates the contact. Among the Delta Chinese, the fact that they hesitate to cross the sexual gap separating them from whites means that whites must take the first step. Since in American society males customarily ask females to go out with them, Chinese girls are asked out, while Chinese boys hesitate to ask out Caucasians; in turn, this is a significant cause of the hypergamous dating patterns now visible in the group. In the North, the fact that dating Negroes is so negatively sanctioned keeps whites from initiating contacts; Negroes possibly initiate most interracial dates; for this reason, black males will be involved more than black females.[20]

Second, it is still unclear to me why sexual imagery is so important in racial segregation or regarding dominance in general. Adams notes that the major reason for the growth of a substantial Caucasian-Hawaiian minority on those islands, in exception to the usual English and American endogamy, is that the immigrants from England and America for the first two or three decades included only males. As soon as families arrived, racial prejudice, expressed sexually, began to be more important.[21] In Chapter 5, we noted the importance of endogamy to racial opposition. It may be that as our theoretical understanding of the more general interconnection of sex and racism advances, the causes of hypergamy and of the exceptions to it will become more obvious.

Present Conflict and Future Prospects

Summary of Theoretical Findings

The story of the rise in status of the "pure" Chinese and of the increase in economic fortune which preceded it has been told in earlier chapters. One of the main reasons for my study of the Chinese was to learn from their case more about the social structure and culture of the Mississippi Delta. Lest that purpose be lost in the narrative, at this point I shall pull together the principal theoretical insights into Mississippi society which their history and presence have provided. Of foremost importance, their interstitial position between black and white served to emphasize the cultural aspects of segregation. Although I had encountered the use of "etiquette system" as applied to segregation before I began this work, it was not a term I previously emphasized. Gradually, however, the importance of the reciprocal norms in the system, each expressing dominance or submission, impressed itself upon me. I would now stress this aspect of segregation above all others.

This is not to say that segregation is not built on a foundation of economic discrimination, nor that psychological matters should be omitted. What it actually is, however, is a system of norms and definitions. As with other normative systems, persons must be socialized into knowledge of it and obedience to it. Like other aspects of culture, it developed slowly, partly without conscious direction. Minor actions such as nouns of address, styles of walking, or ways of looking at members of the other race are specified by the normative code. Deep-seated assertions about the worth or lack of worth of the other person are expressed by these small distinctions in etiquette, which is why their violation stands as a shock to the collective conscience, a betrayal of the "Southern way of life."

When one sees this point of view and the importance of it, many things fall into place. First, it explains how the Chinese could be so successful economically. As outsiders, they were relatively oblivious to the nuances of the segregation code and had an alternate value system which provided them, in the beginning, with different rules on which to base their self-esteem. They could therefore break the Mississippi code. Whites could not, for they possessed no alternative values with which to withstand the condemnation of their peers and neighbors. In addition, since whites presumably know the code and are expected to obey it, violations by whites would be more severely condemned than violations by Chinese. A belief system, and also a social structure, are not threatened by a small group of outsiders who behave as if they do not hold its premises, but even a single turncoat from within the system is a threat, since potentially he could be the first of many deviants.

As outsiders, then the Chinese were subject to less condemnation and were less affected by that which they did receive, at least at first. They therefore established a social identity toward the black side of the color line, as expressed in their store locations, social relations with Negroes, and their courtesy (or etiquette) toward them. It may even be true that after they understood the system, they consciously made use of it for greater profit; for example, naming their stores by their first names, and allowing blacks to call them by first name even when they were not friends, may have been devices to improve customer relations and win more trade. In any event, the etiquette line was clearly involved in the Chinese economic success.

Since the rules of etiquette lie in the mores, they are not often consciously perceived. They appear "natural" and commonplace. Many persons do not think to mention patterns of etiquette, because they do not think of these patterns in the first place, but take them for granted. Thus, although interviewing and participant-observation are the least formal of methods and are the most likely ways to pick up issues not directly asked about, I remained ignorant of the etiquette relation between Caucasians and Chinese for several months. Chinese grocers joke with Caucasians, and Caucasians almost invariably refer to Chinese by their first names. Naively, until late in my research I assumed that this pattern signified close friendship ties between the two groups. Finally, a particularly stereotyped telephone conversation between a lawyer and a grocer in Greenville forced me to realize that the Caucasian was speaking to the Chinese exactly as he would to a Negro. After that experience, since I now knew to ask about the matter, I discovered deep resentment among the Chinese toward the ways whites speak to them. The Chinese have not pressed whites on the matter but have played along in order to seem polite and unthreatening, while focussing on more tangible goods.

Basic assertions about blacks and whites — the furious negation of human dignity referred to by Fanon — are codified by these rules of etiquette. I found many details to illustrate this point, including the feelings of disgust and contempt directed by middle-class whites toward white storeowners in black neighborhoods and the obvious importance of the etiquette concessions whites bestowed upon Chinese-Negroes. Thus it became clear that one of the principal ways American racism keeps blacks down is by cultural oppression: the mounting of a detailed attack on the identity and worth of the oppressed. Eventually many members of the subservient population, as well as most members of the dominant group, come to believe the racist assertions. Thus after the system is established, some blacks have psychological or economic vested interests in its continuance; we saw, for example, that there was muted black criticism of Negro-Chinese marriages.[1]

Also falling into place was the relation between segregation as an etiquette system and the white class structure. Whites who were too closely associated with blacks, such as those who operated stores in "niggertown," were and are considered perverse and deviant by the straight white community and are spoken of with great emotion. Again, this is because they shock the collective conscience; that is, they violate or appear to violate the norms of segregation. And this shows that segregation is not merely a machine for rational exploitation, but is in the mores, is a normative system first of all, and often gets in the way of exploitation.

From previous knowledge of the Delta, I had already concluded that it was highly stratified, both between races and within the white population, but the relative acceptance extended to the Chinese by the working class, compared to the exclusion practiced by middle- and upper-class groups, caused me to rethink the conventional wisdom about the origins of prejudice. My conclusions, in the chapter on opposition, represent the most far-reaching analysis I was able to make on the basis of my research, and constitute, I feel, its most important single contribution to the theory of race relations. Two cautions, however, must be noted regarding the material in that chapter. First, my data are not sufficient to prove the points of analysis raised, but only enough to illustrate them. Second, it is well known that violent racism of the Ku Klux Klan type does emanate from working- and lower-class whites when the chips are down. In the discussion of class and prejudice I was not trying to prove the lower class free of prejudice. Rather, I attempted to show that status pressures impinge upon the lower white strata from the white status structure. Such pressures and definitions tend to filter down through the system, eventually reaching and affecting even the Chinese and Negroes, who then take on some aspects of a colonialized or segregationist mind-set themselves.

In short, in a cultural sense, racism originates in the upper class. The top of society is white, culturally and racially, and the Chinese, at first, were neither. That white society is now beginning to open to them is due in great part to their open acculturation to Caucasian standards and styles. As the chapter on the transition showed, the Chinese came to be defined almost white racially because they made great efforts to appear white culturally.

Young People and Parents

The rapid acculturation of the Chinese has not been accomplished without some strain within the family, between the generations. Chinese families are not exempt from the friction between first and second generations experienced by other immigrants to the United States. And, owing to the sojourning patterns prevailing before World War II, the present population of young people represents the first large group of Chinese children to be born in the state.

In all, there are several hundred Chinese children in the Delta. Along with others in Memphis and across the river in Arkansas and Louisiana, they constitute enough young people to support a substantial Chinese youth subculture. As noted in Chapter 4, they maintain a number of formal activities, supplemented by a continuous flow of informal parties, visits from relatives, and associations with other Chinese at school and church. Chinese who participate actively in these activities form a tight gossip network. Among them, not much can happen in one end of the Delta that is not immediately public knowledge at the other. There is little social privacy. The final product is little private social activity, and in particular, little dating within the group. Most boy-girl contact occurs at the organized events; a Chinese boy graduating from high school, even from college, may be able to count his dates on the fingers of one hand.

Many Chinese girls resent what they consider the social im-
maturity of the boys. They hold the same standards for self-
esteem as their Caucasian counterparts and feel hurt and
humiliated by being ignored. By the end of their freshmen year
of college, most of them have been asked out at least once by a
Caucasian boy, and many have accepted, in some cases over
parental objections. The daughters have adopted the concept
of romantic love, including dating, engagement, and determination of marriage by the couple involved, while their parents
may still emphasize more pragmatic aspects of the match.[2] Although arranged marriages are quite rare now, parents still
may set up a meeting between their daughter and a prospective
husband. Such intervention usually causes the daughter to
lose face in the eyes of her peers, and she may renounce her
parents' action. Many do not find an adult Chinese woman
whom they might take as role model. Many Chinese wives
cannot speak English well enough to answer the telephone
easily. Some of them cannot drive an automobile, which only
increases their isolation. Often in Chinese homes I would be
introduced to the husband and children, but the wife would
come in only to serve coffee or tea. In short, in most Delta
families the wife is markedly less Americanized than her husband. The men have been here longer, have more Caucasian
and Negro contacts through their work, and simply "know the
ropes" better. Within the family, this gives them an edge
which leads to continued male dominance. Their daughters do
not want to assume a similar family position; they much prefer the greater freedom of an American wife. Their brothers
are more ambivalent. They are oriented toward white American forms, but at the same time they admire their fathers'
dominance in the household.

Conflict between sons and parents tends to be centered on
participation in nonacademic Caucasian activities, and it is
specifically focussed on the issue of dating and marriage with
Caucasians: "All my friends are always talking about the
trouble with their parents. You have to comply with your parents, but you know you should get out more, do more things."

The old argument used by parents — "you should be Chinese because you won't be accepted as a Caucasian anyway" — is losing its force, as the children are beginning to be accepted. The first-born is the path-breaker, bearing the brunt of the struggle for freedom and participation. Pressure from the parents is particularly intense if he is a male, for the first-born son is more important to the family than any other child. However, his partial break-throughs make it easier for his siblings to participate more widely.

Often small-town young people are so immersed in activities with Caucasians that they do not want to take part in all-Chinese events, which they consider inferior copies of the white originals. An extremely Americanized girl, whose brothers and sisters were the only Chinese children besides herself in her tiny hometown, expressed this feeling strongly: "I didn't go to the Chinese dances. My parents tried to push us to go, and we resented it. I always tore up the invitations before Daddy saw them. I guess I thought it would be hard to get to know other Chinese people, and I wondered what they would think of me. I mostly know Caucasians. They were my friends, the only people I know." This girl feels guilty about boycotting Chinese activities and about the conflicts with her parents. On the other hand, those who do attend Chinese functions also express ambivalence about their participation and their Chinese heritage. Most Chinese young people, for example, are not really proud of their ability to speak two languages and have made no effort to learn written Chinese. They will not pass on much of the tongue to their children; many of them could not even if they wanted to. Chinese youths do not know much about China, nor have they learned anything of their own family's history in China or Mississippi. Some of them have not even found out their mother's Chinese name. Most are ignorant of the role played by Chinese in California. Nor do they show much curiosity about such matters. Eighteen out of twenty-one respondents at the 1967 Chinese Baptist Youth Conference said they wanted to learn more about China, but only eleven had read even one book about it. Their curiosity seems to be a dutiful questionnaire response rather than a genuine quest.

At a party in Cleveland, I watched as two teenagers, recently arrived from Hong Kong, had a difficult time, while English conversation swirled around them. No one translated for them, and their Delta-born cousins, who had brought them, looked embarrassed by their presence. The white Baptist church is considered "better" in some basic way than the Chinese Baptist Church. One student at Delta State College was aware enough of this general pattern to label it "our Chinese inferiority complex." It is shown in the fact that girls who date Caucasians receive a kind of envy from other Chinese girls. One young adult went even further, saying to me, "I don't *fool* with the Chinese at all!" Such a statement implies that one is no longer Chinese. A young mother, to a question about teaching her children Chinese culture, replied "It's all right, I guess, for kids to know about the customs," but went on to imply that her children would not know them and that she did not mind their ignorance. When young Chinese-Americans from the North or West visit relatives or friends in the Delta, they are appalled at the lack of Chinese consciousness, the expressed feeling of inferiority, the emphasis that white ways are better. History for the young Delta Chinese begins with their own birth. Non-Mississippi Chinese are bitter about this ignorance; they call Mississippi Chinese young people "bananas" — yellow on the outside, but white on the inside!

Cleveland, with its large and fairly close-knit Chinese community centered around the church, has a nucleus of young people, also centered there, who are less Americanized than any other major group in the Delta. But even here, the younger generation converses with each other wholly in English, and it is clear that its members have made a commitment to rather complete acculturation. Once there were several Chinese summer schools in Mississippi, but by 1967, even the school in Cleveland, which persisted longest, had closed, and no schooling in the Chinese language or customs was available anywhere in the Delta, summer or winter. Choir anthems and other parts of Sunday worship at the Cleveland church are in English, without excuse to elders who cannot understand, but when Chinese activities are introduced in church, such as memorization of a Bible verse in Chinese, it is with an air of apology to the students.

The split between Chinese and American ways, between old and young people, should not be overstressed, however, for although the students lack such traditional respect-engendering attributes as age and occupational stature, they have the greater prestige in the family, for their way — the white American way — is admitted to be the course of the future. In other words, the split between parent and child is not an open clash, because parents themselves recognize the inevitability of change. Thus children have considerable status in the family and sometimes socialize their own parents into American customs. In China, children came last in terms of rights in the household.[3] In Mississippi, they definitely do not.

Language is one area in which acculturation will soon be virtually total, but not all areas of culture are changing at the same rate. Seeking areas of resistance to Americanization, I asked grocers and students all over the Delta to tell me what elements of Chinese heritage were being passed on and would most likely endure. Invariably they cited the area of familial relations. Chinese, they said, value strong family ties very highly; divorce is a disgrace and a rare occurrence; above all, respect and responsibility for parents and grandparents are prescribed. Even if the language and other customs are lost, Chinese parents feel sure that the sense of family responsibility is being firmly implanted in the young. Family ties are still stronger here, they felt, than in urban Chinatowns.

They are partly correct. Chinese adolescents do feel that any open clash with their parents should be avoided, and they heed parental advice in many instances when Caucasian children would not. Marriage and children are still important goals, for both sexes. But even in this area of supposed resistance to innovation, ideas are definitely changing. The most graphic demonstration of the change I witnessed was an argument in Memphis between two undergraduates — "James," a foreign student from Taiwan, originally from the Mainland, and "Kenny," a Memphis-born grocer's son[4]: "[James:] Chinese families [in Taiwan] have a large family, you know. Usually two or three generations live together. [Kenny, quick introjection:] That's bad! [James:] No, that's *good!*" Later in the conversation, Kenny argued that the duty children owe aged parents is limited primarily to financial support. Having them in your own household, he argued, would invariably cause friction. Furthermore, the stronger family ties of Delta Chinese, stronger perhaps than those of Northern urban Chinese, are a concomitant of the extremely tight family structure made possible by the close physical and social ties between home and business. As this pattern ends — and occupational choices are shifting now — so will the family closeness it facilitated.[5] And as children plan different work from their fathers', fathers no longer have the promise of the business to hold over their sons' heads; nor does a father's grocery acumen mean much to a budding electrical engineer.

It seems, then, that even this area is eroding, and a few parents glumly agreed with this evaluation. If I am correct, then virtually all aspects of Chinese culture in the Delta are gradually giving way under pressure from American forms. A few individual traits, such as restraining emotion, or offering food to guests with both hands, may persevere, but their continuance will be more a "memory" of a culture than a true element of it.[6]

We have noted that young Chinese do not think or talk about their own cultural heritage. They also avoid discussing the social structure in which they live. In several towns I ascertained from Chinese leaders exactly who had been responsible for white opposition to their progress. Almost invariably, as shown in Chapter 5, upper-class native white Southerners were involved; however, when I asked Chinese students the same question, they usually blamed Italians, Jews, or lower-class whites. They possessed no concrete data to back up their assumptions; indeed, most of the acts of opposition they described took place before their own birth. But they could have professed ignorance, instead of blaming groups which were in fact largely blameless. The causes for this distortion may be instructive, because Negroes, especially those of the middle-class, often similarly blame lower-class whites for the discrimination and opposition Negroes face. The explanation, in the Chinese case at least, seems to be that it is satisfying to believe that the "good" people, those who matter in society, the reference group, really want you, and that only the "white trash" oppose you. This outlook, this mis-knowledge, may even have been actively fostered by Chinese parents, who might not want their children to grow up feeling that educated, high-status people were prejudiced against them.

Race relations, Negroes, Caucasians — these were seldom discussed in my presence, and I do not think this avoidance was due solely to my presence. The difference between Chinese and Caucasian was striking in this regard. My Yankee origin has always caused white Mississippians to bring up race relations, whether their own point of view is reactionary or progressive. Race is simply the number one topic. Some decades ago, a Northern journalist had the same experience, and described it vividly: "When I first went to the South I expected to find people talking about the Negro, but I was not at all prepared to find the subject occupying such an overshadowing place in southern affairs. In the North we have nothing at all like it; no question which so touches every act of life, in which everyone, white or blacks, is so profoundly interested." [7]

This is not so among Chinese young people. Just as their parents are isolated by their racial position from active participation in Mississippi politics, so youth are isolated — perhaps partly *by* their parents — from political deliberations. Group discussion at the Chinese Baptist Youth Conferences seemed to me, and to several of the other participants, to be rather irrelevant and sterile, due in part to the apparent wish of the conference's adult leaders to be noncontroversial. Even on the Sunday after Martin Luther King's assassination, set aside for discussion of race relations by President Johnson, there was no mention of the topic in the Cleveland Baptist Church, even in vague "brotherhood" terms. Nor did the student-run Sunday school ever take up that topic, or any other major social controversy, seriously.

Political passiveness is rooted deep in Chinese culture. But the social noninvolvement and lack of political awareness on the part of young Chinese is primarily a result of their unsure social position. Other groups of ambiguous racial status, such as the part-Indian peoples in the Atlantic Coast states and elsewhere, have withdrawn even more, in the face of a social and political structure which allowed them no real participation.[8] As is shown later in this chapter, the primary response of the young Chinese to their difficult position is to leave the state, and it is impossible to say they are wrong. They do not, after all, have the power to change it.

Civil Rights and the Chinese

Sociologists traditionally predict that groups or individuals on their way up feel special need to look down upon those away from whom they have just risen. According to this style of thought, the higher scores of Polish- and Irish-Americans on prejudice tests are easily explained, for ethnic groups are insecure in their status; in addition, they often face competition from Negroes or other groups below them. Agreeing with this argument, Oliver Cox predicted that the Delta Chinese, once admitted to the ranks of the dominant race, would be especially likely to be racist: "Should the Chinese make the necessary response [i.e., eliminate Chinese-Negro relationships], we should expect them to show an even greater hatred for Negroes than that of the whites." [9]

Certainly the extraordinary rise of the Chinese in racial status might be expected to have great effects upon their own attitudes about race relations. Therefore, I made special efforts to get data on their present views on civil rights, segregation, and the Negro population. In addition to broaching the topic carefully in interviews and conversations, I included relevant items on a five-page questionnaire given to twenty-six Chinese college-age students from all over the Delta and to seventy-four Caucasian students at Mississippi State University.[10] Respondents were asked to agree or disagree with eighteen statements, according to the following scale:

+1 Agree slightly   −1 Disagree slightly
+2 Agree in general   −2 Disagree in general
+3 Agree strongly   −3 Disagree strongly

The most interesting results are summarized in Table 5. They prove Cox entirely wrong. The Chinese are not more racist than Mississippi whites; on the contrary, they are the most equalitarian population, besides Negroes themselves, in the entire Delta. The operative question is item 3, which asserts that within ten years Mississippi should completely integrate its schools. This issue has been publicly debated for many years and is therefore an area in which opinions may have real bases and unusual permanence. No other question so divides white and Chinese replies. Chinese students moderately agree with the statement (+1.62), while Caucasians moderately disagree (−1.30). The difference, nearly three points, is extremely large, for the ends of the scale are only seven points apart. Even more vivid is the fact that only four of twenty-six Chinese show any disagreement with the item, while fifty-six of seventy-four whites are segregationists, most at the extreme (−3) position. Item 3 is confirmed by the replies to item 6, "it is all right to have Negro foremen over whites." Here the difference is less striking (1.51) but is significant at much better than the .01 level.[11]

Interviews with Chinese college and high-school students confirmed their questionnaire responses. I raised the topic with at least two dozen students at three Mississippi schools and found only one segregationist, even though I broached the issue from a neutral or conservative stance. Clearly, being in a racial minority makes a major difference in one's think-

Table 5. Questionnaire Responses of Chinese and Caucasian College Students

	Means	
Item	Chinese	Caucasian
2. In ten years there will probably be essentially complete school integration throughout the South, including Mississippi.	2.08[a]	1.22
3. In ten years, there *should* be essentially complete school integration . . .	1.62[a]	−1.30
6. It is all right to have Negro foremen over whites.	1.23[a]	−0.28
7. If left alone by Northern agitators, the Southern Negro wouldn't really care very much about the segregation of races.	1.12	1.16
8. The Negro must prove himself to be responsible and educated before political equality should be given him.	2.54[b]	1.89
10. The growing Puerto Rican problem in NYC indicates that immigration from that island should be placed under limitation like immigration from other nations.	0.46[a]	1.50

[a] Statistically significant at .01.
[b] Statistically significant at .05.

ing about other minority groups and their treatment. A typical respondent drew the parallel explicitly: "Being Chinese [pause], I really don't like to see people discriminated against. I really can't see why they won't let Negroes go to school with us. There seems to be some natural animosity between whites and Negroes in the South." Or as a girl from Greenville put it: "I'm here; why shouldn't they be? I know that some Chinese, not many, are prejudiced. That always surprises me — that one nationality group should be prejudiced against another."

Interracial dating has led some of the more thoughtful Chinese to an extremely equalitarian position. I remember talking with a sophomore coed in a dormitory lounge at the University of Mississippi. She had expressed her difficulties with her parents and with her own identity when she first began to date Caucasian boys. In a very soft voice, so that passing whites could not overhear, she asked me what I thought about intermarriage. "How do you think?" I replied. "Well, I favor it," she answered. I agreed, saying that one should marry whomever one really liked, without regard to race, and she went on to say: "But then, you know, if you feel that way about Chinese-white intermarriage, you have to think that way about Negro-white marriage too." Again I agreed, and I observed that black-white couples in Boston seemed to be working out all right. She then said: "Yes. Some of them are smarter than we are, anyway. How do Mississippians think the way they do — do you know?" Almost no white Ole Miss students would have expressed such attitudes in 1967. So Cox is wrong; Delta Chinese have not followed the path of the Irish or Poles in northern cities. Instead, like Jews, they remind us that not every immigrant group responds to similar structural situations in the same way.

Since the younger Chinese are more acculturated than their parents and are more oriented toward full participation in white society, we might expect that their parents would be even less influenced by Mississippi's way of thinking about segregation and civil rights. This is not so, however. Almost no Chinese feels that Negroes have been treated justly or given an equal opportunity by the Mississippi social system. But among the older Chinese there is a substantial sprinkling of segregationists. The Chinese grocer sees mostly lower-class Negroes who are illiterate and unemployed, and this clientele does not win his respect. For when Chinese evaluate each other, two virtues are central — family responsibility and economic enterprise — and these are precisely the areas of greatest Negro failure.[12] Furthermore, the Chinese need to rationalize their increasingly favorable treatment by whites, contrasted to the continued oppression faced by blacks. Like most Americans, they tend to explain their own good fortune by reference to personal characteristics, such as drive and hard work; conversely, the low place of the Negro is ascribed to his "laziness" and "lack of ambition." Older Chinese, then, exhibit considerable unreflective racism.

In the period of transition, it was plain that white pressure caused the Chinese to clamp down on Chinese-Negro intermarriage, and it is clear that Caucasians lie behind much of what racial antipathy the Chinese now exhibit. This is clearly if subtly shown in the following comment, made by a grocer who extends little courtesy to his black customers: "Those Negroes come in here, call Chinese by first name; don't do that in white store. They think they can get away with it to a Chinese. Sometimes they call another Negro 'Mr. Something,' and then say 'Jim, Jim!' to me!" In fact, there is a reciprocal relationship between white racism and its Chinese subsidiary. After a Chinese grocer has picked up antipathy toward blacks, he may demonstrate it by an anti-Negro joke or remark. Caucasians then react with great approval and repeat the remark to other whites later, for such a comment, coming from a non-white, possesses greater significance than if uttered by a white. Whites are thus "confirmed" in their racism by an "outside observer," and the Chinese learn that such remarks not only earn white approval but at the same time act to separate themselves still further from blacks in the eyes of whites.

Nevertheless, most Chinese adults are far more liberal than Mississippi Caucasian adults. Many, like their children, are explicit integrationists for all races. Some even reject the easy rationalizations about individualistic qualities and upward mobility and do not draw the insidious comparison between Chinese and Negro methods of advancement. For instance, one individual pointed out to me: "If you say to a Negro, 'you can have your rights, but just don't come in to *our* society,' you're just being stupid, because whites have all the power." A Greenwood merchant surprised me with his unusual evaluation of the chance of a black riot there: "We don't have riots, but in a way we'd be better off if we did! There'd be more chance for the Negro." Usually the Delta Chinese keep their views on race relations carefully hidden and do not act on them, but Negro political leaders in Greenville expressed satisfaction with the voting patterns of Chinese on that city's interracial advisory boards.

Not only the Chinese but also Lebanese and Jewish minorities in the Delta have been more liberal on civil rights than have old-line Protestant Americans. The Italians vary more: I met several harsh segregationists among them, but the mitigating influence of their church, oriented toward national and international Roman Catholic tenets, has been substantial. In the town of Shaw, Italians have been slow to participate in the Citizens Council or to enroll in the private segregated school, according to Frank Hough, a founder of both organizations. Nevertheless, the other minorities, even the Lebanese, are less progressive in thought than are the Chinese. This I believe is because nonracial ethnic minorities can look toward complete assimilation and complete equality, especially as far as racial status is concerned. But no matter how high the Chinese rise economically, they can never merge racially with the upper caste, except through the distant and unpopular possibility of complete intermarriage. In the meantime, racial distinctiveness, unlike cultural diversity, is an immutable and immediately visible characteristic. Chinese therefore have a constant reason to fear racial discrimination, even when it is directed against others, and even when they themselves are on the dominant side. "What could happen to Negroes could happen to Chinese," was a repeated refrain in interviews with both students and adults.

Indeed, the Chinese have maintained an uneasy balance on

a racial tightrope. Relations with white Mississippi are of great importance to them, for they have now been defined white and their children attend white schools. At the same time, rapport with blacks must be maintained, for the black community provides the bulk of their customers in most stores. In the period 1955–67, which was dominated by the Citizens Councils and white reaction to the Supreme Court at first and by black action in the civil rights movement later on, this tightrope became increasingly difficult to walk. Caucasians intimidated Chinese grocers to show solidarity with the white "cause," and several grocers did join the Citizens Councils, especially in Greenwood. Later some of the same merchants and others were asked by civil rights leaders to allow signs to be placed in their display windows or to support the cause financially, and intimidation was often involved in these requests, also. The Chinese of course tried to keep their Citizens Council membership hidden from their black clientele and their civil rights contributions secret from the white power structure. In some towns, the grocer was never approached by either group, and in general, until the spring of 1968, the Chinese were able to stay quietly in the "middle" without much friction.

During the years since 1963, the racial unrest, court decisions, and general discussions accompanying the civil rights movement have definitely worked in the favor of the Chinese. For example, Greenville hired a Chinese woman to teach school in 1966, after earlier refusing her, and both Chinese and Caucasian informants believed the intervening civil rights pressure was a factor in the reversal. A Chinese graduate student from Clarksdale said: "Civil rights has improved attitudes a lot. It has helped the Chinese. As Caucasians begin to have doubts about their treatment of Negroes, they begin to have doubts about whether their treatment of Chinese is fair." [13]

As the confrontation between white and black has sharpened, whites have felt ideological pressure to include the Chinese more definitely on their side. Greenville High School in 1969 elected a Chinese boy president of the student body, a step which would have been unimaginable two years earlier. An observer said to me that "the kids were trying to be liberal," and their action quite definitely was in response to the attitude changes caused by the civil rights movement. As a result, even those Chinese who are avowed segregationists have ambivalent feelings toward civil rights, for they recognize the benefits the Chinese have reaped as its fruits.

Black Migration and Black Power

In addition to changes wrought by civil rights action, vast alterations of Delta life are now taking place under the twin pushes of farm mechanization and urban industrialization. The Delta slumbered until about 1950, operating much as it did in the last century, as basically a cotton economy dominated by large planters. But in the last twenty years transformations have occurred. This is not the place to summarize the entire recent history of the region, but several changes are directly relevant to the position of the Chinese.

First of these is black depopulation. Agriculture has been overwhelmingly mechanized: cotton is now picked by machines and weeded by chemicals, and three tractor drivers may do the work of several dozen families. As a result, the Negro population in Bolivar County, for example, dropped 44.4 percent in the 1950's alone! [14] The decline is continuing. Figure 5 shows less than half the expected number of Negro males in the young-adult age brackets and a smaller but still striking absence of young Negro women.

As a result, once profitable Chinese stores in tiny towns like Alligator and Schlater have become losing ventures. During the 1967 summer, two Chinese stores closed in rural Coahoma County alone. Small-town grocers are following their clienteles to Clarksdale, Greenville, and Memphis or are leaving the South entirely. More substantial towns, including Cleveland, Indianola, Clarksdale, Greenville, and others, have thus far resisted the trend. Many of their Negroes have moved

North but have been replaced by new intracounty migrants from the surrounding farmland. The rural areas are beginning to bottom out, however, and several of the larger towns will begin to experience absolute decreases in their black populations.

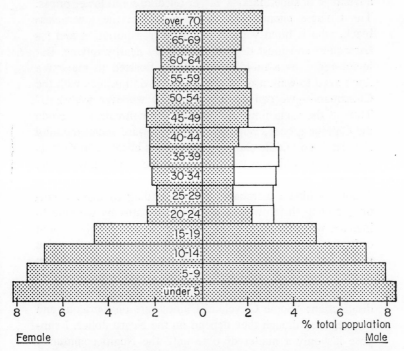

% total population

Female   Male

Open bars for ages 20-44 show percentage of the entire United States population, male, in those age categories.

5. Age and sex of Negro population, Bolivar County, 1959.

In some towns, industrialization will halt the decline: the Delta Council reported a 658 percent rise in industrial payrolls in the Delta for the ten-year period ending in July 1967.[15] As a result of federal legislation, Negroes are securing some industrial jobs; thus many of those who remain in the cities, working in industry or employed by the school systems or poverty programs, will have higher incomes. In turn, they will have different buying habits. The ramifications of the Negro class system upon shopping decisions have already been discussed. The middle-class black avoids Chinese groceries in order to exact courtesy from white clerks and to take advantage of supermarkets' larger selections and lower prices. The Chinese clientele has been based on the lower-class black, who is often without adequate transportation and refrigeration and must depend upon daily nearby buying. But increasingly, as a middle-class Negro boasted to me: "We don't *need* to walk around the corner to do business with the Chinaman — we can do business with whoever we want." Thus at the same time that outmigration threatens to erode the Chinese grocer's population base, upward social mobility may lead the middle-class segment of his clientele to shift its patronage to white-owned stores or to stores which are white in image.

Some Chinese merchants are responding to these conditions and to their own drive for white status by working to increase white trade. They may change to a cash-only basis in order to discourage black customers, and frequently they give whites better courtesy. But in turn, their differential courtesy alienates the black community. A civil rights leader made an ominous prediction to me in 1967 about the outcome of this disaffection: "Some Cleveland Chinese are discourteous and hostile, even though they depend on the Negro dollar. I suppose it's only a matter of time until the Negro community rises up against the Chinese grocers, some of them, unless they begin to try to recruit some support in the community."

Within a year, his prediction was proved correct. After Rev. Martin Luther King, Jr., was murdered, what must in the context of Watts and Newark be termed a minor riot hit Memphis, and vandalism remained at a high level for several days. Chinese stores seemed especially singled out for attack. The disturbances spread rapidly to towns in the Delta; in Cleveland, a harsh curfew was ordered after fire bombs were used and looting broke out. Again, stores owned by Chinese were affected, as were white-owned stores in the black area.

Considerable discrimination seemed involved in the initial target selection. Two Chinese stores faced each other on Chrisman Street in Cleveland. One merchant had remodeled, with a brick front and modern windows, so that his store resembled a small supermarket on the outside. Inside, its prices and selection still made it a small grocery, and especially apparent was the rude and even hostile treatment given by the merchant and his family to their customers. Change was slapped down on the counter, rather than placed in customers' hands, and discussions of prices were usually curt and unpleasant. The other grocer allowed a more relaxed atmosphere. He provided benches in front for his customers and did not mind if they spent more time than money inside. In the first wave of disturbances, directly after the assassination, his store was left untouched, while across the street his neighbor's mini-supermarket was hit twice by bricks and firebombs.

Since then, the discourteous merchant has been forced out to another location, but both stores have been hit. Numerous groceries in Greenville and other Delta towns have also been affected, and it has not always been discourteous or exploitative merchants who were singled out. Indeed, in some towns, Chinese in general may have become the target: in Greenville, Caucasian merchants seem to have received less trouble than Chinese. Perhaps in some Northern ghettoes Jews may have received more opposition than W.A.S.P. proprietors. In short, we need a theory of target selection in racial disturbances, for the choice is not always based on such rational grounds as previous discourtesy or exploitation.

A first consideration is that the Chinese stores are located directly in black areas. White-owned stores are mostly downtown, in the central business district. Rioters usually stay in their own neighborhood, where they know the turf and can remain more anonymous than if they venture outside. In addition, because whites, too, are still prejudiced against the Chinese, Chinese stores are perhaps a safer target than businesses owned by Caucasians. The Chinese cannot mobilize the police or other forces of repression against vandals as effectively as white merchants could. Chinese merchants in Greenville have complained publicly that little action has been taken by police there to aid them.

Moreover, black action against Chinese in a sense unites blacks with whites. I have heard some blacks disparage Chinese in terms very similar to those used by white segregationists against the Chinese. One black political leader even suggested to me that whites may have planted the idea deliberately, so as to keep Negroes and Chinese from coming together in common cause. This is false, but it is possible that some of the motivation for anti-Chinese actions may be cultural, coming from white society but picked up and acted upon by blacks. At the same time, the Chinese, while easier to hit than whites, stand in as satisfactory surrogates for them. Just as Chinese-Negroes may be good marriage partners partly because there is something "white" about them, so the bombing of Chinese groceries represents a symbolic attack upon the white community, which is the ultimate target.

Finally, it may be that the Chinese as a group are now singled out because Negroes are particularly enraged by the irony of their gain in racial status. White grocers were always white. Chinese, however, were once in approximately the same position as blacks, were once brothers in oppression. Now, however, they have been allowed to join white institutions, move into white neighborhoods, and send their children to white schools, and they have lost no time in taking advantages of these opportunities. Blacks may feel a sense of betrayal in the action of the Chinese. In addition, it is sadly ironic that the most visible result of the black liberation movement in the Delta has been the elevation of the Chinese to near-white status, leaving blacks more alone in their oppression. The new white status of the Chinese is obviously beneficial to them, but it is also perceived by blacks, who are consequently losing any sympathy they may have felt with the grocers. Black militant youths in Cleveland have developed an explicit ideology that the Chinese are exploiting their neighborhoods economically and are driving home with the profits in order to buy status in the white community. Hence to such youths it is an act of black patriotism to loot a Chinese store, regardless of such "minor" considerations as the owner's courtesy or civil rights contributions.

Of even more ominous significance for the Chinese business future is the economic dimension of black power. Racial solidarity is increasing among Delta blacks. In Claiborne and Jefferson counties, just south of the Delta, three black-owned cooperative groceries have opened, as a consequence of political organization and economic boycotts there, and are proving successful. In Greenwood, Chinese and Caucasian-owned groceries have been under almost continuous boycott for several months, and a black co-op supermarket has been established. In Chicago and Harlem, black storeowners are beginning to enjoy some assets, as well as the traditional liabilities, in their struggle against white competitors. If this ideological revolution sweeps the Delta, it may completely outmode the analysis of the causes of Chinese economic success outlined in Chapter 2. The black cooperative may take away the lower-class black trade, while the middle-class black is already switching to white-owned supermarkets.

Relations between Chinese and Negroes have become even more tense as the Chinese have been forced, because of the desegregation of the public schools, to make their choice of white schools and white society more obvious. In 1966 and 1967 Negroes were irritated in Clarksdale and Indianola by the successful evasion by Chinese of school-zoning ordinances which worked to keep Negroes in segregated schools. Even though the merchants live behind their stores in the heart of the black community, many were able to establish white addresses or in other ways managed to continue sending their children to the white schools. When full desegregation came in 1970, whites pulled out *en masse* from Indianola and some other systems, and Chinese students enrolled with them in hastily enacted all-white private "academies." To blacks, this is one more example of Chinese racism, and store courtesy not only cannot make up for it but makes the merchant appear more hypocritical.

Depopulation, the changing status of blacks who remain, and the growing polarization of the races in Mississippi have all worked to increase the precariousness of the Chinese position, at the same time that the civil rights controversy has improved it. Balancing on the racial tightrope is becoming ever more difficult. Therefore, a majority of Chinese parents are no longer urging their children to remain in Mississippi when they grow up, and Chinese young people are not staying in the state after they graduate from college. Thus changes in the Chinese population are even more striking than among Negroes.

The Future of the Chinese Population

For almost a century, the Delta has been a good place for the Chinese to make money. As long as they were sojourners in the system, financial success was their primary goal within it, for money was the key to winning the esteem of their peers in China. As their orientation shifted to Mississippi, however, money no longer sufficed as a general goal; like other groups, the Chinese now want to engage in occupations which reward them with status and win approval from their Mississippi and American peers. Nor is this change in outlook peculiar to Mississippi; Moench noted the same transition among younger Chinese in Tahiti: "Influenced by their education and associations with French and Tahitians, and aware that the characteristic industriousness and frugality of Chinese is far from universally admired by non-Chinese, their attitudes show ambivalence toward their parents' slavish devotion to making money. They recognize in it a sacrifice directed toward their own benefits, yet are unwilling to accept it as representing a satisfactory life." [16]

Operating a grocery, even a large supermarket, is not a high-status occupation in the Mississippi Delta. Consequently, few young Chinese now enter it. One young adult who did, and who already owns one of the Delta's largest supermarkets

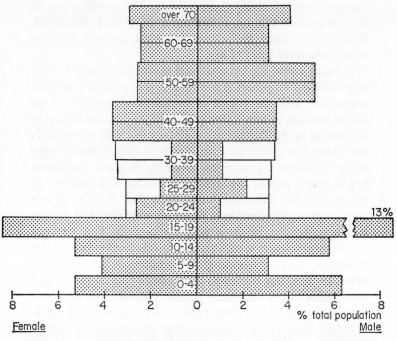

Open bars for ages 20-39 show percentage of the entire United States population in those categories.

Bolivar County data are from field census by the author, summer, 1967.

6. Age and sex of Chinese population, Bolivar County, 1967.

and is in an excellent position financially, complained bitterly of his situation: "I don't like groceries, but as long as I'm in it, I'll *make* myself like it. But I'm going to make damn sure my children aren't in it." Most of his age mates — in fact, more than 95 percent of all Chinese high school graduates since 1950 — have gone on to college. Usually they enter "five-year" fields — occupations such as engineering and pharmacy which require five years of study and then confer quick professionalization and relatively high starting pay. And they do not practice their engineering or even their pharmacy in small-town Mississippi; all but a handful have left the state after receiving their diploma. The resulting gap in the young-adult cohorts, both male and female, is incredible. Figure 6 indicates the almost complete dropout between twenty and forty years of age.

In many cases, the occupational choice itself leads to out-migration, but in others it does not, and in general it is more accurate to view the choice of work as an outgrowth of an earlier decision to move. For in a sense the Chinese are again sojourning in the Delta; only now their place of reference is not China, but the western and northern United States, especially the urban metropolises. Even eighth-grade youngsters beg to spend part of the summer vacations with relatives in Houston or San Francisco, and by the time they are in college, their career selection is based on what they feel are the best opportunities in those geographic areas. This new sojourning orientation is also related to the development in the students of a new reference group: students in the North and West. In turn, this relates to their questioning of Mississippi segregation mores and their greater progressivism in racial attitudes compared to their parents. In response to a questionnaire item, Delta Chinese college students chose Robert Kennedy as their first choice for President by a two-to-one margin over any other candidate; George Wallace, who was chosen by the majority of white Mississippi State University students, received not a single vote.

There are several reasons for the shift of the young Chinese away from Mississippi. First, the declining Negro population and the corresponding decrease in store volume have caused an exodus of some Chinese adults and a feeling among others that selling to blacks is hardly an occupation of great promise for their children. In addition, during the clampdown on civil liberties in Mississippi that followed the 1954 Supreme Court school decision, Chinese became very apprehensive about their own position; they envisioned such a radical polarization that they would be forced to choose sides completely, thereby losing either their white social rights or their black source of livelihood. Therefore, according to two

Chinese informants, some sent their children to out-of-state colleges and began to consider moving away themselves. These problems are beginning to be a matter of the past, however, even in the Delta, and in any case they do not explain why even future pharmacists and schoolteachers elect to leave Mississippi.

Having shifted from their parents' definition of what constitutes the good life, young Chinese adults want a more extensive social life than they can experience in the Delta. They still cannot participate completely in the social world of their Caucasian contemporaries, especially after eighth grade, when coeducational activities have assumed paramount importance. But the Chinese population is too small to offer a fully satisfactory substitute. Dating within the group is hampered by its tight gossip network, which makes any gaffe immediate public knowledge. Further stifling dating and courtship is the fact that Chinese must be exogamous by family name. Since perhaps half the group is named "Joe" or a variant, and another 20 or 30 percent are Wongs, the pool of potential mates or dates, already small, is cut down still more. Many young people deliberately choose Houston, San Diego, or another Western city with a large Chinese minority, in order to find a mate.

Probably the most important single reason for leaving is the continued discrimination the race still faces in Mississippi. Several Chinese girls, after graduating from teacher-training programs at Delta State College or Mississippi State College for Women, have tried without success to get an appointment in a Delta school system. Professors of education at both schools reported to me that Chinese teachers still have to go out of state to be employed.[17] In religion, the situation is the same. Faced with its first Chinese applicant for the ministry in 1966, the Mississippi Methodist hierarchy turned him down. The minister responsible told me: "I couldn't come out and say 'we don't need you because you're a Chinese,' but I could foresee complications because he was Chinese." Chinese parents feel that barriers preclude occupational success in other fields, such as law or medicine, and therefore they urge their children to enter engineering and other lines of work in which ability counts more than social connections or racial ascriptions. Moreover, discrimination is broader than occupational exclusion. Chinese continue to be rankled by their still uncertain racial status in general. Even the most well-meaning Caucasians sometimes subtly slur them. For example in conversation with me a Baptist official in Bolivar County said: "There are a few of the Chinese who attend some of our white churches — I mean, our *other* white churches, I don't want to imply that the Chinese aren't white, they're some of the most gracious people . . . [breaks off in confusion]."

Chinese students and adults invariably use "Caucasian" to refer to whites, but this term is almost unknown to Mississippians; as one girl complained, Delta whites think there are only two races in the world and do not know what to do with the Chinese. In Mississippi, to be considered not quite white means to be judged perhaps somewhat black, and we have remarked often enough what a disaster that is. It constitutes a basic attack on one's self-esteem as a person and is the reason why one woman told me: "My kids went North as soon as they could. They hate the South." I asked a Greenville couple if they wanted their children to leave Mississippi. Their answers emphasized the two basic reasons underlying the Chinese exodus:

> [Wife:] Yes sir! I don't want them to stay here. There ain't no money here.
> [Husband:] It's not only the money, it's the dignity of man. If you haven't got *respect,* you haven't got nothin'.
> [Wife:] My little boy and Johnson's little boy were inseparable. They went everywhere together. One day a bunch of them were going to the YMCA, and Johnnie said, "Why can't I go?" I said, "No, you can't go." "Why?" "No." Finally I said, "OK, go." He was turned away. I still don't know how to explain it to him.

The Mississippi Constitution should be changed — regarding school, marriage, everything. . . .
White people come in the store, they say "Elaine!" [18]
"you!" — never "Mrs. Wong." It doesn't bother me, though, not really. I'm so glad my children will soon be grown and can move away.
[Husband:] Up North, they are more liberal; they do not segregate us as strong as they do down here. But we never talk about those things, you know — no use.

A rather Americanized boy in Memphis gave evidence that the role of unobtrusive grocer no longer appealed to him on political grounds: "We want to be not only in American society, but also to be a *part* of it, help define it, and change it." As yet, this kind of role is impossible for Chinese in the Delta — their status, though white, is simply far too precarious. A college student from Cleveland summed up his position, and that of his race, perfectly: "Sometimes I feel as if my skin is just a shade darker than white, and sometimes that it's just a shade lighter than Negro." That feeling, I believe, is the key to the outmigration of the race.

The depopulation process among the Chinese has partly been countered by some continued immigration of older couples from Hong Kong, but the tide cannot be turned or even appreciably slowed. At one time there were fifty-six Chinese stores in Greenville; now only thirty-four remain. Table 6 shows the number of Chinese in Bolivar County from 1880 to 1967 and projects, on the basis of the age and sex statistics presented in Figure 6, the population through 1975. After about that date, the drop will become even more precipitous, for there will come a time of "critical mass," when a Chinese community in any sense of the word will prove unmaintainable. The older families will move out to the West Coast or Houston in order to be near their sons and daughters. The missions and the Chinese Baptist Church will close their doors, and even a remnant of social life within the Chinese group will prove impossible to maintain. A handful of very

Table 6. Bolivar County Chinese Population, 1880–1967, with Projections to 1975

Year	Chinese population
1880	0
1890	20
1900	36
1920	83
1940	180
1960	212
1967	186
1970	180
1975	148

Sources: 1880–1960 data from U.S. Census of Population; 1967 figure from field census by author, summer, 1967; 1970 and 1975 projections based on 1967 census and life table (see Figure 6).

Americanized families will remain, but the unusual saga of the Asian traders in the plantation South will be at an end.

The Chinese first found a niche in the Delta because of its system of racial segregation. Over the decades, that system had vast repercussions on their own social organization and led to efforts to escape it by acculturation. Now segregation itself is gradually breaking down, and the Delta Chinese will not long outlast its demise.

Appendices, Notes, and Bibliography

Appendix A. Historical Record of the Chinese Entry

Various published sources have put forth different speculations concerning the date and manner of the first entry of Chinese into Mississippi, and still other stories were given me by Chinese residents in the state itself. In his master's thesis at the University of Mississippi, George Rummel admits that "why they came to Mississippi is not known," [1] but he lists the possibility that they came: (1) as domestic servants, brought in from New Orleans by a steamboat captain, to work in his Greenville home; (2) as steamboat laborers; and (3) as grocers from the beginning. His first hypothesis was apparently supplied by a white informant. I could find no data supporting it. Possibly an isolated individual may have entered the state in this way, but I cannot confirm it, either through word of mouth or in newspapers and manuscript censuses of the time.

A similar story about household help was printed by the *Hinds County Gazette* on November 10, 1877: "Coahoma County, although it has a colored population of three to one over the white, is wretchedly off for 'house help,' and just received a consignment of Chinese girls from San Francisco."

Other rumors about new "shipments" of Chinese sporadically made newspaper headlines from Vicksburg to Memphis during the 1870's, and their publication is not sufficient warrant for belief. The Coahoma County story is almost surely false. Its premise — that domestic help was so scarce that importation of women over a distance of 2000 miles was cheaper than hiring local Negroes — is extremely dubious. Furthermore, San Francisco in 1877 had a male-female population ratio of at least seven to one; Chinese *men* predominated in personal service occupations in that city; the few girls were already engaged as wives or prostitutes. Finally, even if the story were true, the women (or men) would not have been the first Chinese to enter the Delta.

Rummel's second hypothesis is more plausible. A Chinese merchant interviewed by Virginia Lee for the Memphis *Commercial Appeal* in 1937 backed it up, but admitted he was only guessing: "In New Orleans they were offered work on interior boats plying the Mississippi. They must gradually have drifted inland from the river." [2] Joe Ting, a Greenville merchant, gave me a different steamboat story. About a hundred years ago, he said, Chinese were working in a fishery in New Orleans. They took passage as crew laborers on a steamboat bound to St. Louis, but the boat caught fire and burned near Hollandale, Mississippi. They swam ashore and, stranded without funds, worked as sharecroppers until they were able to start small groceries in a little town. The story seems plausible because of its vivid detail. However, a cursory check of Greenville newspaper files failed to unearth any steamboat burning in the right time period, and an older member of the Joe family did not confirm the tale.

Ray W. Joe, a leader of the Joe family in Greenwood, told me that Chinese worked their way to New Orleans on the railroad and then worked up to the Delta as construction gangs on the Yazoo and Mississippi Valley Rail Road, now the Illinois Central. Other Chinese informants confirmed his account, emphasizing the role of the railroad. Unfortunately, the Yazoo and Mississippi Valley was not built until 1883, while Delta Chinese appear in tax records and in the United States Census in 1880. This error points to a general problem in evaluating verbal accounts passed on in the Chinese population. Since sons were born in China to merchants in Mississippi, there was a very rapid turnover of personnel in the Delta during the sojourning period. In the process, historical details were lost, and over time, mere supposition has solidified into "knowledge."

Although I am not able to disprove Rummel's second hypothesis, then, nor Joe Ting's variant of it, I can find neither written data nor any other verbal reports to confirm either. Rummel himself opts for his third hypothesis, on the extraordinary grounds that it "fits most logically into sociological knowledge regarding Chinese migration." He then proceeds to embellish an account written by Robert O'Brien in *Social Forces* in 1941. As Rummel tells it: "A Mr. Wong, the first Chinese who came to the Mississippi Delta, arrived in San Francisco from Canton, China. He looked for work in the California gold fields and on the labor crews of the transcontinental railroad. Finding conditions extremely difficult, he returned to the ship he had come over on and contracted to work until it made its next port — New Orleans. There he began working on a river boat steamer operating between that city and the small river port of Rosedale, Mississippi. He worked on the paddle wheel steamer until he had saved enough money to open a small independent grocery store in Rosedale in 1875." [3] However, Rummel's discussion of West Coast happenings is completely undocumented. In personal discussion with me, he cited only Reverend Ira Eavenson, founder of the Cleveland Chinese Mission, as a source for it, but Evaenson gave me no confirmation himself. Furthermore, Rummel's account lacks verisimilitude. It is unlikely that the same ship plied two such different routes and completely dubious that it would still be in port after Mr. Wong had checked out two fields of work, which in those days would have required several weeks. Furthermore, if the transcontinental railroad had not been completed, Wong could have found work on it, for workgangs were in short supply until the last spike was driven. If it was finished, in 1869, then he would have traveled to New Orleans over it, for until the completion of the Panama Canal in 1914, and even thereafter, almost all internal migration within the United States from 1870 on was by rail. Finally, Rosedale was founded in 1872 as a political headquarters for the Republican party in Bolivar County under the name "Floreyville"; "Rosedale" was not adopted until after Democrats gained control of the state in 1876.[4] Very probably Rummel's story is an imaginative reconstruction to make good magazine copy; since it was published in a student magazine at the University of Mississippi, Rummel perhaps felt that it would do little harm to the historical record.

Less excusable is the account in *Social Forces* on which it is based. According to O'Brien: "A Mr. Wong was the first member of the group to settle in Mississippi. He left Canton to engage as a contract laborer on the railroads in California," [5] and then, via New Orleans, arrived in "Rosedale" in 1875 to found a store. Neither Rummel nor I place much faith in O'Brien's research, however; much of it seems closely based on Lee's article in the *Commercial Appeal,* without citation, and his account of the Chinese entry is probably drawn from the following paragraph from that source: "The oldest Chinese inhabitant of the Delta now is 92 years old. His name is Wong. Wong remembers coming to the Delta some 62 years ago (1875). There was only one or two Chinese here ahead of him." [6] O'Brien's evidence can therefore, I believe, be discounted.

There are two formulations of the Chinese entry which do have solid evidence behind them. First, it can be proved from the historical record not only that plantation owners agitated during the late 1860's and early 1870's for Chinese immigration but also that they did receive some Chinese laborers and employed them as farm workers. By 1870, and perhaps even earlier, Chinese farm laborers were active on plantations in Mississippi, Louisiana, and Arkansas.[7] Second, several Chinese sources independently confirmed to me an account of the first Chinese resident in Mississippi whom they know to be connected with their group. According to them, several Chinese men were working on sugarcane plantations and "shrimp-farms" in Louisiana after work ended on the transcontinental railroad in 1869. The fact that there were too many workers and not enough work prompted eight or nine to book passage (as paid passengers, not crewmen) on a steamboat to Greenville, to work for a plantation owner near Stoneville in Washington County. The plantation did not pay them what they had been promised, so as soon as they could they opened tiny stores, first in Sunflower, Mississippi, and then in Greenville and elsewhere. The last of them died in 1943, at the age of 99 (this would be Mr. Wong, the "oldest Chinese inhabitant of the Delta, now 92 years old," cited by Virginia Lee in 1937 in the *Commercial Appeal*.) I believe this story, but I doubt that these eight or nine initial settlers antedate the plantation work gangs; the *Commercial Appeal* story would set the date at about 1875.

In any event, it is demonstrated that Chinese entered the system in about 1870 as plantation sharecroppers. If the present Chinese inhabitants of the Delta are not related to these first settlers, they do trace their group to other pioneers, also originally sharecroppers, who entered Mississippi in about 1875.

Appendix B. Methods

Interviewing of Chinese, Negro, and Caucasian adults and students was the most important single research method used. Subjects were not chosen to represent all groups in the population proportionally but were selected because of their particular connections with or knowledge about the Chinese and their relations with whites and blacks. More whites were interviewed than members of any other race because they were more heterogeneous occupationally, and individual whites were selected because of their particular structural connections with the Chinese. Therefore, interviews with whites were concentrated among school officials, ministers, businessmen, and grocers, which left planters, small farmers, and workers somewhat underrepresented.[1]

Among the Chinese, I emphasized my student status in becoming friends with a number of college and high school students,[2] and I began my work by interviewing Chinese undergraduates at Mississippi State University, Mississippi State College for Women, and the University of Mississippi. Although the attitudes of the younger generation are surely not representative of the entire population, their information about a wide variety of topics proved invaluable. The Chinese sample was also somewhat biased toward more acculturated long-term residents and away from women and new arrivals, especially those with little knowledge of English. This selection was helpful for understanding Chinese-white interaction, since it included the individuals most knowledgeable about that interaction, but attitudes cannot be projected onto the entire Delta Chinese population on the basis of my sample alone.

Among Negroes, those interviewed included members of all relevant categories, although the sample in each was not large. I was able to compensate somewhat for the small sample by developing close rapport with several individuals, making them into near informants.

My own background proved helpful in establishing rapport with members of each group. Substantial interaction with white Mississippians, including a part of my undergraduate education at Mississippi State University, gave me empathy and a specific institutional reference which markedly facilitated interviews with whites. Interaction with both middle- and lower-class Negroes, including individuals active in and alienated from the civil rights struggle, coupled with a summer of work at Tougaloo College, gave me an orientation and institutional reference which was useful for interviews with Delta blacks. Finally, for the Chinese, my best reference proved to be my connection with Harvard University, for the Chinese are nationally oriented and are aware of and impressed by Harvard's reputation, so that an air of "scholarly" legitimation was lent to what otherwise might seem an unusual and threatening activity. In addition, my coming from outside the system minimized certain threats I might otherwise have represented to them and made confidences placed in me seem less dangerous.[2]

Objective facts of past and present interaction were usually the point of inquiry, and since these were checked by multiple sources from different racial groups, the interview data are perhaps more than usually trustworthy. I interviewed a total of 321 different people. They are listed by race and occupation in Table 7.

Table 7. Persons Interviewed, by Ethnic Group and Occupation

Chinese...	98
College and high school students and recent graduates..	45
Grocers..	42
Others...	11
Chinese-Negroes[a]...................................	17
Negroes...	38
Political leaders and civil rights workers..............	8
Middle-class professionals..........................	16
Grocers..	5
Poor people and youth..............................	9
Whites[a]..	163
Businessmen and Chamber of Commerce officials	
(excluding grocers and realtors)...................	24
Grocers and food wholesalers.......................	14
Realtors...	4
School officials...................................	30
City officials, judges, etc..........................	11
Newspaper editors, reporters.......................	10
Lawyers, doctors, hospital administrators.............	10
Ministers..	23
Planters...	14
Misc., including workers...........................	23
Indians and Mexicans.................................	5
Total interviewed....................................	321

[a] Several minority groups, including Jews, Italians, and Lebanese, 18 persons in all, are represented in the "white" category.

A great deal of my information, from vague impressions to controlled observations, came from participation and observation in Chinese and Caucasian homes, stores, churches, parties, school events, and other institutional settings. Evidences of what I learned from the participant observation are scattered throughout the book. However, in addition to interviews and participation, I did utilize several more formal sources of data, which should be briefly noted here. The few published items on the Delta Chinese consist mainly of a page or two in books on other topics and are included in the bibliography. Such material as W.P.A. histories, newspaper archives, court records, legal case histories, tax records, and United States Census material, proved more valuable. In Greenville and Clarksdale, school board minutes and correspondence were obtained. Finally, I made some use of a miscellany of other sources, including clippings held by the Chinese Baptist Church of Cleveland, cemetery tombstones, and private manuscripts.

Current records provided "hard data" sources with which to check some of the impressionistic statements given me in interviews. Included were Chamber of Commerce membership rolls, church bulletins and donation lists, and newspaper accounts of youth activities. High school yearbooks, with their lists of organizational memberships after each senior's name, were particularly informative, as were class-day programs and student newspapers. Mississippi State University kindly supplied grade averages anonymously for all recent Chinese graduates, as well as overall student averages for comparison.

In order to survey attitudes of Chinese Mississippians on a variety of topics, I constructed a five-page questionnaire, and at a conference of Chinese college students held in late August 1967, distributed it to about thirty-eight individuals. Because of scheduling problems and because several students from Cleveland did not fully trust my intent, only twenty-seven were returned.[3] For comparison, I was able to get replies from seventy-four Caucasian students in introductory sociology classes at Mississippi State University.[4] The two questionnaires, which differ in some details, can be found in Appendix C of my doctoral dissertation, "The Mississippi Chinese," Harvard University, 1968.

Notes

Introduction

1. Throughout this book, "race" and racial terms are used as social labels, not biological assertions, and do not impute genetic racial "purity" to those so labeled.

2. Included were 98 Chinese, 38 Negroes, 163 Caucasians, and 22 others (Chinese-Negroes, Indians, Mexicans). Appendix B contains a general discussion of the methods used in this study, including an outline of the strengths and weaknesses of the interview process and of the sample of interviewees.

1   Entry of the Chinese

1. William F. Gray, ed., *Imperial Bolivar* (Cleveland, Miss., 1923), p. 17. See also Florence W. Sillers, compiler, *History of Bolivar County, Mississippi* (Jackson, Miss., 1948).

2. Maurice Elizabeth Jackson, "Mound Bayou — A Study in Social Development," unpub. thesis, University of Alabama, 1937, p. 28, paraphrasing Walter Sillers, Sr., in Gray, ed., *Imperial Bolivar,* and David L. Cohn, *God Shakes Creation* (New York, 1935).

3. William C. Holley, Ellen Winston, and T. J. Woofter, Jr., *The Plantation South, 1934–1937* (Washington, D.C., 1940), pp. xvii–xix, 44, 55–57. All these figures save sharecropper income should be moderately increased for the Delta, because in the Delta

statistics, several other areas with somewhat smaller farms, poorer soil, and lower agricultural production were included.

4. A descriptive comparison of the two counties is offered in Donald J. Bogue and Calvin L. Beale, *Economic Areas of the United States* (New York, 1961), pp. 369–370, 638–639.

5. Both axes are divided into percentages of total population or income, respectively. The key provision is that individuals with more income are placed successively further to the right. Thus richer persons fall in the higher percentiles on the population axis. Since they possess proportionately more income, as plotted on the vertical axis, the slope of the curve is constantly rising. A quick intuitive grasp of the Lorenz technique can be gained by considering that a society with complete equality would be represented by the diagonal line itself, since each unit increment on the population axis would be accompanied by a unit increment in income. The Gini Index is the ratio of area enclosed between the curve and diagonal to the total area under the diagonal. In the case of complete equality it would equal 0.00. In contrast, a society of total inequality — all families penniless save one with *all* the income — would be portrayed by a horizontal line from "0" to nearly "100" on the population axis, connected by a nearly vertical line to "100, 100," a line completely bowed out toward the perimeter of the right triangle. Its Gini Index would be nearly 1.00. In other words, the more bowed out the curve and the greater the Gini Index, the greater the inequality in the system. H. R. Alker, Jr., supplies a general introduction to Lorenz curves in Chapter 3, "Measuring Inequality," of his *Mathematics and Politics* (New York, 1965).

6. Data are from *United States Census of Population, 1960,* vol. I., *Characteristics of the Population.* Census data are available only for income groupings. To construct the curve, it was assumed that all households in a given income classification, such as $1000–$1999, earned the midpoint income, in this case $1500. Such a process makes line segments out of what in reality is a continuous and more bowed-out curve. The difference in Gini Index is not large, however, and can be shown to be less than 0.02, even for the county with the greater inequality. Thus Bolivar County's true Index falls between 0.534 and 0.550, and Livingston County's between 0.389 and 0.400.

7. "Social class," used narrowly, is by no means a purely economic term based solely on relation to productive enterprises.

Marx was clear on this point, although not all Marxists have been. See for example the first two-thirds of Marx's *The Eighteenth Brumaire* (New York, 1963); see also a careful discussion of class by Lawrence Stone, *The Crisis of the Aristocracy, 1558–1641* (London, 1965), pages 56–64. The term does have a good deal more precision, however, when used narrowly, than status groupings such as "upper middle." As I mean it, a social class is a group of people (the units are families) who are in social discourse with each other on a level of rough equality and who at least occasionally act in concert to affect other groups. In turn, concerted action and social intercourse imply further conditions. A common style of life is required, because socialization into that style builds up a set of similar attitudes which are inseparable from the common purpose underlying concerted action. Life style also becomes an important means of identifying those with whom one interacts socially and excluding those beneath. Institutional memberships in such organizations as Rotary, the Delta Council, and First Baptist or Methodist Church, provide sites for communication, solidarity, and further identification and certification. Finally, in at least some situations there must be common interests or a common purpose, which make it in individuals' perceived self-interests to act as a group. This purpose can derive from parallel economic positions or from parallel political positions (vis-à-vis poor whites or Negroes, for example). It also results from intermarriage and commensality, as in the case of the planter, who can count on the support of businessmen and professionals.

8. Buried in Robin Williams' *Strangers Next Door* (Englewood Cliffs, N.J., 1954), p. 42, in a study of attitudes in Savannah, Georgia, and three northern cities, is a supportive finding: in the South there is much less anti-businessman reaction among all classes than in the North.

9. Georg Simmel has written an excellent and subtle analysis of processes involved in a dominant-subordinate relationship. See "Conflict," in *Conflict and the Web of Group Affiliations* (Glencoe, Ill., 1955), chapter 3. He stresses that as soon as the relationship ceases to be one of absolute coercion, it becomes at least partly one of social *inter*action, meaning that each party must to some degree take into account the attitudes and desires of the other and the effects of his own actions upon those attitudes and desires. Such a process intrinsically implies that the other person

is an equal, or at least a person, to be reckoned with as well as utilized. Dollard notes that the planters also suffered "a sharp narcissistic wound; their gratification in owning and controlling Negroes so completely was taken away by force." See John Dollard, *Caste and Class in a Southern Town* (Garden City, N.Y., 1957), p. 186.

10. As usual in Southern history, the threat was seen to be also sexual, and many writers warned of the peril faced by Southern white women in such an overwhelmingly black population. This theme underlies much of David Cohn's *God Shakes Creation,* for example, one of the most famous interpretations of Delta life.

11. William M. Burwell, "Science and the Mechanic Arts against Coolies," p. 558 of *De Bow's Review* (July 1869), pp. 557–571. Note that the argument depends upon the assumption, in the last sentence, that the political influence of the Negro was an accomplished fact; although this assumption seemed perfectly reasonable in 1869, it was unfortunately negated within a decade.

12. Cf. Bert James Loewenberg, "Efforts of the South to Encourage Immigration," 33 (October 1934), 363–385.

13. Vicksburg *Times,* June 30, 1869, "The Coming Laborer."

14. For the record, there is yet another way in which the Chinese were linked, before their arrival, to the Negro and Caucasian in the South. Southern Congressmen, in return for support of their anti-Negro position, voted with California Democrats to pass laws restricting Chinese immigration and citizenship.

15. Powell Clayton, *The Aftermath of the Civil War in Arkansas* (New York, 1915), p. 208.

16. Vicksburg *Times,* June 30, 1869, "The Coming Laborer."

17. In later years, Italians and Mexicans were imported to the Delta for similar reasons. See Robert L. Brandfon, *Cotton Kingdom of the New South* (Cambridge, Mass., 1967), chapter vii, and Carter G. Woodson, *The Rural Negro* (Washington, D.C., 1930).

18. See Clayton, *Aftermath of the Civil War,* pp. 208, 213; *Jackson Semi-Weekly Clarion,* August 2, 1870, "More Chinese Coming," and August 30, 1870, "Labor in Louisiana"; United States Works Progress Administration, *Arkansas, A Guide to the State* (New York, 1941), p. 346.

19. Pao Yun Liao, *A Case Study of a Chinese Immigrant Community,* page 15.

20. Evidence on this point, and a full discussion of all data relating to the entry of the Chinese into Mississippi, is presented in Appendix A.

21. A. D. Kirwan, *Revolt of the Rednecks* (Gloucester, Mass., 1964).

22. Even today many planters will admit they still prefer Negroes as tractor drivers and farm workers to whites, for they are less troublesome and can be fired, if necessary, with fewer repercussions. The preference for black labor, and the shutting out of working-class whites, was one of the grievances expressed by the Alliance and subsequently by the Populist Party in the South near the end of the preceding century.

23. For the record, a few Mennonites entered the Delta two decades ago and were farm laborers for a time, but this represented no serious immigration movement among the planters.

24. Ta Chen, *Emigrant Communities in South China* (New York, 1940), pp. 59, 82–83, 89. It should be noted that this reference deals not with the precise area from which Mississippi Chinese and most other Chinese in the United States came but rather with an area of Kwangtung and Fukien somewhat farther up the coast. Probably Chen's findings are applicable, but we do not know for sure.

25. This is particularly evident in Vicksburg, in the relations between resident Chinese grocers and visiting Chinese research scientists, usually Mandarin-speaking.

26. J. K. Fairbank, *The United States and China* (Cambridge, Mass., 1958), p. 28.

27. The Mississippi Chinese was not different from some of his counterparts in Southeast Asia and elsewhere. Many Chinese entered Thailand, Malaysia, and other countries as plantation laborers, hoping to switch to independent businesses as soon as possible, and planning in the long run to return to their families in China.

28. This pattern was reported by Dorothy Hyde Bracey in "Effects of Emigration on a Hakka Village," unpub. diss., Harvard University, 1967. No evidence on the matter could be adduced from the present study; probably Bracey's argument is valid for the Mississippi Chinese.

29. It goes almost without saying that Negroes in Mississippi have faced even more negative evaluations from whites; and of

course they have not been able to maintain their original culture as have the Chinese sojourners.

30. Paul C. P. Siu, "The Sojourner," *American Journal of Sociology*, 58 (1952–1953), 34. Much of the present discussion relies upon this clear and valuable essay.

31. Jackson *Weekly Clarion*, August 12, 1870.

32. Ibid., November 20, 1873, "John in the South."

33. Clayton, *Aftermath of the Civil War*, p. 214.

2 Economic Success

1. See Leon Friedman, ed., *Southern Justice* (New York, 1965), for a recent study of contemporary operation of legal systems in Mississippi and other Southern states.

2. Chapter 3 offers a more extended discussion of the legal situation faced by the Chinese.

3. For the record, the eight exceptions include two families jointly engaged in TV sales and repair, an insurance agent, two pharmacists, and three planters. In addition, two or three grocers also farm.

4. Nationally, in 1950 only 20.1 percent of all employed Chinese were classed in the broad category "proprietors, managers, and officials." Of these, probably less than one in four, or less than 5 percent of the total Chinese labor force, operated groceries. Data from Rose Hum Lee, *The Chinese in the United States of America*, table 10.

5. Edward J. Ryan, *The Value System of a Chinese Community in Java*, unpub. diss., Harvard University, 1961, p. 20.

6. Other than this general sanctioning of independent business enterprise in the cultural heritage of the immigrants, many had no actual business experience before their arrival in Mississippi.

7. Compare Ryan: "It is common, of course, for immigrants upon first arriving in Indonesia to be employed by a kinsman . . . Such a position, however, is never a significant goal; it is . . . instrumental to establishing an independent business. It is a means for the individual either to accumulate sufficient capital and strike out on his own or to establish his reputation as hard working and honest and develop credit which enable him to achieve the same end." *The Value System of a Chinese Community*, p. 21.

8. An even clearer example of this process can be seen in

Jamaica, where the British colonial view of what constitutes an honorable occupation lingers on. In about 1964, Smith asked a sample of Jamaican schoolboys, "What work do you want to do when you leave school?" Artisan and professional occupations were the overwhelming favorites; only 0.2 percent chose retail business. M. G. Smith, *The Plural Society in the British West Indies* (Berkeley, 1965), p. 202. Broom concludes that "the Chinese in Jamaica would not have gained control of the grocery trade so quickly if the educated colored had not become committed to the professions and the civil service as status-bearing occupations. It is ironic that British colonialism, which historically has been so heavily influenced by commercial interests, should have implanted a disdain of commerce among many colonial peoples." Leonard Broom, "The Social Differentiation of Jamaica," *American Sociological Review,* 19 (1954), 125. The insight that status systems codify this sort of information originated most forcefully with Thorstein Veblen. *The Theory of the Leisure Class* (New York, 1953), especially pages 37–38 and 86. For a recent restatement, see Talcott Parsons, "A Revised Analytical Approach to the Theory of Social Stratification," in *Essays in Sociological Theory* (New York, 1964).

9. Richard Wright tried it, in a Yankee-owned establishment in south Mississippi, with disastrous results. See his *Black Boy* (New York, 1951), pp. 202–212.

10. Paul K. Edwards, *The Southern Urban Negro as a Consumer* (New York, 1932), pp. 125, 138, my italics.

11. Ibid., page 140. I do not know why these percentages total more than 100. Enough Negro-owned groceries existed, incidentally, for customers to have shopped at one except for the problems of selection and store appeal, noted above, and other problems to be considered below.

12. Frantz Fanon, *The Wretched of the Earth* (New York, 1966), p. 203.

13. Such views almost always filter down, not up; see Veblen, *Theory of the Leisure Class,* p. 81.

14. In the context of emerging black solidarity and awareness, however, these patterns may not last much longer. The discourteous merchant was hit by a minor firebomb attack in the wake of the assassination of Rev. Martin Luther King, Jr., in 1968; discourteous Chinese and Caucasians in Clarksdale and elsewhere

have faced boycotts in recent years. See Chapter 7 for a more detailed account of these developments.

15. Proverbs 14 : 20.

16. Richard Moench, "Economic Relations of the Chinese in the Society Islands," unpub. diss., Harvard University, 1970, pp. 61–62. Romanzo Adams made a similar observation in Hawaii; see his *Interracial Marriage in Hawaii* (New York, 1937).

17. Andrew W. Lind, "Adjustment Patterns among the Jamaican Chinese," *Social and Economic Studies,* 7 (1958), 154.

18. To use the Parsonian pattern-variable.

19. In *The Mark of Oppression* (New York, 1951), p. 316, Abram Kardiner and Lionel Ovesey go further, claiming that "every Negro who is higher than lower class has a sense of guilt to other Negroes because he considers success a betrayal of his group and a piece of aggression against them."

20. Dollard, *Caste and Class in a Southern Town*, pp. 341–342.

21. David Cohn, *Where I Was Born and Raised* (Notre Dame, Ind., 1967), p 87. This idea is a pervasive theme throughout Cohn's book.

22. Once again, there is a close parallel between the Chinese experience in Mississippi and in colonial Southeast Asia. W. L. Cator, for example, cites similar competitive advantages enjoyed by the Chinese in Indonesia versus European businessmen. See his *The Economic Position of the Chinese in the Netherlands Indies* (Chicago, 1936), p. 56. The parallel points up the similarity between the Chinese sojourners in each society but also make starkly evident the extent to which the social systems were alike. When black leaders refer to their followers as a colonized people, at least regarding the Mississippi Delta, they do not exaggerate.

23. Hodding Carter, *Southern Legacy* (Baton Rouge, La., 1950), p. 118.

24. Ibid., p. 116.

25. Veblen, *Theory of the Leisure Class,* pp. 41–42. In *The Lazy South* (New York, 1967), David Bertelson argues strongly that the ideology of work avoidance even predated and partly caused the spread of slavery itself.

26. Robert H. Silin, "A Survey of Selected Aspects of the Chinese in Jamaica," unpub. master's thesis, Harvard University, pp. 16–17. In Thailand the situation was much the same; see Richard

J. Coughlin, *Double Identity: The Chinese in Modern Thailand* (Hong Kong, 1960), pp. 12–16.

27. The foregoing analysis is not anti-Marxist. On the contrary, an adequate explanation of the social system of the Mississippi Delta will necessarily rely so heavily upon Marxist assumptions, theory, and methods that it will fall directly under the rubric of post-Marxist sociology. However, as any of his case studies shows, Marx did not maintain that only the lower classes possess false consciousness, while the ruling class (or classes) acts in its own rational self-interest. Nor did he claim that ideas and ideologies possess no life of their own. His argument was that the means of production influence the social relations of production in a dialectical process, both in turn affecting the cultural superstructure of the time. The ideology of the upper class represents at least in part an attempt to explain the success of its own members in morally acceptable terms. This ideology then influences the actions and choices of its adherents, most obviously by setting the definitions of what constitutes class interest, so that what is perceived by an actor to be in his own interest may in fact work to subvert or not to enhance his class position.

28. In Chapter 5, an anti-Chinese incident in Clarksdale is reported. About thirty white merchants and their peers signed a petition opposing Chinese school integration in 1941. The driving force behind the movement was a small grocer, E. C. Cagle; significantly, none of his supporting petitioners, so far as can be ascertained, was even close to membership in the upper class. Most of the signers could be considered as *lumpen-bourgeoisie,* like Cagle himself.

29. Robert E. Park and Ernest W. Burgess, *Introduction to the Science of Sociology* (Chicago, 1921), p. 621.

30. R. D. McKenzie, "The Oriental Invasion," *Journal of Applied Sociology,* 10 (1925), 120–130.

31. Following the line of thought of Park and McKenzie, Shibutani and Kwan have elaborated a theory of ethnic accommodation similar to my argument above. See their *Ethnic Stratification, A Comparative Approach* (New York, 1965), especially chapters v, vii, and xii. In *Toward a Theory of Minority-Group Relations* (New York, 1967), p. 81, Hubert M. Blalock, Jr., makes the same point with specific application to middleman minorities.

3 Social Status Before 1940

1. This orientation originated with Robert E. Park; see, for example, "The Etiquette of Race Relations in the South," in *Race and Culture* (New York, 1964), pp. 177–188.

2. A startling example was related to me by a Chinese grocer in Greenwood. He wanted to hire a Negro butcher for his meat department. But whites complained, threatening a boycott, because they "didn't want a nigger" handling the meat they took home to their family. The implication is that Negroes are diseased and unclean, but when white families eat out, the restaurant's cook, much more closely involved with the food's preparation than any butcher, is invariably black. The explanation is that in Greenwood, the job of butcher is usually held by whites. The "unclean" rationale, though not a conscious hoax, is corollary to the basic intent of keeping Negroes out of a Caucasian occupation. "Cook," on the other hand, in keeping with Southern traditions, is domestic labor, to be avoided; it has always been a Negro job, and the cleanliness argument somehow is never brought up.

3. John Dollard, a Yankee, repeatedly elicited such reactions among his Southern white associates. See *Caste and Class,* pp. 48, 345–350.

4. For the record, the third group need not be racially distinct. Sporadic attempts were made to keep Italian children in separate schools during the first two decades of this century (see Brandfon, *Cotton Kingdom,* chapter 7, and Woodson, *The Rural Negro,* p. 78, note). Mexicans have suffered similar discrimination since then (see *The Greenville Delta Democrat-Times,* Sept. 6, 1945, "Mexican children in county have no school facilities"). In both of these cases, however, many members of the minority were initially in the same occupational class as Negroes and had the same low income. To a greater extent than with the Chinese, then, the discrimination was based on economic grounds. And with regard to the Italians, after a few individuals had risen in economic and occupational stature, the rationale against them broke down and the oppression began to lift. That Chinese are distinctive *racially,* an ascribed characteristic of great visibility and greater immutability, meant that they had to be treated as a group, even though their economic status was higher and more differentiated from Negroes almost from the beginning.

5. William Alexander Percy, *Lanterns on the Levee* (New York, 1941), p. 18. The statement about violence is not borne out by interviews with police chiefs or editors of the period nor by a survey of the newspaper archives in Greenville and Cleveland. Percy's dismissal of the threat to whites ("except to the small white store-keeper") confirms the analysis of the preceding chapter regarding the place of the petty-bourgeoisie. Note finally the use of "breed" to refer to Chinese-Negro sexual relations — a dehumanizing verb choice reminiscent of slave breeding and cattle breeding.

6. Robert W. O'Brien, "Status of the Chinese in the Mississippi Delta," *Social Forces*, 19 (1941), 390.

7. As colonial Southeast Asia became more commercial, the Chinese played a similar go-between role. See, for example, Richard J. Coughlin, *Double Identity; The Chinese in Modern Thailand* (Hong Kong, 1960), especially chapter 1.

8. White Mississippi, having placed Chinese in the social position of the Negro, didn't care if the two races "fornicated" amongst themselves. "[No section in the Code] prohibits any marriage or social relations between the negro [*sic*] and Mongolian races, and they are left free to maintain such social, including marriage, relations as they see proper to enter into." (Supreme Court majority decision, *Rice et al. v. Gong Lum et al.*, Mississippi Reports, vol. 139, 1925, p. 780.)

9. This discussion is partly based on Bracey, "Effects of Emigration on a Hakka Village."

10. G. W. Skinner, "The Chinese of Java," in M. H. Fried, ed., *Colloquium on Overseas Chinese* (New York), 1958, p. 2.

11. Maurice Broady, "The Chinese in Great Britain," in *Colloquium on Overseas Chinese*, p. 33.

12. M. H. Fried, "The Chinese in the British Caribbean," in *Colloquium on Overseas Chinese*.

13. Mississippi Code, 1942, recompiled, vol. one A-1956, section 459. The penalty is imprisonment of up to ten years. For avoiding the statute by going out of state to marry, the penalty is the same, and mere advocacy of intermarriage carries a maximum punishment of a $500 fine and six months' imprisonment.

The definition of the crime and its punishment has been essentially the same since the Code of 1892 (section 2859). It did not become a dead letter until July 1967, while the field research for this thesis was underway, as the result of a decision of the United States Supreme Court on a case originating from Virginia. Delta Chinese were definitely aware of this decision, which received attention from the national news media, and spoke of it with satisfaction.

14. See Chapter 6 for a fuller treatment of the theory of interracial marriage.

15. Arthur F. Raper, *The Tragedy of Southern Lynching* (Chapel Hill, N.C., 1933), p. 102; Clarksdale data from school board minutes and notes.

16. "In the absence of proper provision of schools at state expense, Tougaloo University stood as the one institution where the young Negroes of Mississippi might obtain competent training." — Vernon L. Wharton, *The Negro in Mississippi, 1865–1890* (Chapel Hill, N.C., 1947), p. 255.

17. Mrs. Harry Ogden (*nee* Florence Sillers), untitled manuscript on the Chinese in Rosedale, 1933.

18. United States Reports, vol. 275, 1927, *Gong Lum et al. v. Rice et al.*, p. 80.

19. Ibid., pp. 80, 81.

20. Ibid., p. 79.

21. Mississippi Reports, vol. 139, 1925, *Rice et al. v. Gong Lum et al.*, p. 763.

22. United States Reports, vol. 275, *Gong Lum*, p. 78.

23. This argument was probably bypassed by Brewer and Flowers because the court had held in earlier post-Plessy decisions that equal facilities need not be identical as long as they were similar in form and purpose.

24. It was soon confirmed by additional adverse judgments; cf. 148 Miss. 462, *Bond v. Tij Fung.*

25. Mrs. Harry Ogden, untitled manuscript on the Chinese in Rosedale, also confirmed by her in interview.

26. Kung-Chuan Hsiao, *Rural China: Imperial Control in the Nineteenth Century* (Seattle, 1960), p. 9.

27. A handful of working-class whites even married Chinese men during the 20's and 30's. See Chapter 6.

28. Paul C. P. Siu, "The Sojourner," pp. 34–35.

29. Negroes, of course, in far larger numbers, are burdened with the same negative definition system, without much chance of escaping via acculturation or image change. Many Southern

whites told me, with real compassion, of the indignities suffered by the Delta Chinese in past decades, failing completely to see the simple fact that the Negro suffers equally or worse even today, that treatment of blacks in fact provided the model of the mal-treatment of Chinese.

30. Compare the politics of Malayan Chinese, as summarized in Victor Purcell, *The Chinese in Malaya* (London, 1948), pp. 146–150. Support for the Kuomintang during the 1930's and 1940's does not constitute an exception to the general noninvolve-ment of Mississippi Chinese, for their contributions were similar to the aid sent by Delta Jews to Israel during the 1967 Arab-Israeli war; that is, in both cases aid was sent by immigrants to a country with which they wished to express solidarity, but which was no longer their permanent home.

4   Transition

1. Robert W. O'Brien, "Status of the Chinese in the Mississippi Delta," p. 390.

2. This assertion is supported in the next chapter.

3. But see Chapter 6.

4. Chinese-Negro marriage, unlike Chinese-Caucasian, was no formal violation of Mississippi law, and in many communities the relationship would have been ignored. Note 18 discusses the rea-sons for the Hollandale reaction.

5. A grocer who broke up his family to avoid ostracism did not usually end all communication with them, especially with his chil-dren. He sent money regularly and actively supported their college educations. In general, the Chinese male recognized and assumed responsibility for his half-breed offspring far more than do most whites in similar position. And of course in some cases he refused to give them up, even at the cost of complete exclusion from white and Chinese social life. Such families are described more extensively in Chapter 6.

6. In Mississippi, caste lines are often given class terms, so that "low-class" Chinese usually refers to Chinese with Negro fami-lies, regardless of their economic stature.

7. George A. Rummel, "The Delta Chinese: An Exploratory Study in Assimilation," unpub. M.A. thesis, University of Missis-sippi, 1966, p. 35.

8. Their endogamy is no pose, put on for white consumption; parents who want their children to retain some Chinese identity are deeply opposed to their intermarriage, even if it takes place outside Mississippi.

9. Surveying Tsarist parents after the Bolshevik revolution, Alex Inkeles observed a similar phenomenon: "Parents . . . seek to raise their children differently from the way in which they were brought up, purposefully adapting their child rearing practices to train children better suited to meet life in the changed world as the parent now sees it." "Social Change and Social Character: The Role of Parental Mediation," in Cohen, ed., *Social Structure and Personality: A Casebook* (New York, 1961), p. 137.

10. Cleveland, Miss., *Bolivar Commercial*, March 19, 1937.

11. The Cleveland church, on the other hand, is more Chinese. At most of its services, which are still held on Sunday afternoon to accommodate store hours, no Caucasians are present. The sermon is alternately in Chinese and English, and the hymns are sung in both at once. This is a requirement, since many children and college students know very little Chinese, while their parents and especially their grandmothers may speak only rudimentary English. But even these services are subtly more American than Chinese: announcements are sometimes made only in English, and parts taken by young people are almost never in Chinese.

12. The speaker is white, a close friend of the Chinese since the 1920's.

13. Less than 8 percent of all Chinese in the United States are Christian, according to S. W. Kung, *Chinese in American Life* (Seattle, 1962), p. 55. But at least 25 percent of the Delta Chinese are church members; in Cleveland over 50 percent belong to a church, and this is probably a good guess for the Delta as a whole.

14. In the Caribbean, where Chinese racial status in the 1920's was also precarious, improvement was attempted by similar non-direct means — suppression of vices, donations to the YMCA, etc. — and a similarly high percentage of the Jamaican Chinese converted to Christianity. See W. M. Cousins, "Chinese in the Caribbean," *The Living Age*, 332 (1927), 20.

15. Kenneth Scott Latourette, *The Chinese, Their History and Culture* (New York, 1928), p. 203.

16. Chinese $N = 5$; Caucasian $N = 12$. Because of these small samples the results are statistically significant only at the .1 level

(t test). However, they are confirmed by similar data from Green-ville High School and by figures comparing Italians and Protes-tants in Shaw. Interview data from Rosedale, Greenville, Green-wood, and Cleveland also support the conclusions in this para-graph.

17. These clusterings are statistically significant at better than the .01 level. Using Chi-square approximations, dangerous be-cause of the low N, each of the examples shows clumping differ-ent from chance at about the .001 level. Computing an approxi-mation of the exact probabilities of these distributions or more extreme variants, the three cases combined would occur by chance fewer than 5 times in 1000.

18. This is ironic, because most of the larger towns — Clarks-dale, Cleveland, Vicksburg, and Greenville — have prided them-selves on their progressive racial policies compared to rural areas. It is true that Delta counties without the mitigating influence of large towns, including Tallahatchie, Sunflower, and Humphries, have oppressed civil rights activities particularly severely. How-ever, small towns even in the homogeneous Delta vary greatly in their patterns of racial accommodation. Two small towns on opposite sides of Mound Bayou in Bolivar County, for example, have quite different reputations among Negroes and old-time planters: Shelby is a "good" town to be a Negro in, while Meri-gold is to be avoided.

Delta small towns also vary in their treatment of mixed Chi-nese-Negro relationships. Two different processes seem to operate, with divergent outcomes. First, in larger towns, whites could look the other way when such relationships were contracted, asserting to themselves that what the Chinese did "over there in niggertown" was of no consequence. But in a smaller community, since every-body "knows" everybody else, ignorance cannot easily be claimed, as a way of dealing with a troublesome situation. Furthermore, since in such towns whites from the beginning occasionally shopped at Chinese stores, a breach of the taboo could not easily be ignored. And so, incidents of hostility toward interracial cou-ples, such as that reported in the first section of this chapter, did occasionally occur.

That everyone knows everyone else in small towns can produce quite a different result, however. It can lead to a relaxation of the rigidity of racial etiquette forms, because a violation of them need not represent a symbolic violation, hence a threat to the patterns themselves, but can easily be construed as a sheer exception, excusable for idiosyncratic reasons. For example, in a town too small to support two cafes, white and Negroes may eat together, from different parts of the same counter. In a larger town, where such details cannot be so thoroughly disseminated, the symbolic significance of the etiquette violation would take precedence and make the act impossible.

Similarly, then, in small towns like Rolling Fork or Coahoma, the symbolic hostility between "pure" Chinese and Chinese-Negro families can be relaxed. Since everyone knows which is which, there is no need to expend effort to further demonstrate the point. Whites in turn need not worry about being too cordial to a Chinese merchant who turns out to be part-Negro or to be married to a Negro, for they have full information beforehand. Ironically, they can then afford to be relatively cordial anyway, for the mixed relationship itself becomes defined as "the — family," an exception, and presents no generalized or symbolic threat to miscegenation mores.

19. In Cleveland several members of the Joe family opened the first air-conditioned self-service market in the Delta, "The Modern Store," in 1938. It soon won the trade of the town's leading citizens, and several Cleveland Caucasians cited it in interviews as a significant cause of further Chinese social mobility.

20. Greenville *Delta Democrat-Times,* April 27, 1945.

21. "We feel that they are a distinct and particular Chinese family," said a petition in Clarksdale.

22. Letter from Reverend N. D. Timmerman and others, to Board of Trustees, Clarksdale Public Schools, Feb. 21, 1941.

23. Robert Michels, *Political Parties* (New York, 1915), pp. 244–245.

24. In recent years, with mechanization, low-wage farm labor has become less central to the plantation system. The social effects of this radical development remain to be seen.

5 Opposition

1. Integration is not really the term at issue. Rather, Negroes (and Chinese) are increasingly working for an equal life chance; this may or may not involve "joining" white society in its current

structure. It does necessitate sharing in the present white dominance over political, economic, and educational goods.

2. Since prejudice is a structural act, we can expect to find it distributed nonrandomly over social structure. Regional differences in levels of prejudice are well known, of course, although they are usually ignored by psychological prejudice theories. More interesting would be surveys of the distribution of prejudice over urban or rural areas, analogous to Faris and Dunham's ecological study of mental illness in Chicago. Or, to switch from a spatial to an organizational focus, the changes in prejudice levels over the life cycle should be reinvestigated, with an emphasis on reference-group theory. Attitudes within a group could also be examined as they vary over roles. Such studies would provide a much-needed corrective to the present genetic emphasis.

3. The older way of looking at the matter, and the concentration on prejudice rather than discrimination, also fits with a habitually American ascription of importance in human affairs to the inner feelings of the individual common man. Thus in response to the summer riots of 1967, the American President designated a Sunday to be set aside for prayer and contemplation toward the goal of racial harmony in the nation. As with the President, an element of bad faith is connected with the emphasis in sociological literature upon feelings of prejudice at the expense of studies of discrimination. Discrimination is harder to analyze, because structural methodology lags behind survey techniques and because by definition exposing discriminatory practices offends the status quo. Studies of discrimination, furthermore, often seem more journalistic, more muckraking, even "pop," compared to the elegant socio-psychological theorizing in prejudice analyses. Thus discrimination research has been harder to fund and proves less occupationally rewarding to the sociologist academician.

4. See Appendix B.

5. One in Vicksburg, one in Cleveland.

6. Rummel, *The Delta Chinese*, pp. 34–35. From context, the businessman probably lives in Clarksdale.

7. Quote from a white minister in Shelby, corroborated in the same conversation by a white teacher of Italian origin.

8. See Chapter 3 for this case. There is no doubt that the school board decisions were not based on law but were due to personal influence. The dissident petitioners included not one name

of real "substance." Therefore, the board did not accede to the grocers' request.

9. Data are from Clarksdale city directories for 1939 and 1946, confirmed by reminiscences from a long-time school secretary.

10. Davis and the Gardners believe that something in the position of a small storeoowner or clerk leads to abnormal racial antipathy; they hypothesize that the quasisubordination such people endure in their relation with Negro customers may make them feel a greater need to assert status, self-worth, and dominance over minorities. See Allison Davis, B. B. Gardner, and M. R. Gardner, *Deep South* (Chicago, 1941), pp. 56–57.

11. These marriages were against state law, of course. Compulsively statistical sociologists will be pleased to note that, given the occupational distribution in the white population, the observed concentration in the lower (and "working") class would occur randomly less than one time in a hundred.

12. Elin L. Anderson, *We Americans: A Study of Cleavage in an American City* (Cambridge, Mass., 1937), p. 246.

13. This ideological view of working-class whites, if I am correct in imputing it to them, is utterly accurate. In Clarksdale, the school system has been under court order to desegregate by establishing reasonable geographic boundaries for each of the two public high schools. Influenced by those who usually influence such decisions, the school board drew the line so that not one Negro attends the white high school. In the process, several working-class whites had to be zoned in the Negro district in an effort to avoid a gerrymander charge. These whites were unable to influence the decision in their favor and now provide lucrative transactions to realtors by their individualistic efforts to escape its consequences.

14. See, for example, Cohn's extremely crude portrait of the Chinese in *Where I Was Born and Raised,* p. 20. See also Percy, *Lanterns on the Levee,* pp. 18–19.

15. "Introduction," in Council of Federated Organizations, ed., *Mississippi Black Paper* (New York, 1965).

16. During and directly after Reconstruction, Democratic newspapers, between attempts to turn working-class whites against Republican or Populist programs by waving the bloody shirt of racial solidarity, were full of exhortations to the Negro that he too would vote Democratic if he knew his true friends. The "conserva-

tive Delta statesmen" — great planters like Charles Scott, LeRoy Percy, William Alexander Percy, and Walter Sillers, Sr. — repeatedly asserted that they were the voices of racial moderation, opposing such violent racial demagogues as Vardaman and Bilbo. Albert Kirwan makes clear the hypocrisy of this view: "It has been contended frequently that Vardaman was the first of the 'demagogues' in Mississippi. If he was a 'demagogue' . . . he cannot have been the first one . . . The pleas for 'white solidarity,' so insistently urged by all leaders, from Lamar through . . . Percy, and Williams, were nothing but appeals 'to prejudice and passion,' just as Vardaman's crusade was . . . Each of them [Vardaman and his opponents] climbed to power and maintained himself there by appeals to racial prejudice." (Kirwan, *Revolt of the Rednecks,* p. 310.) Kirwan goes on to dismiss sardonically the claim put forth by LeRoy Percy's son that at least Percy himself was a true statesman, aghast at Vardaman's ideas.

17. Delta counties, which more than hill counties are influenced by an upper class, have been more violent in recent years against civil rights "agitators." Such counties as Tallahatchie, Sunflower, Yazoo, and Leflore, and even Coahoma, Issaqueena, and Tunica, have built up an awesome reputation among civil rights workers for violent intransigence, unmitigated by counter-pressure from the law enforcement machinery, and in fact often directly instigated by deputies and police. Hill counties vary much more; several have been surprisingly free from repression. Furthermore, although Neshoba and some others provide strong exceptions, some of the hill counties which were violent have also been dominated by large plantations, including Grenada and Madison, and have a social structure somewhat similar to Delta counties.

18. Dollard, *Caste and Class in a Southern Town,* pp. 74–83. Dollard's class analysis, despite the title, is sketchy, as he himself confesses in the preface to the paperback edition (p. ix). Dollard admits to very little knowledge of lower-class whites: "Very conspicuous in this account of economic gain has been the absence of data on the lower-class white people . . . My research has yielded *no direct data* on this point . . . There are few lower-class whites in Southern town; so the chance did not exist to study them in the town itself" (p. 130, my italics). His class descriptions are also questionable, "There seem to be very few upper-class . . . Whites in Southern town," he writes (p. 95). But a

Lorenz curve of income for a typical Delta County (Chapter 1, Figure 2) belies this claim, as does the 1937 government survey (Holley, Winston, and Woofter, *The Plantation South*), of the plantation system. By "upper class," Dollard apparently means a status category including only those individuals who might be accorded "national" upper-class status in New York or Chicago; accordingly he finds it to be a very small group, "less bound by the Southern mores and folkways" (pp. 82–83). He would have constructed a more powerful analysis had he defined class on the basis of occupational, political, and status position within the Mississippi social system. But if the necessary transformation is made, so that much of Dollard's "middle" class is recognized as part of the upper-class establishment, it is clear that his analysis of the sources of discrimination supports my own.

19. Davis, Gardner, and Gardner, *Deep South,* p. 52.

20. Wharton, *The Negro in Mississippi,* p. 225.

21. Veblen, *Theory of the Leisure Class,* p. 81.

22. The same linking of moral authority and status superiority, cemented by conspicuous consumption standards set by the upper class, partly explains the disproportionate societal influence wielded by large slaveholders before 1860. As Eugene D. Genovese puts it: "The high propensity to consume luxuries, for example, has always been functional . . . in aristocratic societies, for it has provided the ruling class with the facade necessary to control the middle and lower classes . . . In this manner, every dollar spent by the planters for elegant clothes, a college education for their children, or a lavish barbecue contributed to the political and social domination of their class." *The Political Economy of Slavery: Studies in the Economy and Society of the Slave South* (New York, 1965), p. 18.

23. Oliver C. Cox, *Caste, Class, and Race* (New York, 1959), p. 524.

24. Lillian Smith, *Killers of the Dream* (New York, 1961), pp. 175–191.

25. Ibid., p. 178.

26. Ibid., p. 188.

27. Cox, *Caste, Class, and Race,* p. 522.

28. Michael H. Schwartz, "Populism and the State: The Organizational Forms of Radical Protest," unpublished manuscript.

29. Davis, Gardner, and Gardner, *Deep South,* p. 50.

30. If the movement grew to be a serious threat, it could no longer be put down with mere status pressure, and upper-class whites would assuredly resort to fraud and violence, as they did against the Populists in the 1890's.

31. After this analysis was written, I came upon one observer who had reached the same conclusion some thirty years earlier: W. J. Cash, author of the distinguished study, *The Mind of the South* (New York, 1960). In an article in the Baltimore *Evening Sun*, August 29, 1935, Cash discussed lynchings, prototypical acts of racial violence usually blamed upon and performed by poor whites. "The force which really lynches everywhere in the South," he wrote, "is the force of public opinion. And when one says public opinion, one shifts the ultimate responsibility straight back upon the 'best people' — the ruling class. For these people everywhere very largely determine public opinion, of course. And they do so with particular effectiveness in the South. . . . [Moreover], the great body of the master class does favor [lynching]." Cash goes on to show that upper-class attitudes are clearly indicated by the invariable complicity of local police, who have "a very accurate sense of the realities of their world." This article is reprinted in *W. J. Cash: Southern Prophet, A Biography and a Reader*, ed. Joseph L. Morrison (New York, 1967), pp. 216–219.

32. John Dollard includes an excellent discussion of the contemptible place of the Delta poor-white in *Caste and Class in a Southern Town*, p. 94 and elsewhere. The very term used to refer to the poor-white — "peckerwood" — carries far more negative connotations than the hill equivalent, "redneck."

33. Sociologists have often argued that the threat of job competition faced by working-class whites, should job discrimination end, constitutes the basic reason for their antiblack sentiments. The difference in "rational" economic threat potentially posed by black as contrasted to Chinese integration is tremendous, but the societal dynamics outlined in this chapter provide a better explanation of working class attitudes. In addition, the basic dialectic in the system is between top and bottom — between white upper class and black lower class. The white upper class is the class with basic interests, both economic and ideological, at stake, for it alone makes money off the black population. Only correlatively is the working class bothered by the competitive argument, though it is thus bothered.

34. "The operation of the courts and the activities of the police also reflect the same conscious or unconscious maintenance of control by the superordinate white caste." Davis, Gardner, and Gardner, *Deep South*, p. 13.

35. Dollard, *Caste and Class in a Southern Town*, pp. 82–84.

36. Davis, Gardner, and Gardner, *Deep South*, pp. 50–51.

37. Cox, *Caste, Class, and Race*, pp. 537–538.

38. So it is that white Mississippians call those white grocers (and white civil rights workers) who operate in Negro areas "perverts," "degenerates." And they are not dissimulating. They believe what they say.

39. Stanley M. Elkins, *Slavery, a Problem in American Institutional and Intellectual Life* (Chicago, 1959).

40. Myrdal, *An American Dilemma*, especially pp. 84–89.

41. Ibid., pp. 87–88, his italics.

42. Ibid., p. 88.

43. Dollard, *Caste and Class in a Southern Town*, p. 343.

44. Myrdal, *An American Dilemma*, p. 598.

45. Anderson, *We Americans*, pp. 22–23.

46. Katrin Norris, *Jamaica, the Search for an Identity* (London, 1962), p. 68.

6 Interracial Families

1. There are also perhaps two dozen "fragments" of Chinese-Negro relationships — widows, widowers, or children — still living in the Delta.

2. Chinese merchant married to Negro woman.

3. Cf. the popular song: "If you're white, all right; *if you're brown, stick around;* but if you're black, get back, get back, get back!" (my italics).

4. See "Black Natchez," National Educational Television documentary film, for a record of the process as it happens.

5. Research on the relation between color and intelligence within the black population is of two kinds. Liberals deny, with scanty data, that there is any relation. Racists claim a relation but say it proves that whites are inherently more intelligent than blacks. I believe both of these positions are absurd. The relation exists, I believe, and is caused by and indicative of the extreme cultural racism permeating American society, especially in the

South, so that light-skinned blacks are perceived to be more white and are expected to be more intelligent and are treated differently, by both whites and blacks. Such an independent variable is both diffuse and subtle; hence it is hard to observe and quantify and requires in-depth longitudinal research to demonstrate its true importance. No such study has yet been done. Rosenthal's work on the effect of expectation on performance comes closest, although no racial variables were involved. Therefore investigations which claim to explain racial differences in school performance, I.Q., etc., are still incomplete. See Robert Rosenthal and Lenore Jacobson, *Pygmalion in the Classroom* (New York, 1968).

6. Kingsley Davis, "Intermarriage in Caste Societies," *American Anthropologist* 43 (1941) 376–395, and F. G. Bailey, "Hypergamy," in Gould and Kolb, eds., *A Dictionary of the Social Sciences* (New York, 1964), supply general introductions to this topic.

7. Romanzo Adams, *Interracial Marriage in Hawaii* (New York, 1937).

8. Frank E. Smith, *Congressman from Mississippi* (New York, 1964), p. 22.

9. Bailey, "Hypergamy," p. 308.

10. Moench, *Economic Relations of the Chinese in the Society Islands,* p. 88. Silin, *A Survey of Selected Aspects of the Chinese in Jamaica,* p. 49.

11. Davis, "Intermarriage in Caste Societies."

12. Robert K. Merton, "Intermarriage and the Social Structure: Fact and Theory," *Psychiatry* 4 (1941) 361–374.

13. Louis Wirth and Herbert Goldhamer, "The Hybrid and the Problem of Miscegenation," in Otto Klineberg, ed., *Characteristics of the American Negro* (New York, 1944), 249–369.

14. Davis, "Intermarriage in caste societies," pp. 379, 381, 393.

15. Wirth and Goldhamer, "The Hybrid and the Problem of Miscegenation," pp. 289–292; Robert Roberts, *Negro-White Intermarriage: A Study of Social Control,* unpub. M.A. thesis, University of Chicago, 1940, especially page 41; Merton, "Intermarriage and the Social Structure: Fact and Theory," pp. 366–370.

16. Roberts, *Negro-White Intermarriage,* pp. 62–81.

17. See Wirth and Goldhamer, "The Hybrid and the Problem of Miscegenation," pp. 281–294.

18. Calvin C. Hernton has suggested some interesting hypo-

theses in this area; see his *Sex and Racism in America* (Garden City, N.Y., 1966).

19. Merton constructed an elaborate paradigm to deal with the issue, but in the same year, Wirth and Goldhamer destroyed it with empirical results which contravened nearly every prediction he made.

20. This argument cannot be pressed far, however, for in modern America, the female often initiates the relationship.

21. Adams, *Interracial Marriage in Hawaii*, p. 53.

7   Present Conflict and Future Prospects

1. Another purpose of the detailed normative code may be to handle potential guilt within the white population. Freud and others have noted that people who hold complex ambivalent feelings toward others in a given situation develop a strong and extensive set of norms developed to deal with them. When a close relative dies, for example, the funeral and ancillary events provide the family with established ways of behaving. Thus no one need examine his feelings toward the deceased to determine how to act toward his death. Actions and therefore to a degree feelings are prescribed culturally in such a case. With regard to race relations, then, the etiquette code may be so completely programmed partly in order that whites need never ask themselves "who am I dealing with? How should I act?" when confronting a black. Once exploitation was established, whites could not admit to themselves that blacks are *not* inferior; hence they could not allow the question to be raised, but had to have every detail of racial interaction arranged in its ordered normative place.

2. Courtship and marriage have been the most important areas of disagreement between parent and child in mainland China, according to Francis L. K. Hsu. See "The Family in China: The Classical Form," in Anshen, ed., *The Family: Its Function and Destiny* (New York, 1959), p. 132.

3. Francis L. K. Hsu, *Americans and Chinese, Two Ways of Life* (New York, 1970), p. 76.

4. Names have of course been altered.

5. William H. Newell, "Some Problems of the Chinese Family in Treacherous River, Province Wellesley, Federation of Malaya,"

unpub. manuscript, makes a similar argument regarding extra-familial sources of male dominance and family cohesion.

6. Chinese-Americans on Long Island seem headed similarly toward total acculturation, according to Chia-Ling Kuo, "The Chinese on Long Island — A Pilot Study," *Phylon,* 31 (1970), 282–283, 287.

7. Roy Stannard Baker, *Following the Color Line* (New York, 1964), p. 249.

8. See Brewton Berry, *Almost White* (New York, 1963), for a discussion of these groups.

9. Cox, *Caste, Class and Race,* pp. 349–350.

10. Details on the sampling procedures and populations can be found in Appendix B.

11. Item 7 does not differentiate the two populations and is in a sense not an attitude question but a factual assertion. Responses to item 8 are informative: the Chinese agree strongly because this type of individualistic thinking, blaming Negro backwardness on lack of education and responsibility, meshes with their ideology about their own rise.

12. In Thailand, "the Chinese, who value highly a stable, well-ordered society, are continually repelled by what they regard as the extreme instability . . . of the Thai people." Coughlin, *Double Identity; the Chinese in Modern Thailand,* p. 85.

13. This trend is national. See, for example, "Orientals Find Bias Is Down Sharply in U.S.," *New York Times,* December 13, 1970.

14. A complete grasp of this migration can be gained from only two references. "The Black Immigrants," by Ben H. Bagdikian (*Saturday Evening Post,* July 15, 1967, pp. 25–29, 64–68), portrays in detail the move of one Bolivar County family; Ellen S. Bryant bolsters his firsthand account with demographic data in *Changes in Mississippi County Population, 1950 to 1959: Some Hypotheses* (Starkville, Miss., 1960).

15. Greenville *Delta Democrat-Times,* June 23, 1967.

16. Moench, *Economic Relations of the Chinese in the Society Islands,* p. 107.

17. Since 1966 Greenville has been an exception. In 1969, Clarksdale followed suit.

18. Here and elsewhere in the book, names have been changed to avoid specific identification.

Appendix A

1. Rummel, *The Delta Chinese*, pp. 23–24.
2. Virginia Winkleman Lee, "For the Delta—Nation's First Chinese Community-education Center," *Memphis Commercial Appeal*, Feb. 14, 1937.
3. George Rummel and Betty Price, "A Vanishing Culture," *Mississippi Magazine*, 5 (1965), 14.
4. Sillers, *History of Bolivar County, Mississippi*.
5. O'Brien, "Status of the Chinese in the Mississippi Delta," p. 386.
6. Lee, "For the Delta."
7. In addition to the evidence cited in Chapter 1, see also U.S. W.P.A., *Arkansas, A Guide to the State*, p. 346.

Appendix B

1. But see the first section of Chapter 5 for discussion of another biasing factor among whites.
2. For a lengthy discussion of this phenomenon, see Georg Simmel, "The Stranger," pp. 402–408 of *The Sociology of Georg Simmel* (Glencoe, Ill., 1955). At the time, I was a third-year graduate student in sociology at Harvard University.
3. Shortly before the conference, a rumor circulated among Chinese grocers in Cleveland that I was a civil rights worker, only ostensibly interested in the Chinese themselves.
4. Dr. Gerald Globetti of the Department of Sociology and Anthropology at Mississippi State University was kind enough to agree to and help with the distribution of this questionnaire.

Bibliography

Adams, Romanzo. *Interracial Marriage in Hawaii.* New York, Macmillan, 1937.

Adorno, T. W., *et al. The Authoritarian Personality.* New York, Harper, 1950.

Alker, Haywood R., Jr., *Mathematics and Politics.* New York, Macmillan, 1965.

Anderson, Elin. *We Americans: A Study of Cleavage in an American City.* Cambridge, Mass., Harvard University Press, 1937.

Bagdikian, Ben H. "The Black Immigrants," *Saturday Evening Post,* July 15, 1967, 25–29, 64–68.

Bailey, F. G. "Hypergamy," in Julius Gould and William L. Kolb, eds., *A Dictionary of the Social Sciences.* New York, Free Press, 1964.

Baker, Ray Stannard. *Following the Color Line.* (1908). New York, Harper Torchbook, 1964.

Barnett, Milton L. "Kinship as a Factor Affecting Cantonese Economic Adaption in the United States," *Human Organization,* 19 (1961), 40–46.

Barth, Gunther. *Bitter Strength: A History of the Chinese in the United States, 1850–1870.* Cambridge, Mass., Harvard University Press, 1964.

Berry, Brewton. *Almost White: A Study of Certain Racial Hybrids in the Eastern United States.* New York, Macmillan, 1963.

Bertelson, David. *The Lazy South*. New York, Oxford University Press, 1967.

Berthoff, Rowland T. "Southern Attitudes toward Immigration, 1865–1914," *Journal of Southern History*, 17 (1951), 328–360.

Blalock, Hubert M., Jr. *Toward A Theory of Minority-Group Relations*. New York, Wiley, 1967.

Bogue, Donald J., and Calvin L. Beale. *Economic Areas of the United States*. New York, Free Press, 1961.

Bowman, M. J. "The Analysis of Inequality Patterns: A Methodological Contribution," *Metron*, 43 (1956), 3–20.

Bracey, Dorothy Hyde. "Effects of Emigration on a Hakka Village," unpub. diss., Harvard University, 1967.

Brandfon, Robert L. *Cotton Kingdom of the New South: A History of the Yazoo Mississippi Delta from Reconstruction to the Twentieth Century*. Cambridge, Mass., Harvard University Press, 1967.

Broady, Maurice. "The Chinese in Great Britain," in M. H. Fried, ed., *Colloquium on Overseas Chinese*. New York, Institute of Pacific Relations, 1958, pp. 29–34.

Broom, Leonard. "The Social Differentiation of Jamaica," *American Sociological Review*, 19 (1954), 115–125.

Bryant, Ellen S. *Changes in Mississippi County Population, 1950 to 1959: Some Hypotheses*. Starkville, Mississippi, State University Agricultural Experiment Station, 1960.

Carter, Hodding. *Southern Legacy*. Baton Rouge, Louisiana State University Press, 1950.

Cash, W. J. *The Mind of the South*. (1941). New York, Knopf, 1960.

Cator, W. L. *The Economic Position of the Chinese in the Netherlands Indies*. Chicago, University of Chicago Press, 1936.

Cattell, Stuart H. *Health, Welfare and Social Organization in Chinatown, New York City*. New York, Department of Public Affairs, Chinatown Public Health Nursing Demonstration Unit, 1962.

Che, Wai-Kin, "The Young American-Chinese in New Orleans in the 1960's," unpub. M.A. thesis, Mississippi College, 1966.

Chen, Ta. *Emigrant Communities in South China*. New York, Institute of Pacific Relations, 1940.

Clayton, Powell. *The Aftermath of the Civil War in Arkansas*. New York, Neale, 1915.

Cleveland, Mississippi, Bolivar Commercial, various issues.

Cohn, David L. *God Shakes Creation.* New York, Harper, 1935.

—— *Where I Was Born and Raised.* (1948). Notre Dame, Ind., University of Notre Dame Press, 1967.

Coolidge, Mary. *Chinese Immigration.* New York, Holt, 1909.

Coughlin, Richard J. *Double Identity; the Chinese in Modern Thailand.* Hong Kong, Hong Kong University Press, 1960.

Council of Federated Organization (COFO), ed. *Mississippi Black Paper.* New York, Random House, 1965.

Cousins, W. M., "Chinese in the Caribbean," *The Living Age,* 332 (1927), 1621.

Cox, Oliver Cromwell. *Caste, Class and Race: A Study in Social Dynamics.* New York, Monthly Review Press, 1959 (1948).

Davis, Allison, Gardner, B. B., and M. R. Gardner. *Deep South,* Chicago, University of Chicago Press, 1941.

Davis, Kingsley. "Intermarriage in Caste Societies," *American Anthropologist,* 43 (1941), 376–395.

De Bow's Review, various issues.

Dollard, John. *Caste and Class in a Southern Town.* 3rd ed. Garden City, N.Y., Doubleday Anchor, 1957 (1937).

Drake, St. Clair, and Horace R. Clayton. *Black Metropolis: A Study of Negro Life in a Northern City.* New York, Harcourt, Brace, 1945.

Edwards, Paul K. *The Southern Urban Negro as a Consumer.* New York, Prentice Hall, 1932.

Elkins, Stanley M. *Slavery, a Problem in American Institutional and Intellectual Life.* Chicago, University of Chicago Press, 1959.

Fairbank, John K. *The United States and China,* Cambridge, Mass., Harvard University Press, 1958.

Fanon, Frantz. *The Wretched of the Earth.* (1961). New York, Grove, 1966.

Frazier, E. Franklin. *Black Bourgeoisie: The Rise of a New Middle Class in the United States.* Glencoe, Ill., Free Press, 1957.

Fried, Morton H., ed. "Colloquium on Overseas Chinese, 12/29/57," in M. H. Fried, ed., *Colloquium on Overseas Chinese.* New York, Institute of Pacific Relations, 1958.

—— "Some Observations on the Chinese in British Guiana," *Social and Economic Studies* (University College of the West Indies), 5 (no. 1), 1956.

—— "The Chinese in the British Caribbean," in M. H. Fried,

ed., *Colloquium on Overseas Chinese.* New York, Institute of Pacific Relations, 1958.

Friedman, Leon, ed. *Southern Justice.* New York, Pantheon, 1965.

Futrell, Robert F., "Efforts of Mississippians to encourage immigration, 1865–1880," *Journal of Mississippi History, 20,* 1958, 59–76.

Geertz, Clifford. *Peddlers and Princes.* Chicago, University of Chicago Press, 1963.

Genovese, Eugene E. *The Political Economy of Slavery; Studies in the Economy and Society of the Slave South.* New York, Pantheon, 1965.

Gray, William F., ed. *Imperial Bolivar.* Cleveland, Mississippi, *Bolivar Commercial,* 1923.

Greenville, Mississippi, Delta Democrat-Times, and predecessors, various issues.

Hayner, Norman S., and Charles N. Reynolds. "Chinese family life in America," *American Sociological Review, 2* (1937), 630–637.

Hernton, Calvin C. *Sex and Racism in America.* New York, Grove Evergreen, 1966.

Holley, William C. Ellen Wilston, and T. J. Woofter, Jr., *The Plantation South, 1934–1937.* Washington, D.C., U.S. Government Printing Office, 1940.

Hsiao, Kung-Chuan. *Rural China: Imperial Control in the Nineteenth Century.* Seattle, University of Washington Press, 1960.

Hsu, Francis L. K. *Americans and Chinese, Two Ways of Life.* New York, Schuman, 1953.

———— "The family in China: the classical form," in Ruth Nanda Anshen, ed., *The Family: Its Function and Destiny.* New York, Harper, 1959, pp. 123–145.

Inkeles, Alex. "Social change and social character: the role of parental mediation," in Yehudi A. Cohen, ed., *Social Structure and Personality: A Casebook.* New York, Holt, Rinehart, and Winston, 1961, pp. 135–144.

Jackson, Maurice Elizabeth. "Mound Bayou — a Study in Social Development," unpub. M.A. thesis, University of Alabama, 1937.

Jackson Weekly Clarion, 1869–1873, especially 6/3/69, 7/15/69, and 11/20/73.

Kardiner, Abram, and Lionel Ovesey. *The Mark of Oppression.* New York, Norton, 1951.

Kirwan, Albert D. *Revolt of the Rednecks; Mississippi Politics: 1876–1925.* (1951). Gloucester, Mass., Peter Smith, 1964.

Kung, S. W. *The Chinese in American Life.* Seattle, University of Washington Press, 1962.

Kuo, Chia-Ling. "The Chinese on Long Island — A Pilot Study," *Phylon,* 31 (Fall 1970), 280–289.

Latourette, Kenneth Scott. *The Chinese, Their History and Culture.* Vol. 2. New York, Macmillan, 1938.

Lee, Rose Hum. *The Chinese in the United States of America.* Hong Kong, Hong Kong University Press, 1960.

Lee, Virginia Winkleman. "For the Delta — Nation's First Chinese Community Education Center," *Memphis Commercial Appeal,* February 14, 1937.

Liao, Pao Yun. "A Case Study of a Chinese Immigrant Community," unpub. M.A. thesis, University of Chicago, 1951.

Lind, Andrew W., "Adjustment Patterns among Jamaican Chinese," *Social and Economic Studies* (University College of the West Indies), 7 (1958), 144–164.

Loewen, James W. "The Mississippi Chinese," unpub. Ph.D. thesis, Harvard University, 1968.

Loewenberg, Bert James. "Efforts of the South to Encourage Immigration, 1865–1900," *South Atlantic Quarterly,* 33 (October 1934), 363–385.

Lyman, Stanford Morris. "The Structure of Chinese Society in 19th Century America," unpub. diss., University of California, 1961.

Marx, Karl, *The Eighteenth Brumaire of Louis Bonaparte.* (1852). New York, International Publishers, 1963.

McKenzie, R. D. "The Oriental Invasion," *Journal of Applied Sociology,* 10 (1925), 120–130.

McNeily, J. S. "War and Reconstruction in Mississippi, 1863–1890," *Publications of the Mississippi Historical Society,* Centenary Series, 1918, pp. 165–535.

McWilliams, Carey. *Brothers under the Skin.* Boston, Little, Brown, 1951.

Merton, Robert K. "Intermarriage and the Social Structure: Fact and Theory," *Psychiatry,* 4 (1941), 361–374.

Michels, Robert. *Political Parties.* New York, Eden and Cedar Paul, 1915.

Miller, Eric J. "Caste and territory in Malabar," *American Anthropologist*, 56 (1954), 410–420.

Mississippi Code, 1942, Recompiled, vol. one A-1956.

Moench, Richard. "Economic Relations of the Chinese in the Society Islands," unpub. diss., Harvard University, 1963.

Morrison, Joseph L. *W. J. Cash: Southern Prophet: A Biography and a Reader*. New York, Knopf, 1967.

Myrdal, Gunnar. *An American Dilemma*. New York, McGraw-Hill, 1964 (1944).

Newell, William H., "Some Problems of the Chinese Family in Treacherous River, Province Wellesley, Federation of Malaya," preliminary typescript, 1963.

Nolen, Claude H. *The Negro's Image in the South*. Lexington, University of Kentucky Press, 1968.

Norris, Katrin. *Jamaica, the Search for an Identity*. London, Oxford University Press, 1962.

O'Brien, Robert W. Status of the Chinese in the Mississippi Delta," *Social Forces*, 19 (1941), 386–390.

Ogden, Florence Sillers. Unpublished ms. on Chinese in Rosedale. Rosedale, Mississippi, 1933.

Park, Robert Ezra. *Race and Culture*. New York, Free Press, 1964.

———— and Ernest W. Burgess. *Introduction to the Science of Sociology*. Chicago, University of Chicago Press, 1921.

———— and Herbert A. Miller. *Old World Traits Transplanted*. New York, Harper, 1921.

Parsons, Talcott. "A Revised Analytical Approach to the Theory of Social Stratification," in *Essays in Sociological Theory*, rev. ed. New York, Free Press, 1964, pp. 386–439.

Percy, William Alexander. *Lanterns on the Levee*. New York, Knopf, 1941.

Purcell, Victor. *The Chinese in Malaya*. London, Oxford University Press, 1948.

Raper, Arthur F. *The Tragedy of Southern Lynching*. Chapel Hill, University of North Carolina Press, 1933.

Roberts, Robert. "Negro-White Intermarriage: A Study of Social Control," unpub. M.A. thesis, University of Chicago, 1940.

Rohrer, John, and M. S. Edmonson, eds. *The Eighth Generation Grows Up*. (1960). New York, Harper and Row, 1964.

Rosenthal, Robert, and Lenore Jacobson. *Pygmalion in the Classroom*. New York, Holt, Rinehart and Winston, 1968.

Rummel, George Albert, III, "The Delta Chinese: An Exploratory Study in Assimilation." Unpub. M.A. thesis, University of Mississippi, 1966.

—— and Betty Price. "A Vanishing Culture," *Mississippi Magazine*, 5 (1965), 14–16.

Ryan, Edward J. "The Value System of a Chinese Community in Java," unpub. diss., Harvard University, 1961.

Schumpeter, Joseph A. "Social Classes," in *Imperialism and Social Classes*. Cleveland, World Meridian, 1962, pp. 101–179.

Schwartz, Michael. "Populism and the State: The Organizational Forms of Radical Protest," unpublished manuscript.

Shibutani, Tamotsu, and Kian M. Kwan. *Ethnic Stratification, A Comparative Approach*. New York, Macmillan, 1965.

Silin, Robert H. "A Survey of Selected Aspects of the Chinese in Jamaica," unpub. B.A. thesis, Harvard University, 1962.

Sillers, Florence W., compiler. *History of Bolivar County, Mississippi*. Jackson, Hederman Brothers (Miss. Delta Chapter, D.A.R.), 1948.

Simmel, Georg. "Conflict," in *Conflict and the Web of Group Affiliations*. Glencoe, Ill., Free Press, 1955.

—— *The Sociology of Georg Simmel*, trans. and ed. by Kurt H. Wolff. Glencoe, Ill., Free Press, 1955.

Sitterson, J. Carlyle. *Sugar Country, the Cane Sugar Industry in the South, 1753–1950*. Lexington[?], University of Kentucky Press, 1953[?].

Siu, Paul C. P. "The Sojourner," *American Journal of Sociology*, 58 (1952–53), 34–44.

Skinner, G. William. "The Chinese of Java," in M. H. Fried, ed., *Colloquium on Overseas Chinese*. New York, Institute of Pacific Relations, 1958, pp. 1–10.

Smith, Frank E. *Congressman from Mississippi*. New York, Pantheon, 1964.

Smith, Lillian. *Killers of the Dream*. (1949). New York, Norton, 1961.

Smith, M. G. *The Plural Society in the British West Indies*. Berkeley, University of California Press, 1965.

Somers, Robert. *The Southern States Since the War, 1870–1871*. (1872). Tuscaloosa, University of Alabama Press, 1965.

Staples, Thomas S. *Reconstruction in Arkansas, 1862–1874*. (1923). Gloucester, Mass., Peter Smith, 1964.

Stein, Maurice. *Eclipse of Community: An Interpretation of*

American Studies. Princeton, N.J., Princeton University Press, 1960.

Stone, Lawrence. *The Crisis of the Aristocracy, 1558–1641.* London, Oxford University Press, 1965.

Thomas, William. "Magnolia Drum Song," *Memphis Commercial Appeal, Mid-South Magazine,* February 11, 1968.

Uchida, Neosaku. *The Overseas Chinese: A Bibliographical Essay Based on the Resources of the Hoover Institution.* Palo Alto, Calif., Hoover Institution on War, Revolution, and Peace, Stanford University, 1960.

United States Bureau of the Census. *Population,* 1860 through 1970, by decades.

United States Department of the Interior, Bureau of Indian Affairs, Choctaw Agency. *The Mississippi Choctaw Indians.* Philadelphia, Mississippi, mimeo., n.d.

United States Reports. Cases Adjudged in the Supreme Court at October Term, 1927, *Gong Lum et al. v. Rice et al.,* 275: 78–82. Also 139 Mississippi 760, *Rice v. Gong Lum,* appeal to Mississippi Supreme Court. Also 148 Mississippi 462, *Bond, State Supt. of Education, v. Tij Fung et al.,* appeal to Mississippi Supreme Court.

United States Works Progress Administration. *Arkansas, a Guide to the State.* New York, Hastings House, 1941.

———— Federal Writers' Project. *Bolivar County History,* no. 19, "Schools of Today," typescript, 1937. No. 6, "Folk Customs and Superstitions," typescript, 1936. No. 5, "Roster of the Colored Troops of Bolivar County," typescript, 1936.

———— *Washington County History,* "Chinese living in Washington County," and "Chinese, continued," typescript, 1936. No. 19, "Schools of today," typescript, 1937.

Veblen, Thornstein. *The Theory of the Leisure Class.* (1899). New York, New American Library Mentor, 1953.

Vicksburg, Mississippi, Post, various issues.

Vicksburg, Mississippi, Times, 1869.

Vicksburg, Mississippi, Weekly Herald, 1869–1870.

Warner, W. Lloyd. *The Status Systems of Ethnic Groups.* New Haven, Yale University Press, 1941.

Wharton, Vernon Lane. *The Negro in Mississippi, 1865–1890.* Chapel Hill, University of North Carolina Press, 1947.

Williams, Robin. *Strangers Next Door.* Englewood Cliffs, N.J., Prentice-Hall, 1964.

Wirth, Louis, and Herbert Goldhamer. "The Hybrid and the Problem of Miscegenation," in Otto Klineberg, ed., *Characteristics of the American Negro.* New York, Harper, 1944, pp. 249–369.

Woodson, Carter Goodwin. *The Rural Negro,* Washington, D.C., Association for the Study of Negro Life and History, 1930.

Wright, Richard. *Black Boy.* (1937). New York, New American Library Signet, 1951.

Young, Donald. *American Minority Peoples.* New York, Harper, 1932.

Index

Harvard East Asian Series